NORTH

TO THE FUTURE

The Alaska Story, 1959-2009

Photo right: Fourth Avenue, Anchorage, circa 1956.
Anchorage was named an All-American City in 1956, 1965,
and 1984, emerging as the center of commerce for Alaska.

N★RTH
TO THE FUTURE

The Milepost

The Alaska Story, 1959-2009

DERMOT COLE

Foreword by Michael Carey

ALASKA BOOK
ADVENTURES™
Epicenter Press

www.EpicenterPress.com

Epicenter Press is a regional press publishing nonfiction books about the arts, history, environment, and diverse cultures and lifestyles of Alaska and the Pacific Northwest.

Publisher: Kent Sturgis
Acquisitions Editor: Lael Morgan
Photo research: Jill Shepherd
Appendix research: John de Yonge, Sam Travis
Proofreaders: Melanie Wells, Sherrill Carlson
Indexer: Constance Angelo
Cover & text design: Victoria Michael
Printer: Edwards Brothers

The Alaska Historical Society was a sponsor of research for this publication; however, the author is responsible for all statements herein, whether of fact or opinion. Readers are encouraged to bring to the publisher's attention any errors found in this book. Email info@epicenterpress.com.

Cover photos—front, from top to bottom: a joyous statehood celebration in Washington, D.C. in July, 1958, Alaska State Library; commercial fishing harvest, Fairbanks Daily News-Miner; highway damage caused by the 1964 earthquake, U.S. Geological Survey; trans-Alaska pipeline, Fairbanks Daily News-Miner; Fairbanks protest against federal land policies in 1978, Fairbanks Daily News-Miner; back—Kotzebue celebration, Ernest H. Gruening Papers/Elmer E. Rasmuson Library, UA Fairbanks.

Library of Congress Control Number: 2008934627
ISBN 978-0-9800825-3-1
First Edition, Trade Paperback original, October 2008
10 9 8 7 6 5 4 3 2
Printed in the United States of America

To order single copies of NORTH TO THE FUTURE, mail $14.95 plus $5.00 for shipping (WA residents add $1.80 state sales tax) to Epicenter Press, PO Box 82368, Kenmore, WA 98028; call us at 800-950-6663 day or night, or visit www.EpicenterPress.com. Contact info@EpicenterPress.com about volume discounts.

green press
INITIATIVE

The text of this book was printed on recycled paper with 100% post-consumer content.

To Sister Elizabeth Eugene, my aunt,
and to the memory of
William P. Cole, my father.

The tumult and the shouting dies,

the captains and the kings depart;

still stands thine ancient sacrifice,

an humble and a contrite heart.

Lord God of Hosts, be with us yet,

lest we forget - lest we forget!

RUDYARD KIPLING

Second Avenue, Fairbanks, mid-1950s. Military construction drove the city's economy in the years leading up to statehood.

FOREWORD

W RITTEN HISTORY HAS one distinct advantage over life as it is
lived. History has a narrative, life does not. We can only construct
the narrative of our lives afterwards, in retrospect.

North to the Future is all that the best history should be—clear, accurate,
informative, complex, and subtle, with an appreciation of the influence of
individuals. And an appreciation of chance, which gave Alaska the largest
oil field in North America at Prudhoe Bay and produced the Anchorage
earthquake of 1964 and Fairbanks flood of 1967.

When Dermot Cole's narrative begins fifty years ago at statehood, Alaska
had 220,000 people, as many as 20 percent of them serving in the military.
North to the Future is the story of events that shaped the lives of these Alaskans
and those who followed.

The 1950s were a decade of incredible optimism. In the words of Juneau
economist George Rogers, "We had been through the Depression, we had
been through a horrible war, and we were going to change the world. We
were going to produce a brave new world—and we even said it just like
that."

Alaskans believed statehood would free them from stateside
domination—principally the Seattle salmon interests—and allow them
to assume their rightful place among Americans. No more paying taxes
to the federal treasury and serving in the military without the right to
vote for president.

The success of statehood is apparent. Alaskans now enjoy prosperity unimagined a half-century ago. But prosperity did not come easily and old-timers now complain that Alaskans exchanged one master, the salmon industry, for another, the oil industry.

Cole's cast of characters includes those present at the creation of the state—politicians Bill Egan, Bob Bartlett, and Ernest Gruening, publishers Bill Snedden and Bob Atwood, and young men who played minor roles but would go on to greater things, including Ted Stevens, Jay Hammond, and Wally Hickel. It also includes those like Howard Rock, who was present at the start of the Native land claims movement, a revolutionary campaign that transformed Native life, and those present at the creation of the modern oil industry like Tom Marshall, who in 1964 was instrumental in persuading Gov. Bill Egan to select the lands around Prudhoe Bay.

These historical characters are all men, but we must remember women served in early meetings of the state Legislature, and with the passage of time, women began to assume more prominent roles in every facet of Alaska life.

As this story of Alaska statehood unfolds, you will find that the author's dominant character is Alaska itself—ever changing yet eternal, where every day a cheechako crosses the border from Canada or flies north looking for a new future, and says, "This is the place for me. This is the place I have been looking for all my life."

Dermot Cole is a fine storyteller, a match for the sourdoughs who charmed audiences with colorful reminiscences in the lobby of the old Nordale Hotel in Fairbanks during my childhood.

Yet, the old-timers, who loved Alaska as passionately as Cole, held no loyalty to the facts and probability. Every day was the coldest on record, every bear the biggest ever encountered, every bottle of hooch the most potent ever distilled. Cole has too much respect for his audience for that— and when we're finished with *North to the Future*, we respect him for a narrative ever engaging, ever stimulating despite sticking to the facts. The facts of Alaska history are remarkable enough.

—Michael Carey

ACKNOWLEDGMENTS

T HIS BOOK WOULD not have been possible without the assistance of many people.

I would like to thank Marilyn Romano, Kelly Bostian, Rod Boyce, and others at the *Fairbanks Daily News-Miner* for their assistance and encouragement.

I am grateful to the many editors, reporters and managers at the *News-Miner* who have helped me learn more about Alaska over the past three decades.

I also want to thank the Alaska Historical Society for its support and for the work its members do providing Alaskans with insight into our past.

Among the individuals who have helped with suggestions, I want to express my appreciation to Angene Johnson, Olivia Karns, Brittany Karns, Dan Joling, Michael Carey, Kent Sturgis, Jack de Yonge, Jo Antonson, Bruce Merrell, Terrence Cole, Patrick Cole, Jack Roderick, Gay Salisbury, Vic Fischer, and Jack Coghill.

Throughout this project, I have benefited from the advice and philosophy of the members of SCUM, led by Dr. Susan Sugai. They helped keep me on track, especially on Sundays during the cross-country ski season when I could have been doing other things.

Most of all, I would like to thank my family for unwavering love and support. My wife, Debbie, an excellent editor, helped me keep my focus. She, as well as my son Connor and my daughters Aileen and Anne, has taught me more than I can say. Over the years they have added immeasurably to my life in ways that I cannot express, while never failing to forgive my limitations.

TABLE OF CONTENTS

Anchorage residents celebrated U.S. Senate approval of statehood on June 30, 1958 with a bonfire on the city's Park Strip.

INTRODUCTION

T HE CIVIL DEFENSE sirens sounded in Anchorage to herald the joyous news on June 30, 1958. On the other side of the continent, the U.S. Senate had voted 64-20 to admit Alaska as the 49th state. In Anchorage, the city that gave energy to the statehood movement, "unbelieving crowds almost silently walked the streets amid the tooting of automobile horns," Lawrence Davies wrote in the *New York Times.*

The three Anchorage radio stations repeated an invitation to Alaskans from M.R. "Muktuk" Marston, who had led the Eskimo Scouts during World War II, to gather on the Park Strip and "make whoopee." He envisioned a fifty-ton bonfire of scrap lumber and debris: forty-nine tons in honor of Alaska and an extra ton to symbolically support Hawaiian statehood. Alaskans voted by a 5 to 1 margin later that summer to accept statehood, and President Eisenhower signed the official proclamation on January 3, 1959.

One of the many editorial writers who took note of the new state's admission into the Union commented, "Alaska is not so much in the present as in the future." Much has changed during the five decades of statehood, yet Alaska struggles with many issues of long standing, ranging from the regional split inherent in the capital-move controversy to the question of how best to develop enormous natural gas reserves on the North Slope.

The arguments about whether 1958-59 was the right time for statehood came down to judgments about Alaska's ability to afford the burdens of self-government. Supporters said it was more about self-respect than economics. But in the early years, some wondered if Alaska would be a state in name only. A *Wall Street Journal* headline summed up the case this way when the celebrating ended:

ALASKA'S ORDEAL
Problems Pile Up
Fast For 49th State
as It Finishes First Year

For the first decade of statehood, it appeared that the critics might be right and that Alaska could not afford to be a state. Fishing was the largest industry in 1959, but the salmon pack was less than half of what it had been two decades earlier. Gold mining continued to decline and the military construction boom prompted by the Cold War was tapering off. Pulp mills and petroleum held promise, but Alaska had only three producing wells on the Kenai Peninsula in 1959. As state government struggled to assume its new responsibilities in the early years of statehood, the Good Friday Earthquake spread devastation across Southcentral Alaska. Reconstruction funds from the federal government helped rebuild much of Alaska's infrastructure.

Those who believed the financial future of the state was in its land holdings were correct. The Egan administration selected land on the North Slope in and around Prudhoe Bay, which turned out to contain the largest oil field ever found in North America, discovered at a time when the oil industry was about to abandon the search following a series of dry holes.

In these pages, I write of the key challenges and conflicts the state faced and how issues related to land and resources have shaped life in Alaska. Three major land laws approved by Congress not only led to new property lines across hundreds of millions of acres, but also established rules that guide the state's development. With statehood, the Congress granted Alaska the right to select more than 100 million acres of land — enough it was hoped, for the state to build a private economy from mining, timber, fishing, and agriculture.

The discovery of oil and the resulting campaign to build the trans-Alaska oil pipeline added momentum to a growing Native-rights campaign. This brought about the second and the third major land bills: the Alaska Native Claims Settlement Act and the Alaska National Interest Lands Conservation Act. The implementation of these measures created the foundation that is shaping Alaska's future.

For most of the first fifty years of statehood, Alaska was represented in Washington, D.C. by Senator Ted Stevens, the longest-serving Republican in the U.S. Senate, and Representative Don Young, a member of the House since the Nixon administration. Stevens used the power of seniority to direct billions of dollars worth of projects to his home state. Yet Alaska politics were in turmoil in 2008, in large part because of an extended federal investigation of political corruption, the full extent of which remained unclear. The conviction of former state legislators and controversy over hidden dealings on a gas pipeline plan helped Sarah Palin overcome long odds and win election to the governor's office in 2006 as a reformer.

She battled the Republican party establishment, challenged the old order, and helped engineer a major oil tax increase and a state initiative to issue a contract for the long-delayed natural gas pipeline to the Lower 48.

In August 2008, Palin was chosen by Republican presidential candidate Sen. John McCain as his running mate, reflecting her meteoric rise to prominence in American politics. No other Alaskan, with the possible exception of Walter J. Hickel, who served as interior secretary under President Nixon, had the opportunity to play such a pivotal role in national and world affairs.

The first major milestone in state history was the 1967 centennial of the purchase of Alaska. In advance of that celebration, Juneau journalist Richard Peter won a $300 prize by suggesting "North to the Future" as a slogan. The words, once featured on Alaska license plates, became the state motto, a reminder, as Peter said, "that beyond the horizon of urban clutter there is a Great Land beneath our flag that can provide a new tomorrow for this century's 'huddled masses yearning to be free.'"

In its first half-century, Alaska emerged from poverty to become one of the wealthiest states in the union, thanks to the rich oil reserves on Alaska's North Slope. Because of the invisible river of oil flowing south through the trans-Alaska pipeline, Alaskans for nearly thirty years paid no state income tax or other statewide tax. Instead, they received annual dividends from earnings of the Alaska Permanent Fund, which consisted of savings and investments funded by a portion of state oil revenues. It had grown to nearly $36 billion by 2008.

Few topics have generated more speeches than the desire to diversify Alaska's economy, but at the half-century mark oil remained the foundation in both good times and bad. In the late 1990s, oil dipped to near $10 a barrel and it appeared that a financial crunch was at hand.

Fishing and tourism support the economy in Ketchikan, seen in this 1984 photo. The Ketchikan Pulp Mill closed in 1997 after nearly fifty years of operation. Close to one million visitors stop in Ketchikan each year.

By 2003, oil prices had climbed to $32, an increase caused in part by the war in Iraq, and ended 2004 at about $35. A year later the price went to $60. The upward trend continued well past the $100 mark in 2008. Soaring demand in China and India, the declining value of the dollar, worries about terrorism, and the war in Iraq combined to improve the state financial outlook. Alaskans had nothing to do with the reversal of fortune, driven as it was by international political and economic trends beyond their control.

Oil production had been on the decline for nearly twenty years, however, and the unprecedented price hike created uncertainty of its own. No one could say how long the state's latest round of prosperity would last. An increase in oil taxes approved in 2007 after the first wave of indictments in the corruption scandal brought new dreams of multi-billion-dollar surpluses. But if world oil prices dropped to a level that would have been considered exorbitant as recently as 2006, the surplus might dwindle. That could mean a return to a statewide income tax, major spending cuts, or dipping into permanent fund earnings, any of which would be contentious.

There are any number of ways to write about Alaska's first half-century. I have chosen to focus on interesting anecdotes about key milestones and individuals, starting with the creation of a new state government and going on to the earthquake, the North Slope oil discovery, the Alaska Native Claims Settlement Act, the building of the trans-Alaska pipeline, and the carving up of Alaska's lands.

In January, 1959 the state entered the Union with optimism and great hope for the future. But during the weeks that followed President Eisenhower's statehood proclamation, a crisis that no one had anticipated cast a long shadow over Alaska.

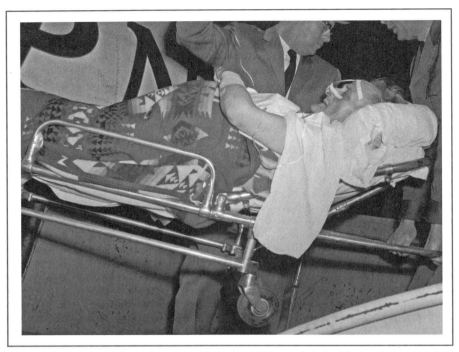

Bill Egan, Alaska's first governor, was flown to Seattle for emergency intestinal surgery just sixteen days after taking office in 1959.

CHAPTER 1
State's first governor fights for life

S IXTEEN DAYS AFTER William A. Egan took office as Alaska's first elected governor, medics strapped him to a stretcher and rushed him from Saint Ann's Hospital to the Juneau airport. A Pacific Northern Airlines crew had removed the forward seats from a Lockheed Constellation to make room for the governor on the flight to Seattle. Egan looked gaunt and tired on that January day in 1959.

"It was a little choppy over Juneau but we climbed up above the rough weather and it was a clear, smooth trip the rest of the way," pilot Dave Schrimer told the *Seattle Post-Intelligencer.* "I've known the governor for thirteen years and he's a good egg. I joked with him and he seemed in good spirits." Dr. C.C. Carter of Juneau and first lady Neva Egan joined Egan on the four-hour flight along the Inside Passage.

At Seattle-Tacoma International Airport, a forklift carried Governor Egan to a waiting ambulance while an attendant administered blood plasma to the stricken governor, who was admitted to Virginia Mason Hospital. At forty-three, Egan was fighting to survive just as the 49th state was coming to life. The Seattle doctors performed emergency surgery to deal with complications stemming from gall bladder surgery that had taken place two weeks earlier in Juneau.

The next night at 10:50 p.m., someone claiming to be Egan's doctor placed a call to KOMO-TV in Seattle, claiming that Egan had died. The TV station and radio station KOL both carried the report, but it turned out to be a hoax and they corrected it minutes later.

The truth was grim enough. Alaska went on a deathwatch. A Juneau reporter had written an obituary for the chief executive that many feared soon would appear on the front pages of Alaska's newspapers: "Death took Governor William A. Egan from one last frontier to another today," it began. In their public statements, the doctors were pessimistic. "He is desperately ill," said Dr. Joel Baker, chief of surgery at Virginia Mason. "I would say his chances are a little less than fifty percent." Later, one of the surgeons said privately that Egan's chances were closer to ten percent. It would be five days to a week before they would know if he would survive the crisis. Egan had directed that the doctors talk openly with reporters about his condition, but the surgeons never mentioned the one-in-ten odds in public, instead referring to Egan as "extremely courageous."

Resting in his hospital bed a day after the surgery, Egan could see from inside the oxygen tent that a nurse had a copy of that day's *Seattle Post-Intelligencer*. It carried a front-page picture of his eleven-year-old son, Dennis, getting off the plane from Juneau. Described by a reporter as "a miniature of his father," the sixth-grader knew his dad was sick, but he didn't understand the seriousness of the situation. The nurse had not read the newspaper, so when Egan motioned that he wanted to see it, she complied. The front-page headline said:

SON OF ALASKA'S GOVERNOR
FLIES TO DAD'S BEDSIDE
Egan in Critical Shape
After 2-hour Operation

The paper carried a nice picture of Egan's son, who wore a suit jacket and a tie, but Egan couldn't bear to read the article. It said the boy had not been told his father might die. "The Alaska chief executive's life hung in the balance," the newspaper reported. Egan read about three paragraphs and threw the paper out of the oxygen tent. He later told Juneau reporter Vern Metcalfe that he knew he had been close to death, but he wouldn't allow himself to think about it.

"Once I recall—perhaps it was only for a minute, maybe longer—that I was in a valley and it was cold. But it seemed that up off to the left was a plateau off the valley wall. It seemed that the sun was always shining there and the grass was green with an abundance of flowers. I remember I was trying to climb the mountain to get to the plateau, but I never could make it," he said. A surgeon told Egan, "We can only do so much and then someone else takes over."

The governor was too ill to read the mail, but letters and notes from across the new state accumulated in his hospital room. Egan was well liked for his person-to-person brand of politics. The messages of support included a telegram from Fairbanks with 150 names.

In Juneau, the transformation from territorial to state government continued in a somber atmosphere. The survival of Egan, a former Valdez storekeeper who had served as president of the Alaska Constitutional Convention, emerged as the biggest worry. No state laws existed yet, as the first Legislature would not convene until the following week, but the constitution contained a provision to deal with a governor's absence. Secretary of State Hugh J. Wade, who held the job that later would be renamed lieutenant governor, took over as acting governor. "I urge all Alaskans of every faith, and his many friends and well-wishers in other states, to ask God to give him the physical strength to pull through this crisis," Wade said.

Wade, fifty-seven, was a former FBI agent and lawyer who once worked for the Eskimo Pie Ice Cream Company in Kentucky and came to Alaska as a federal administrator during the New Deal. He hadn't expected to be leading the new state during its first days, but then again, no one else had either.

A little more than two weeks earlier, government officials and newspaper reporters had gathered on the third floor of the federal building in Juneau for the official birth of the 49th state. They had been told that everything would be official at 9 a.m. on January 3, 1959, but Egan waited for official confirmation from the White House. This was the first time since 1912, when Arizona joined the Union, that a new star would be added to the American flag.

Waiting nervously to take the oath of office that day, the chain-smoking Egan looked pale and thin. He wore a dark blue suit, blue shirt, and blue tie. If he didn't look as hearty as normal, it was understandable, given his gall bladder surgery the month before. On most formal occasions, Egan looked like a "country boy hurriedly and temporarily dressed for Sunday services," a visiting writer once observed.

Egan was a Valdez grocer and former territorial legislator whose political gifts included an uncanny memory. His father, a hard rock miner, died in an avalanche in 1921 when Egan was seven. He went to work in fish canneries

Bill Egan, the middle figure, above, piloted the "Spirit of Valdez," an Eaglerock OX-5 aircraft owned by Owen Meals. To Egan's left is George Gilson; the man on the right is not identified. The photo is believed to have been taken between 1932 and 1935. Neva Egan, seen below in a 1954 photo, worried about Egan's flying and secretly was relieved when a hangar fire in 1939 ended the future governor's flying career.

at age ten. "I got ten cents an hour for putting empty cans on the line and four years later I was at the other end of the line catching full ones for fifty-five cents an hour," he once said. "I thought I had it made." Egan drove trucks for the territorial road commission for a while and worked for bush pilot Bob Reeve as a "bombardier," dropping freight from the back of bush planes. He considered sticking with aviation, but "it didn't look very promising because in those days the aviators were all walking around with holes in their pants."

Egan's formal education had ended in high school because of the Great Depression, but he was a student of politics who admired FDR and did a lot of reading. The work habits he developed in the gold mines, on the docks, the highways and in the store he bought served him well. He believed in working "eight to five," a state commissioner once said, meaning from 8 a.m. one day to 5 a.m. the next. During his years as a territorial legislator, he had earned the nickname "Eagle Bill" for opposing a bill to end the bounty on eagles, arguing that the birds took a toll on the salmon population.

He hitched a ride to Fairbanks in the fall of 1955 to take his place as a delegate at the Alaska Constitutional Convention. His fellow delegates selected him as president and he won praise from all sides for his even-handed rule and ability to instill cooperation. Katie Hurley, chief clerk of the convention, was astounded to learn that he had committed the rules of the convention to memory. For Egan, that wasn't hard.

One of the secrets to Egan's long career in Alaska politics was his ability to put a name with a face. In a profile of Egan, visiting Seattle journalist and historian Murray Morgan said the Alaska governor never stopped meeting as many people as he could, which is why he didn't eat in hotel rooms. When he flew, he had a habit of walking up and down the aisle of the plane to say hello. At one reception, Morgan was astounded when Egan asked, on a first-name basis, about people living in Haines, King Salmon, Atka, Anchorage, Kotzebue, Circle, and Chicken. "He used to embarrass my mother all the time by calling across the street and yelling their name and saying hello," Dennis Egan said. "I don't have a clue how he had the ability to remember names, but it sure was real."

Neva, who had warmed baby formula for Dennis on a hot plate while her husband served as a territorial legislator, said his hobbies included working nights and weekends and talking politics at any hour. "After many years I've discovered that when Bill is talking at dinner with friends he never notices what he is eating. He has many a dish he wouldn't have otherwise touched while engrossed in conversation," she wrote.

Bill Egan, above, president of the Alaska Constitutional Convention, signs the Alaska Constitution at the convention's closing ceremony at the University of Alaska in Fairbanks on February 5, 1956. Below, Christian von Schneidau paints a portrait of Egan.

They had met and fallen in love after she moved to Valdez to teach school. He liked driving her in his car, one of the few in Valdez, and taking her up in his old airplane. "It never looked particularly sturdy to me. In fact, I could never figure out how it held together at all," she said. Neva was ashamed to tell him how afraid she was of flying in his plane, but she always said a prayer and went along. "When his plane burned in a hangar fire in 1939, I was sorry for him for his loss, but I always figured that fire saved his life—and maybe mine."

She was intrigued by his fascination with politics and his depth of feelings about it. She had been raised in a Republican family in Kansas and never argued politics with him. "He had grown up with an intense interest in politics. He had fist fights over issues when he was in grade school," she said. "He started reading the *Congressional Record* for fun when he was in junior high and he had an amazing knowledge of bills and voting records in the Congress." His godfather was Congressional Delegate Tony Dimond, who sent copies of the *Congressional Record* to the Egans. The only time he lost his shyness, she said, was when he argued politics.

They had a daughter, Elin Carol, but she died at seven months in 1941, just as his political career was starting. He served in the Army at Ladd Field in Fairbanks during World War II and returned to Valdez after the war to discover that he had been elected mayor in his absence.

Neva, who did the ironing and darning in the governor's mansion, said that when her husband was in good health an ideal dinner would be a medium steak, with French fries, a salad with French dressing, homemade bread, coffee, and ice cream. But he was not his usual self on that first Saturday in January. All he wanted was to get on with the swearing-in ceremony.

The Associated Press carried the much-awaited news from Washington, D.C. at 9:15 a.m. in Juneau, 12:15 p.m. on the East Coast. James Hagerty, President Dwight D. Eisenhower's press secretary, confirmed that the President had signed the proclamation admitting Alaska as the 49th state. House Speaker Sam Rayburn, seated to Eisenhower's left during the ceremony in the Cabinet Room, looked on as the President signed and dated the document. "Be sure to make it 1959," Rayburn advised. The date of the ceremony had been in doubt for weeks, as the President couldn't act until certification of the results of Alaska's fall election. Gathering the votes by hand in election districts spread across four time zones in Alaska was a cumbersome process.

Vice President Richard Nixon sat on Eisenhower's right and Interior Secretary Fred Seaton stood behind the President. Others clustered near the President were six of the seven Alaskans invited by Ike—*Anchorage Times* Publisher Robert B. Atwood; Mike Stepovich, the last territorial governor of Alaska; Waino Hendrickson, the acting territorial governor; and the first three men elected by Alaskans to Congress—Democrats E.L. "Bob" Bartlett, Ernest Gruening, and Ralph Rivers. Egan was the seventh invitee, but believed he should be in Juneau at the moment Alaska became a state.

The President used twelve fountain pens for the signing ceremony, distributing nine of them as souvenirs to the Alaskans and members of Congress. The visitors had been told to stand in spots marked on the floor, providing order for the official photographs, taken while Eisenhower signed six copies of the documents. Some grumbled later that the White House hadn't allowed spouses of the new Congressional delegation to attend and claimed that the official list of invited guests had been limited for political reasons, leaving out many high-profile Democrats in Congress.

Eisenhower had been a reluctant convert to the statehood cause, influenced by Interior Secretary Fred Seaton and others. Eisenhower had been among those who shared the view that Alaska couldn't afford to pay its way and he worried about the military ramifications. Years later, however, Eisenhower would claim statehood for Alaska and Hawaii as major accomplishments of his administration.

The real suspense in the White House that day was how the Stars and Stripes would be altered to recognize Alaska. The nearly one hundred photographers and TV cameramen gathered for the occasion showed the most interest when Eisenhower turned and unfurled the new flag design. In the months beforehand, about 2,000 people had submitted proposals to redesign the Stars and Stripes to accommodate Alaska, but few people had seen the final 49-star design, which Eisenhower had approved the day before at his farm in Gettysburg, Pennsylvania. The President said he preferred an arrangement with four rows of six stars alternating with five rows of five stars, sketching his idea for a visitor at the ceremony. "But I was overruled by all my advisors," Eisenhower joked to Bob Bartlett, the tireless statehood campaigner who soon would be sworn in with Ernest Gruening to represent Alaska in the U.S. Senate. The new flag contained seven staggered rows of seven stars, but would remain in place for only a year until Hawaii brought the total to fifty.

Fairbanks Daily News-Miner

Alaska State Library

Top photo: President Dwight D. Eisenhower signs the Alaska statehood proclamation on January 3, 1959. Looking on are, from left, back row, Alaska Rep.-elect Ralph Rivers; Sens.-elect Ernest Gruening and Bob Bartlett; Interior Secretary Fred Seaton; acting territorial Gov. Waino Hendrickson; David Kendall; former territorial Gov. Mike Stepovich; and Bob Atwood, president of the Alaska Statehood Committee. To the President's right is Vice President Richard Nixon; to his left, Sam Rayburn, speaker of the House of Representatives.

Bottom photo: Jubilant Alaskans and other statehood advocates gathered happily outside the U.S. Senate chamber on June 30, 1958 after the Senate approved statehood on a 64-20 vote. Visible from left are Ernest Gruening; Sen. Frank Church, Democrat, Idaho; Sen. Thomas Kuchel, Republican, California; former territorial governor Mike Stepovich; Sen. Henry Jackson, Democrat from Washington state who was floor manager of the bill; Wally Hickel; Sen. Arthur Watkins, Republican, Utah; and Sen. Richard Neuberger, Republican, Oregon.

Describing the ceremony, one reporter wrote, "History had been made with a minimum of ceremony and no pomp." The same could be said for the ceremony that took place 3,000 miles and three time zones away in Juneau. The early-morning sun glistened on Gastineau Channel as federal judge Raymond Kelly, clad in a black robe, administered the oath of office to Egan, who put one hand on a Bible presented to his family by the First Baptist Church of Juneau.

As he raised his other hand, Egan took the oath, similar to the loyalty oaths in widespread use in that era: "I William A. Egan, do solemnly swear that I am not a member of the Communist Party or any subversive parties or affiliated with such party, that I do not believe in, am not a member of, nor do I support any organization that believes in or teaches the overthrow of the United States government by force or by any illegal or unconstitutional method, that I will defend and support the Constitution of the United States, and the Constitution of the State of Alaska, and perform all of the duties of the office or position on which I am about to enter, and therein do equal right and justice to all men, so help me God."

Egan and Wade stood in front the Alaska flag of eight stars of gold on a field of blue and a venerable forty-eight-star American flag. Wade wore a gray suit and bow tie.

Alaska's radio stations wasted no time announcing the news that Texas had become the second-largest state. It was shortly after 7 a.m. in Fairbanks and Anchorage and 6 a.m. in Nome. In Fairbanks, cab drivers honked their horns, sirens sounded, and a driver flashed his headlights at the corner of Second Avenue and Lacey Street in the six-below-zero chill. In Juneau, the Post Office opened two hours before Egan was sworn in as collectors lined up to buy the new seven-cent airmail stamp honoring Alaska. E.M. Peck of the Fleetwood Cover Service in Pleasantville, New York purchased the first sheet. Fifty temporary employees helped mail a half-million copies of the new stamp that day. It featured the Big Dipper and North Star of the Alaska flag superimposed on a map of Alaska.

Dignitaries gathered outside the federal building in Juneau to strike a replica of the Liberty Bell forty-nine times. The new governor left the building that soon would be known as the State Capitol, and went to the 20th Century Theater in downtown Juneau to address a crowd of about 800. The Juneau High School Band played "Alaska's Flag" and the Alaska National Guard posted the colors.

As the new leaders of the state walked on the curtained stage, the audience gave a standing ovation. Neva Egan wore a blue dress and jewelry made from Alaska ivory, while her son Dennis "sat on the stage with a dignity and seriousness most uncommon in an eleven-year-old boy," said writer Pat Oakes of Fairbanks. Unlike many politicians, Egan was never comfortable giving speeches. Gathering his strength for his first public pronouncement as governor, he said that almost a century had passed since the purchase of Alaska from Russia and "our apprenticeship is done."

He drew a comparison between the admission of Alaska and the launch of a satellite by the Russians one day earlier, labeling both as historic events. The satellite had been the first object to break free of earth's gravitational pull. He said Alaska now was free from territorial restrictions, proof that "Uncle Sam continues to practice what he preaches."

"We are today full members in that great Union of sovereign states," Egan said. "We shall strive to maintain and enhance this moment's glorious radiance of America's 49th star." The program planners from the Juneau Chamber of Commerce did not make room on the agenda to hear from Wade, who, in the words of one Juneau reporter, "seems destined to setting some sort of a record for being the 'silent man' of the Egan administration."

Egan and Wade took office without pay, their salaries to be set by the first Alaska Legislature, which had yet to meet. Egan didn't even have a state car. The Lincoln that had been the official vehicle for the last three territorial governors remained federal property. One published report said the Lincoln would be headed to Guam or some other federal enclave. The contents of the governor's mansion might have been removed also, but an agreement was reached to "loan" certain furnishings to the new state, and Congress later transferred title to the mansion's furniture and pots and pans.

Before Egan's illness disrupted plans for an inaugural ball, the organizers declared it would be an "Alaska formal" event. "Roughly translated," newspaperman Vern Metcalfe joked, "this means that everyone should wear a suit and tie, preferably with a shirt."

Summing up the day's events, the editors at *Jessen's Weekly* in Fairbanks proclaimed:

SATURDAY WAS GREATEST DAY
IN HISTORY OF ALASKA

The *Juneau Empire* bent the rules of English beyond all reason with a four-inch-high banner:

WE DOOD IT!

It was a momentous day in Alaska's history, but despite the headline writers' enthusiasm, the real celebration had occurred with bonfires, street parades, and parties the previous summer when Congress approved the Alaska statehood bill on June 30. That concluded a political campaign that had dominated public life in Alaska in the 1950s.

The Senate vote was the crucial decision in 1958 because Eisenhower had already signaled he would sign the statehood bill. News of the victory spread quickly to Alaska by telephone and Teletype. Bob Atwood's *Anchorage Times* had prepared a front page for a late afternoon extra edition with what would become the most famous headline in its history. The bold, black letters six and a half inches high shouted:

WE'RE IN

Sirens, fire alarms, and church bells sounded throughout Alaska, motorists honked their horns, lines formed at the bars, and people danced in the street on that summer day. In Fairbanks, Don Pearson dumped dye into the Chena River, hoping to turn it into a temporary river of gold. However, the saltwater dye transformed the water to a bright fluorescent green. "Statehood celebrants jammed Second Avenue," reporter Jack de Yonge remembered. "Conga and Bunny Hop lines snaked in and over and around bodies. City cops and military police refereed friendly fist fights and broke up the others."

In Anchorage, a bonfire burned that night on the Park Strip under the midnight sun. Anchorage resident Frank Adams said the Eisenhower proclamation in January was something like "celebrating a honeymoon years after the wedding took place. I'm happy, but I did all my celebrating when we had the bonfire. That was the real day in Alaska history."

The admission of the 49th state ended a long campaign founded on idealistic notions about the value of self-government and the democratic process. Proponents believed statehood would give Alaskans control over their destiny and end decades of federal domination. This dream of self-government led to an unusual political consensus that gained strength

Although Alaska did not become a state until January, 1959, much celebrating took place the previous June 30 when the U.S. Senate approved statehood. In Juneau, above, Alaskans ring a replica of the Liberty Bell. In Fairbanks, below, children climbed aboard a fire truck that made its way up and down city streets, its siren heralding the historic occasion.

through the 1950s. Year in and year out, Congress had rejected statehood, largely because of political calculations about how expansion of the U.S. Senate might change the balance of power there. In the summer of 1958, statehood forces prevailed, with many crediting the tireless work of Bartlett, who had sold the statehood dream as Alaska's non-voting delegate to Congress.

It was a matter of considerable resentment among some Alaskans that most people in the United States didn't know that Alaskans, as residents of a territory, paid federal income taxes and were subject to the military draft, but were denied representation in Congress. After Congress and the President endorsed the terms under which Alaska would become the 49th state, Alaska voters sealed the deal with a 5 to 1 landslide vote on August 26, 1958. The turnout was so large that many polling places had run out of ballots and had to use samples. For the first time ever, Alaskans would be able to choose their governor, elect a legislature with real power, and vote for president. When the chance to select the nation's leader came in 1960, among the 62,177 who exercised that right was 101-year-old Frank Hart of Tenakee Springs. It was only the second time he had enjoyed the privilege. Back in 1880, before moving to Alaska, he had cast a vote for James Garfield.

"Few contests in Congress in recent history have been more bipartisan," the *New York Times* concluded about the campaign to achieve Alaska statehood. The effort was bipartisan, but sharp regional divisions across the country had played a part in the political mix. Southern senators feared that Alaska's admission would weaken their ability to filibuster civil-rights legislation. Immediately after Alaska entered the Union it became apparent that the power to filibuster would not be eroded by Alaska's senators. Texas Sen. Lyndon Johnson strong-armed Alaska's first two senators and several other new senators who had opposed the filibuster to side with him on a motion that preserved what the South wanted, according to columnist Drew Pearson. Johnson won the backing of Gruening and Bartlett by offering to help them get federal funds for projects in Alaska, part of the most successful "one-man sales campaign" seen in the Senate in a decade, the columnist said.

That Johnson deemed it important to pressure the Alaskans in exchange for future favors was a sign that the state now had power that had been denied the Alaska Territory, which had no voting members in Congress for more than half of the 20th Century. From the time of the first statehood bill in 1916 to the last in 1958, Alaska had witnessed the rise and fall of large-scale gold mining; a military expansion designed to counter the Japanese and then the Soviet Union; improvements in aviation that made roadless regions more accessible; the growth of Anchorage into a community of 80,000; and the increasing recognition that Alaska's natural resources held the keys to its future.

In the Senate, both Bartlett, the former *Fairbanks Daily News-Miner* reporter who had grown up in a working-class family, and Gruening, the former editor of *The Nation*, sought the title of Alaska's "senior senator." Gruening, a New Yorker who had earned a medical degree from Harvard but who never had practiced medicine, was known as a brilliant and combative man whose life was accurately summarized in the two-word title of his autobiography, *Many Battles.*

Bartlett had been elected to Congress seven times when he entered the U.S. Senate. He knew his way around Capitol Hill and felt no need to be treated as Gruening's protégé, though he was seventeen years younger. Because neither man would give way to the other on who deserved to be the junior senator, they flipped a coin. Bartlett won. Gruening, who was nearly seventy-two, became the junior senator. The third member of the delegation was Democrat Ralph Rivers, elected to Alaska's only seat in the U.S. House.

The challenge for Alaska's new elected leaders was formidable. They had to create a state government where none existed and find a way to pay for services in a land of few roads, vast distances, limited industry, and a cost of living up to fifty percent higher than Seattle's. The lifeblood of the Alaska economy was military construction spending by the federal government, but that was in decline. There were those who thought that Alaska always would have to depend on federal largesse for survival. These burdens could have overwhelmed even the most optimistic statehood advocates, but Bartlett and others were inclined to accentuate the positives.

"I'm sure the opponents of statehood will be glad before long that Alaska is the 49th state because we have many contributions to make," Bartlett said.

Tom Stewart, a Juneau attorney who had served as secretary of the Alaska Constitutional Convention, wrote later that beyond the desire for self-government, the "meaning of statehood principally assumes the character of possibilities." Whether those possibilities ever would be achieved depended on what Alaskans would do with their rights of self-government.

Such was the backdrop at the birth of the new state, but there was hardly any time to celebrate before Egan's illness rattled residents from Ketchikan to Barrow. Two hours after he was sworn in as governor, Egan was back in Saint Ann's Hospital in Juneau. He had a four-hour surgery to remove his gall bladder three days later. From his hospital bed, Egan made good on one

Former territorial Gov. Ernest Gruening, opposite page, soon to become one of the new state's first U.S. senators, was one of thousands of Alaskans who voted by an overwhelming margin in August, 1958 to accept statehood. Sen. Bob Bartlett, above, confers with Gov. Bill Egan the following May during the formative early days of the new state.

of the central promises of the statehood campaign and signed an order against the renewal of fish traps.

Fish traps, described by opponents as "Alaska's enemy number one," had long been the most visible symbol of outside domination of Alaska. Companies in Seattle and elsewhere owned most of the traps, which were large contraptions made of logs and large nets that were so efficient catching fish that they put many fishermen out of work. It was a one-sided issue in Alaska. No politician was in favor of fish traps and candidates tried to outdo one another by being as anti-trap as possible. Few other issues would ever again seem to be so clear-cut in the new state.

Within three weeks of taking on his new job, Egan found himself on the critical list in the Seattle hospital. By the end of January the worst was over. As winter turned to spring, he regained some strength and prepared to return to Juneau.

The doctors said his incredible will to survive made a difference. He returned to Juneau in April, thirty-two pounds below his normal weight, but walking on his own. He spoke for ten minutes to the Legislature and received three standing ovations. "I can't begin to express how wonderful it is to be back in Alaska," he said. "I am no longer our ailing governor."

With Egan's recovery, the state of Alaska had survived its first crisis.

ALASKA'S DIPLOMAT

One of the 49-star flags preserved in the Alaska State Museum in Juneau once occupied a prominent place in the chambers of the U.S. Senate until the 50-star model arrived in 1960.

How the historic flag ended up in Juneau reveals something about how Sen. E.L. "Bob" Bartlett

Sen. E.L. "Bob" Bartlett presents to Gov. Bill Egan the forty-nine-star flag that was displayed in the U.S. Senate until admission of Hawaii to the Union in August 1959 required adding a fiftieth star.

solved problems and how he differed from Sen. Ernest Gruening, the other Alaskan who represented the new state in the U.S. Senate.

On July 6, 1960, Bartlett wrote to Burke Riley, an aide to Gov. Bill Egan, about a "sticky situation" regarding Gruening and the Senate's 49-star flag.

Joe Duke, the Senate's sergeant-at-arms, had asked if Bartlett would like to have the obsolete 49-star flag for the Alaska museum in Juneau.

Bartlett said yes. In the meantime, however, Gruening walked into Duke's office and asked for the flag. Duke didn't want to give Gruening the flag, but as a Senate employee he was in no position to refuse.

"Joe does not like Ernest at all, at all," Bartlett wrote in a private letter to Riley. "One of the reasons, and probably the controlling one, is that Ernest bawled Joe out unmercifully one time and another time spoke disparagingly about him on the floor of the Senate."

Gruening had gone onto the floor of the Senate a year earlier and embarrassed Duke by complaining about the lack of a 49-star flag in the Senate chambers. Duke had proposed keeping the 48-star version on display because the flag would have to be replaced the next year anyway, with the 50-star model recognizing Hawaii. While another senator might have tried to solve this quietly, Gruening turned it into a public dispute.

"Sergeant-at-Arms Duke explained to me that this flag cost $175 and that with the admission of Hawaii, a 50-star flag would be needed and that it would be economical to await the 50-star flag," Gruening told his colleagues in a speech preserved in the *Congressional Record*. "But I must register an emphatic dissent from this particular economy. Alaska is entitled to a full year's display of the 49-star flag, which Alaska's admission to the Union brought into being."

Thus rebuked, Duke purchased a new 49-star flag in August 1959 and displayed it in the Senate chambers. When it came time to retire the flag the next summer, he didn't want to do any favors for Gruening. Leave it to Bartlett, who had sharpened his skills representing Alaska for fourteen years as a non-voting delegate to Congress, to think of a way to avoid a direct confrontation and preserve the peace.

Bartlett suggested that Duke write a letter to both senators saying that he wanted to give them the flag, but that he had promised Egan months earlier that he would send the flag to the state museum in Juneau.

Then Bartlett set about to rewrite history. "I told Joe I thought this might be arranged and it would relieve the situation all around," Bartlett told Riley.

Egan was out of town, but all that was needed for the plan to work was for the governor's office to go along with the ruse. "I hope you can do this and I hope you can do it without waiting for Bill's return by back-dating a letter and sending it on to Joe and by forging Bill's name," Bartlett wrote.

Bartlett even wrote the back-dated letter, dated February 17, 1960, purporting to be a request from Egan to Duke for the Senate flag.

The deception worked. Duke had a perfect excuse to send the flag to Juneau, where it remains to this day, a testament to Bartlett's brand of diplomacy, which the senator practiced until his death in 1968.

The new state of Alaska found itself suddenly responsible for various government functions and services, including road maintenance, that previously were overseen by the federal government. In this photo, believed to have been taken in the early 1960s, a Caterpillar tractor struggles to reopen the Richardson Highway after a snowstorm closed Thompson Pass near Valdez.

CHAPTER 2
Organizing a new state government

O N THE DAY Alaska entered the Union, the federally owned Alaska Communications System (ACS) abruptly declared an end to its long-standing practice of providing a fifty percent discount on long-distance telephone and telegram service to Alaska government agencies. Alaska was now a state, and federal law required that it be treated the same as every other state, meaning no discounts. It made no difference, the Army said, that other states didn't use the system. It was a matter of treating every state the same.

Taking note of the anticipated $32,000 annual increase in telegram and telephone costs, the governor's office told state employees to adjust their telephone and telegram habits accordingly and recognize the advantages of first-class mail. "It is noted that mail sent out via four-cent postage will reach most points in Alaska within a day or two," the governor's office said.

Such was the state of communication when the first Legislature convened on January 26, 1959, called to order with the ivory gavel, made by an Eskimo artist, which had been used in every Legislature since the first territorial gathering. With the exception of the gavel and the meeting place, the new Legislature had little in common with those of the past, handcuffed as they were by Congressional restrictions.

A majority of the sixty lawmakers were freshmen, but seventeen men and three women belonged to an exclusive club they called "Omega Alpha," consisting of those who had served in both the last territorial session and

A select group of Alaskans who gathered for the 1959 legislative session, were the "omega-alpha" members who had served in both the last territorial Legislature and first state Legislature. From left, they were, front, William Beltz, Helen Fischer, Earl Hillstrand, Ralph Moody, John McNees, George McNabb, Eben Hopson, Jack Coghill, Richard Greuel; rear, Warren Taylor, Frank Peratrovich, Andrew Hope, James Nolan, James Norene, J. Earl Cooper, Dora Sweeney, Irwin Metcalf, Douglas Gray, Irene Ryan, and Alfred Owen.

Conferring at the start of the first Alaska State Legislature, above, were Sen. William Beltz of Unalakleet, Senate president; Sen. Irene Ryan of Anchorage; and Rep. Warren Taylor of Fairbanks, speaker of the House of Representatives. All three were Democrats. Their party dominated the Legislature, filling eighteen of twenty seats in the Senate and thirty-four of forty in the House.

the first state Legislature. Jack Coghill of Nenana was the only Republican member of Omega Alpha.

The territorial government had been a decentralized operation in which no one could rule with a firm hand. The territory featured more than fifty separate and independent boards, agencies, commissions, and departments. One of them, the Territorial Historical Library and Museum Commission, had not met for ten years, but this didn't seem to matter. The territorial governor appointed by the President, in the words of Ernest Gruening, who held the job for thirteen years, had "merely the power to persuade."

The Territorial Legislature typically resisted giving Gruening or any other governor more persuasive powers, so the standard practice was to create a new board or commission every time a new program came into being. R.N. DeArmond, one of Alaska's leading journalists and historians of the 20th Century, described territorial budget proposals as a "useless mess" in which agencies sometimes asked for twice as much money as they needed. That way, legislators could cut the budget requests in half and believe they were saving money.

The Alaska Constitution, written at the University of Alaska in Fairbanks in 1955-56, created a strong executive to compensate for the lack of accountability in territorial government. One writer later would observe that the constitution gave such power to the executive that it would "make a saber tooth out of Dagwood Bumstead." Egan predicted there would be "no buck-passing in this state government," given the strong powers invested in the governor. Based on the duties vested in the governor by the Alaska Constitution, *Harper's Magazine* headlined a profile of Egan, "The Most Powerful Governor in the U.S.A."

As they gathered in Juneau in 1959, legislators tried to digest a 268-page consultant's report proposing a structure for the state government. The Public Administration Service, a Chicago think tank, said eleven departments should be created with a workforce of about 2,200, roughly twice the size of the territorial bureaucracy. Nearly half of those workers would be in the highway section of the Department of Public Works. Legislators met in the plain brown office building that became the state capitol. It had none of the decorative flourishes of other state capitols, such as a gold dome or rotunda. Forty members of the House crowded into a tight space where twenty-four lawmakers had conducted their business during territorial days, leaving little room for spittoons for those who chewed tobacco.

It was a Democratic crowd, reflecting Alaska's political climate. Alaska was almost a "one-party state," historian Herman Slotnick wrote, though Richard Nixon's victory in Alaska in 1960 was the first sign that the Republicans might have a future in the 49th state. Nenana's Coghill, the youngest senator at thirty-three, was one of only two Republicans in that twenty-member body in 1959. One of his children in Juneau was eight-year-old John Jr. who would grow up to become a GOP legislator as well, serving during an era when Republicans controlled government. "You must make momentous decisions which will shape our course for years ahead," acting Governor Hugh Wade told the Legislature in the first State of the State address, filling in for the ailing Egan. "Yours is a role comparable to that of the constitutional convention and you share with that group the responsibility of 'founding fathers.'"

The largest revenue source was the income tax, which brought in $8 million annually, while the acting governor cautioned that oil revenues, expected to total $3 million, could not be counted on indefinitely. "Sustained production is needed to make this a continuing major item of future income," Wade said.

The senators chose William Beltz, forty-six, an Eskimo from Unalakleet, as president of the Senate, while Warren A. Taylor, a sixty-eight-year-old lawyer from Fairbanks, led the House. Two self-taught men, their backgrounds hardly could have been more different. Taylor had worked on the Copper River and Northwestern Railroad in 1909, served during World War I, and studied law at home. He represented Cordova in the 1930s, Kodiak in 1944, and then Fairbanks. He was the only man elected to the Legislature from three cities. While Taylor was known for an acid tongue and mastery of parliamentary procedure, Beltz used logic and a "minimum of words" to get his ideas across, a reporter wrote. He was a carpenter and union business agent who attended all eight grades in his village school. For the next two years, his grammar school teacher, who believed in his potential, tutored him at night with books that he bought.

The immediate challenge was to write state laws to implement the constitution. "This was a stupendous task," wrote Juneau attorney Mildred Hermann. "No such responsibility ever before confronted any first state legislature. It was accomplished in spite of almost overwhelming pressures from established agencies, boards, and commissions." Hers was a voice of authority, as she had been admitted to the Alaska Bar in 1934, having studied law in the office of pioneer judge James Wickersham. A key proponent of

LEGALIZING THE NENANA ICE CLASSIC

The Nenana Ice Classic, for all of its tradition as Alaska's most popular guessing game, hasn't always been legal.

In 1960, there was a brief time when police seized ice classic tickets at the printer and the state prepared to shut down the operation, setting off a crisis that prompted action by the state Legislature to keep the classic alive.

Betting on when the ice goes out long has been a spring pastime in the North. The custom took root in Dawson, where bars conducted ice pools in which patrons paid $1 a chance to guess the minute of breakup on the Yukon River.

"A ticket on an ice pool, in those early years, was usually a secondary consideration," newspaperman Stroller White wrote. "The prime object in approaching the bar was a drink."

The longest-running ice pool event began in 1917 among Alaska Railroad workers in Nenana. It evolved into a popular guessing game followed closely by Alaskans who didn't worry much about its cloudy legal status.

"Discussion of the legality of the pool in Alaska is strictly bad taste," a reporter for *Collier's* magazine wrote in 1947. "Most Alaskans try to sidestep the issue by pointing out that the mails aren't used for distribution or collection of tickets or money. The tickets are brought to Nenana in sealed cans by individuals, by train, plane, and dog teams."

For years, for legal reasons, newspapers refrained from printing details about the Nenana Ice Classic in editions that went through the U.S. mail. "You know what is available," the newspapers would say about ice-classic tickets.

A year after Alaska entered the Union, Jack Coghill, then a senator representing Nenana, co-sponsored a bill to legalize, among other things, the Nenana Ice Classic and the lower-profile Fairbanks event, the Chena Ice Classic. Coghill's bill was offered in response to an announcement by the state's new Department of Public

Safety and the attorney general that they would begin enforcing anti-gambling laws, putting an end to the ice classics and charity raffles.

The debate that followed was about how far was too far in legalizing gambling.

As the Legislature and governor considered the issue, a Methodist minister brought the question to a head. The Rev. Richard Heacock of the Juneau Methodist Church signed a complaint before the U.S. commissioner in Juneau that led to the seizure of ice-classic tickets, posters, and reporting forms.

Heacock and two policemen appeared with a warrant at the offices of Empire Printing in Juneau one afternoon and the policemen confiscated 3,000 tickets. Heacock signed the complaint, he said, because "gambling is wrong and illegal."

Meanwhile, the police chief in Fairbanks said he would hold off on a crackdown on the ice classic and bingo games until the Legislature made a decision on the gambling issue.

Fairbanks Daily News-Miner

Volunteers raise the tripod for the Nenana Ice Classic in March, 1973. It took a special act of the new state legislature to save the classic in 1960.

The situation was complicated by Governor Egan's belief that the proposed legislation went too far in allowing raffles and other gambling activities and that the door would be opened to high-stakes gambling. When the Legislature approved Coghill's bill, Egan vetoed it. The Legislature overrode the veto just twenty minutes after Egan signed the veto.

The Nenana Ice Classic was saved.

Alaska statehood, she had served as a delegate to the constitutional convention.

Lawmakers created a dozen departments to carry out the functions of state government, outlining duties for each one. Despite the state's creation of the new Department of Fish and Game, the federal government retained power to manage fish and game for the first year of statehood. That created considerable resentment, foreshadowing the arguments between the state and federal governments about control and access of resources, which would inflame a debate about subsistence hunting in the decades to come.

Some of the names of the departments have changed, but the basic structure approved in 1959 remained in place a half-century later. "By this action the first state Legislature rightly takes its place with the delegates of the Constitutional Convention who wrote and agreed upon the executive section," said Hermann, called the "Queen Mother" of the constitutional convention by some.

The first Legislature also created a court system that she believed would become a model for the rest of the country. But this long-time observer of Alaska politics wasn't totally satisfied with what happened that year. "The casual way in which almost $30 million of taxpayer money was appropriated, we found actually shocking. If there was a treasury watchdog, he slept in his kennel throughout the entire session," Hermann said.

In her view, the House needed "a couple of muzzles" for emergencies and she objected to the tendency toward "extravagant salaries." The territorial legislators had received $15 per day plus $20 per day for expenses. The first state Legislature raised that to $40 per day for expenses while in session, plus a flat annual salary of $3,000. Lawmakers also voted to allow each member to receive one first-class airline ticket to Juneau for each session and an allowance for fifty pounds of excess baggage.

Hermann believed that Jay Hammond, an independent from Naknek, had emerged after the first month as a politician with promise. Some started to call him the poet laureate of the Legislature, recognizing the tortured poetry he wrote that occasionally ended up in the state's newspapers. He made fun of other lawmakers, various state officials, and himself, offering pointed observations in poems that would have been difficult to express openly as prose. Hammond, who was to become governor fifteen years later, made an early venture into poetic politics with this offering over the $3,000 salary and $40 *per diem* spat:

Now boys, it's really outrageous,
for you to try to persuade us,
that to live in a manner not sporty,
it takes 3,000 and forty.

On that bill we just couldn't back you,
but the reason we're forced to attack you,
is really not because we're so thrifty.
Heck, we want 6,000 and fifty.

All sixty legislators ran for office the preceding year without knowing how much they would decide to pay themselves. Legislators defended the $3,000 rate, saying it was about what apprentice carpenters were making, but less than plumbers and electricians. The governor's office received 509 letters and telegrams, five of which supported the pay plan.

Fairbanks Democratic Sen. George McNabb said he had weighed the telegrams opposing the pay measure and they only weighed 9.5 ounces. "Not one working man of this state has protested," he said. Anchorage Democratic Sen. Ralph Moody said the pay rates should be high enough to attract good people to run for office. "If we have big problems to solve then we ought to have people down here with the ability to solve them," he said. Arguing for a $365 annual pay rate, Coghill said a token salary was "all we can expect from the new state." Agreeing with Coghill, Democratic Rep. Earl Hillstrand of Anchorage said that paying people money was no guarantee of integrity, courage, or dedication. "The quality the people of Alaska want and must have in the Legislature cannot be bought," he said.

However, the majority argued that low pay would mean that only wealthy Alaskans could afford to serve as legislators, or that the lower pay would open lawmakers to influence by pressure groups with money. Most Alaska newspapers attacked the pay plan, but one editor defended it. Vern Metcalfe, writing in the *Juneau Independent*, said "Even at $3,000 per year and $40 a day a man should be measured for a fright wig if he wanted to change places with the members of the 1959 legislature."

The legislative pay bill was the first law enacted by the Alaska State Legislature, an action that allowed lawmakers to collect their first paychecks after seventeen days on the job. Wade and the hospitalized Egan had to wait until March to get paid. The Legislature approved a $25,000 salary for the governor and $18,000 for the secretary of state, among the highest in the country for those positions.

Two years later, when the forecast for state revenues was decidedly more pessimistic, lawmakers cut their annual pay to $2,500 and trimmed the daily expense payments to $35, rates that remained in place until 1967. But the first session of the new state Legislature did much more than create a framework for the new Alaska government and argue about salaries.

Lawmakers changed the age of majority, so that residents would be full-fledged citizens at age nineteen instead of twenty-one. The House asked that the annual fair at Palmer be recognized as the "Official Alaska State Fair" for 1959 and the honor be given to the Tanana Valley Fair in Fairbanks for 1960. They created the Governor's Committee on Local Hire to promote hiring of residents. They appropriated $1,335 to buy three IBM typewriters, established design standards for the stars on the state flag, deciding that the background be the same shade of blue as on the American flag. They also approved a bill calling for building seasonal roads to mining prospects, using the cheapest construction methods available.

They enacted legislation allowing females to serve liquor in restaurants but prohibiting female bar employees from soliciting customers to buy drinks. Lawmakers declared their support for "Highway 97," the numerical designation for the road that some people hoped one day would extend from Fairbanks to Nome.

In an attempt to protect blind pedestrians, legislators made it unlawful for anyone except a blind person to carry "in a raised or extended position a cane or walking stick which is metallic or white in color or white tipped with red."

Beyond such specifics, broader questions about the implications of statehood in a land with few roads, little investment capital, and a tiny population spread out over hundreds of thousands of square miles, presented breathtaking challenges.

Jay Rabinowitz of Fairbanks, who served for more then thirty years on the Alaska Supreme Court as one of Alaska's most distinguished jurists, worked in Juneau under Attorney General John Rader as the state legal machinery was assembled. "Those were fantastic days," he recalled. "It is hard to convey the excitement in that office at that time. There was a whole new legal system to administer. The first legislature was busy passing bills establishing the various courts, structuring the probation office, and setting up the parole system, and we were charged with the responsibility for administering it all."

When he became a judge in 1960 in Fairbanks, the Army Air Corps veteran of World War II felt that same sense of excitement. "When I was named to the Superior Court, there had not been a criminal trial and there had been only one civil trial in the district since statehood," Rabinowitz said. "It is an amazing thing to be in a position where everything you do establishes a precedent of sorts. It makes you choose your words and actions carefully."

In the executive branch, the Department of Administration was the first cabinet-level agency to open for business. Floyd Guertin, forty-five, was sworn in a few minutes after the department was created, filling a gaping hole left in the bureaucracy when the finance chief with check-signing privileges retired.

Alaska entered the Union with a financial security blanket—a promise from the federal government for five years of grants to help smooth the way. But the grants masked the anemic economy of the state. "For the most part, its people make a living taking in each other's wash," wrote Joe Rothstein, the political editor of the *Anchorage Daily News.*

To some, it wasn't the 49th state at all. It was the "maybe" state. Maybe there would be oil lease money. Maybe the federal government would relax the rules on Bristol Bay fishing. Maybe an income tax would produce more money. Maybe tourism and mining would prosper. The statehood boosters proclaimed that good times were ahead, if only Alaska could be free to reach its potential in drilling for oil, digging coal, cutting timber, and damming rivers to generate electricity.

Statehood gave citizens a voice in determining the course of things to come, but the euphoria gave way to an attitude described by Anchorage banker Elmer Rasmuson as "a sense of awe in recognition of the great task ahead." In a 1959 analysis, the *Fairbanks Daily News-Miner* outlined what it called the "Alaska Blueprint."

"Population will double, living costs will drop because of the development of new resources, oil will be discovered, transportation will be improved and made more inexpensive, and new sources of payrolls will appear all over Alaska," the newspaper predicted. An opposing view came from the *Ketchikan Daily News*, which warned that lawmakers appeared to be trying to "loot the new state of Alaska." Editor Bud Charles said that his paper had fought statehood "to the bitter end," believing that the territory couldn't afford to pay for services that had been provided by the federal government. "Now that we have become a state, Uncle Sugar has turned over many of these heretofore federal operations with the resultant costs attached," he said.

The first few years of Alaska statehood were difficult because of the economic troubles that became obvious once the focus shifted from the campaign of getting statehood—an effort that bore some resemblance to a religious revival—to the more mundane chore of establishing a bureaucracy, writing budgets, and figuring out how to pay for it all. It took one political mindset to give speeches about civil rights and freedom and another to decide how many accountants, mechanics, and teachers should be on the payroll.

Opponents of statehood, with cold logic on their side, had argued that the territory could not afford self-government. But Congress allowed the new state to select 103 million acres of land as state property, hoping that a land grant equal to the size of California would provide the foundation for a new economy. The unprecedented land grant, however, brought with it unprecedented responsibilities.

The state had to decide what lands it wanted. This required planning, forethought, and administration. The single act that did the most to make the state a financial success was the decision by Egan's administration to select lands at Prudhoe Bay on the North Slope. Had that land not been under state control in 1968 when the largest oil field in the history of North America was discovered two miles underground, Alaska's future would have taken a decidedly different course.

Statehood did not bring immediate economic prosperity to Alaska. Wages might have been higher than those in the Lower 48, but Alaskans had to contend with what some referred to as the "FCL" or the "Fearful Cost of Living." The cost of living was as much as fifty percent higher than in Seattle.

After a little more than a year as a state, the fiscal apprehension prompted a *Wall Street Journal* article headlined:

ALASKA'S ORDEAL
Problems Pile Up Fast for
49th State as It Finishes First Year

Starting a new court system, establishing local governments, equipping schools, selecting lands, managing fish and game resources, running airports, maintaining highways and taking over other tasks from the federal government was a huge task and came at a high price. "The honeymoon is over," a legislator told the *Journal* reporter. The growing financial appetite of the new state rapidly ate into the nearly $30 million in transition money received from the federal government.

The public works commissioner referred to the difference between the need for money and supply of money as a "slight gaposis." By 1962, Egan would say, "Alaska is beset by problems as awesome as its geography." Gaposis didn't begin to describe the challenge of providing services to communities and regions spread over an area twice the size of Texas, with a total population of fewer than 250,000. The federal government remained the largest landowner and the biggest player in the economy. The feds had spent about $1 billion in Alaska during World War II and continued a military buildup after the war because Alaska was seen as a strategic center for waging the Cold War with the Soviet Union.

Yet, the trend in the early 1960s was for shrinking military construction budgets, which led to layoffs and unemployment and the first emergence of the fiscal gap. Combined with lackluster results in fishing, timber, and mining, this left Alaska with a weak economy at a time when the demands for public services were soaring. Before it went out of business, the territory had about 750 employees and a budget of $18 million. Within four years, the state budget was triple that amount and nearly 4,000 people were on the payroll.

This growth coincided with regional political divisions that had grown more pronounced, inflamed in part by the decision of *Anchorage Times* publisher Bob Atwood to campaign for moving the capital out of Juneau.

In this gloomy environment, a *Saturday Evening Post* feature in 1963 raised the question of whether the state ever would become more than "an invalid ward of the federal government." The article appeared under the shocking headline:

ALASKA
Can it survive as a state?

The *Post* reporter pondered the possibility that Alaska would be crippled by economic problems and dependent for almost everything on the federal government.

"As a territory we were spoon-fed," said Martin Underwood, a former FBI agent who became Alaska's first public safety commissioner. "Our status was second-rate, static, and demoralizing, but it was comfortable."

Opposition to statehood had centered on the question of costs and taxes, and the anti-statehood sentiment was most pronounced in Southeast Alaska. The opponents were correct in predicting that higher taxes would come with self-government. Proponents of statehood had argued that Alaska could not afford to remain a territory given the limitations and failings of government without representation.

Complaints that the new state wasn't doing enough to promote economic development were misplaced, according to Senator Bartlett, who said that everyone knew Alaska would have to endure lean financial years after statehood. "Personally, I doubt very much whether there would be any substantial inflow of capital if all taxes for new investments were wiped out across the board and even if the Legislature would provide a bonus arrangement for companies coming in," he said. "I have always thought this talk about tax rates scaring off industry to be less than sound."

The problems of attracting industry had more to do with transportation costs, lack of financing, a small population, distance from markets, and the economics of scale. It was unrealistic to think that change would happen overnight. Yet, every discussion in a public place focused on what might be done to attract new industry. In the late 1950s the forest products industry had expanded in Southeast, but as economist George Rogers noted, "Alaskan lumber mills have led very erratic existences."

"With adequate hydroelectric energy in the Southeast, production of newsprint there would be a real possibility," the federal Department of Commerce said in a 1959 handbook on Alaska's development. "In fact, one or two waterpower plants at any of several sites near cities on the seaboard would be a powerful magnet to metallurgical, paper, and other industries. Under favorable conditions, mining of certain metallic ores could greatly improve the state's economy almost overnight."

In the state's second year, a planning group reported that the needs for schools, hospitals, highways, state offices, and other facilities would overwhelm the new state and cost $325 million. "Truly, a financial crisis looms ahead," the State Planning Commission declared. To make ends meet, the Legislature authorized the revenue commission to hire a collection agency to go after outside companies that owed taxes—a token step, but a revealing one. There also was a proposal in 1961 to cut in half the expense of providing license plates by requiring just one plate per car.

The state survived its early years on a small surplus it had accumulated from oil leases and federal transition grants. The lease revenue could not be counted on to continue, and the transition grants were due to run out in 1964. Without a fresh influx of federal funds or some other breakthrough, the state would face a crippling deficit. "If we do nothing about our future, we are doomed to a slow economic death," warned George Rogers. Rogers said the state was on a "thin knife-blade edge" and had perhaps six years before the drop in military construction would be catastrophic. "If we don't develop our natural resources, we're sunk. If we do the job well, I think we'll do all right," he said.

Republicans denounced the planning commission report as unnecessarily gloomy. "It is this type of backward thinking that can deter our growth and wreck our economy," said Jack White of Anchorage, regional GOP chairman. "I suggest the entire report be dumped into the Gastineau Channel before anyone else hears about it."

A state official in Juneau told the *Wall Street Journal* in 1960 that optimism was justified based on past performance—something would come along. "Something always happens to help Alaska," he said. "Economically, you can't even justify Alaska's existence, but it's here—just like Washington, D.C."

As the financial problems worsened, some suggested that maybe statehood was a mistake after all. But it was too late to go back. As a reporter for a London newspaper had written in 1958, with considerable foresight, "The first fruit of statehood is almost certain to be disappointment for, though statehood will stimulate change and investment, it will take years to show effect."

In the early years after statehood, the economy of Southeast Alaska lived and died on timber and fishing. Later, tourism provided some diversity. This photo, taken in 1989 or 1990, shows a mill operated near Sitka by the Alaska Pulp Corp., owned by Japanese interests. The company closed the mill in 1993. The next year, the U.S. Forest Service terminated Alaska Pulp's long-term contract to harvest timber in the Tongass National Forest, an arrangement that had existed since 1953 and represented one of the first large foreign investments made by Japanese industry after World War II.

CHAPTER 3
Life on America's Last Frontier

A LASKA NEVER HAS been short of big thinkers. In 1959, Anchorage Mayor Hewitt "Hoots" Lounsbury confirmed his place among them when he predicted, "The city has a potential for being the largest metropolis in the Pacific Northwest. I can conceive it outstripping Seattle."

The mayor was closer to the mark in his prediction that Anchorage could become a "winter sports Mecca" and that the Port of Anchorage could become a major point of entry. "There is no dream that can't become a reality if the people get behind it," he said.

A visiting writer describing Anchorage in 1959 found that the most commonly heard story was of the rich capitalist who arrived two decades earlier carrying his extra shirt in a paper bag. "There's just enough truth to keep the legend alive and to keep on luring simple souls north with the dream of riches in their eyes," William Worden wrote in the *Saturday Evening Post*.

The leading 20th Century example of the man who arrived with nothing and made something of himself was a Kansas transplant named Walter J. Hickel. Two days after his twenty-first birthday in 1940, Hickel discovered he would have to wait three months for a visa and a passport to travel to Australia. Where could he go without a passport, he asked the White Steamship Company in Los Angeles. Alaska was the most attractive option, so he bought a steerage ticket from Seattle to Seward for about $40 on the S.S. *Yukon*. Hickel was nearly broke when he reached Seward, so he borrowed

THE LAND OF THE 59ERS

Few people moving to Alaska ever departed their former homes with the fanfare afforded the motley crew of Detroit residents who dubbed themselves the "59ers" and joined a motorized wagon train headed north in 1959.

With reporters watching, they left the Motor City intending to homestead in Alaska, attracted by the prospect of "free land" and the chance to escape the economic slump in Michigan. The group consisted of twelve married couples, fourteen children, three single men, and one single woman.

In 1959, Alaska had about 2,500 patented homesteads covering 327,640 acres. Most of the land had not been developed for agriculture, as the homestead program intended, or even cleared.

Referring to homesteaders who came north at about the same time as the 59ers, one author said their preconceptions centered on "idealized living by trapping, hunting, and fishing."

On the Kenai Peninsula, a 1955 study found that only ten percent of the homesteaded land was occupied by those who planned to farm and only one percent of the land was cleared for crops. Homesteading, as a general rule, didn't create a farming industry in Alaska. Most homesteads became rural residential property and the residents found other ways to make a living.

Under the federal land laws then in effect, the 59ers could homestead 160 acres, but first they had to identify the land, file papers with the federal Bureau of Land Management, and clear a portion of the land within three years.

"Success of these people is important to every Alaskan," the *Anchorage Times* editorialized. "They are symbolic of the thousands of others who want to come here and make a home. If the 59ers succeed, their venture will be a boon to the development of Alaska's population. Alaska needs people."

The 59ers pulled into Anchorage with a police escort, complete with sirens, speeches, folk dancing, and a musical performance by the Western Ramblers from Elmendorf Air Force Base featuring a song written for the occasion by Sergeant Gardner B. White Jr. to the tune of "Geisha Girl." The chorus was:

Ain't a gonna wander,
ain't a gonna roam.
Ain't a gonna look no further,
for I found myself a home.

I'll build a little cabin
that I can call my own.
I will stay forever,
in my new Alaskan home.

The city rolled out the red carpet in front of city hall. "You are the first pioneers of the new state," Anchorage Mayor Hewitt Lounsbury told the weary travelers.

The newcomers had talked of homesteading on the Kenai Peninsula, but couldn't find enough land there, so they opted instead for the Susitna Valley and settled near what is now known as Trapper Creek.

Alaskans were skeptical, noting that jobs were almost impossible to find and the dream of living on remote land and finding work nearby was not practical. A Valdez resident said that people often wrote her asking what they needed to homestead on 160 acres. "Plenty of cash," was her response. The Carpenters Union in Alaska had sent a letter the preceding year to union halls in the Lower 48 warning people not to come. "If you still insist on coming to Alaska seeking work as a carpenter we advise you to bring money and your fishing rod," the union warned. "You'll need the first to live and you'll have all the time in the world to use the second."

Of the original party, only thirteen were still in the Susitna Valley a year after their arrival. Many returned to Detroit. Others moved to Anchorage and elsewhere in Alaska. In 1971, when a *New York Times* reporter checked back, Marino and Carol Sik were among the small group who had remained. He said they agreed with the statement, "You don't have to be crazy to homestead, but it helps."

The new Parks Highway connecting Fairbanks and Anchorage went right through the couple's property. "At least now we can get out when we have to," Marino Sik said.

$10 (which he repaid the following summer). The cost of breakfast and a railroad ticket left him with thirty-seven cents. Within an hour, he had a loaf of bread, bologna, and two cents.

By the age of thirty-nine, Hickel was described in one of the many books about life in the new state as "Alaska's number one young businessman." Listening to what he called the "little man" inside him, Hickel made his fortune in construction, starting with homes and branching off into hotels, including the Travelers Inn hotels in Anchorage and Fairbanks. At the dawn of statehood, Hickel talked about his next project, a high-rise hotel to be built on Fourth Avenue in downtown Anchorage. "The Captain Cook Hotel will do credit to any city of half a million people," Hickel said. "Relatively speaking, there will be nothing like it on the American continent." However, his vision languished until after the 1964 earthquake. Hickel scoffed at the idea that downtown Anchorage should not be rebuilt in the same location because of unstable ground, arguing "you can't run from natural disaster."

Hickel told author Herb Hilscher that he saw a prosperous future for the 49th state by 2009. He didn't predict that he would serve two terms as governor, thirty years apart, or that he would be appointed U.S. interior secretary, but he did offer a forecast that oil would be as important to Alaska as it was to Calgary and Edmonton. "Before my time is up," he said, "I expect to see a billion dollars of new American capital profitably invested in the new state, a million people living here, and Anchorage truly a northern window looking out on the world."

Hickel's brand of opportunity found many ready believers in Alaska in 1959, a state on the cusp of major change. With the military buildup during World War II, Southeast Alaska was no longer the dominant region. Coastal towns in Southeast lived and died on fishing and timber, while Anchorage attracted a diverse mix of oil speculators and drillers, entrepreneurs, pilots, military personnel, construction hands, and office workers.

Tourism was in its infancy, but businessmen could see potential in Alaska's scenery. "In all of Alaska, there are less than 500 rooms with private baths," said Chuck West, who founded Westours. "This certainly isn't much when you consider that the Olympic Hotel in Seattle alone has 1,000 rooms." Travelers needed good spare tires and an adventuresome spirit to survive a trip on the unpaved Alaska Highway. The industry received its first major boost with the state's creation of the Alaska Marine Highway System in 1963, which offered an alternative route north. Backed by a statewide bond

Alaska long has attracted dreamers and doers, such as Wally Hickel, who was both. Hickel arrived in the territory in 1940, broke, after buying a steerage ticket on a steamship from Seattle to Seward. Hickel built the Captain Cook Hotel in Anchorage and later served two terms as governor and as secretary of the interior under President Richard Nixon.

issue, the *Malaspina,* the *Taku,* and the *Matanuska* soon were sailing the Inside Passage and providing new ferry access to isolated communities.

"The lumber mill just had its best year because it could ship out on the ferry," Lew Williams Jr., publisher of the *Petersburg Pilot,* told a visitor from *National Geographic* in 1964. "We even have a parking problem now. Thanks to the ferry, we can afford to bring in cars."

Juneau writer Mike Miller said the ferry system had done wonders in making Juneau and other towns in Southeast more accessible. "When the *Malaspina* made the first trip late in February 1963, every person in town not bedridden by incurable disease turned out for its 10 p.m. arrival," he said. "The outside world had come to our doorstep. We all wanted to cry— and some did," he said.

Improved access was not limited to Southeast. In the late 1950s, Alaska Airlines and other airlines advertised pressurized DC-6 service with flight times of less than six hours between Seattle and Fairbanks. Everything began to speed up in 1960. In March of that year, Pan American World Airways began flying Boeing 707 jets with a one-way fare of $99 on the Seattle-Fairbanks route. The Fairbanks runway was not long enough to handle the jet traffic, so Pan Am initially used the runway at Ladd Field, later to become Fort Wainwright. Northwest Airlines followed that summer with DC-8 jet service to Anchorage, cutting the flight time to Seattle nearly in half.

By 1963, there was talk that with the expected arrival of supersonic travel, Anchorage soon would be two and a half hours from New York City and three hours from Paris. "Our own studies have already led us to believe that Alaska holds one of the keys, if not the single most important key, to future success in the era of supersonic transport," Samuel Pryor, vice president of Pan Am, told the Anchorage Chamber of Commerce.

Environmental opposition and economic woes kept that supersonic vision from ever getting off the ground in the United States, but international air traffic from Asia and Europe did justify the notion that Anchorage wasn't a sleepy city in the most remote part of North America, but rather, as the chamber of commerce put it, the "Air Crossroads of the World." The Scandinavian Airlines System, SAS, was the first airline to use Anchorage as an international stopover, followed by Air France, KLM Royal Dutch Airlines, Japan Air Lines, and others. SAS had twenty crew members in Anchorage on a typical day and a staff of seven in the city.

THE OUTSIDE WORLD LOOKS IN

As half of the *Huntley-Brinkley Report* on NBC and one of America's leading journalists, David Brinkley was no stranger to controversy.

When he devoted a half-hour of his weekly news program, *David Brinkley's Journal* to Alaska in January 1963, he was denounced roundly by anyone who was anyone in Alaska—even before anyone in the 49th state had seen the show.

Alaskans learned from news reports that Brinkley described Alaska as the "biggest, emptiest, coldest state in the Union and quite possibly the happiest." It was a state, he reported, that had come into the Union hoping for a financial boom that had not materialized and it remained heavily dependent on military spending.

Alaska is a "place where it is cheaper to import oil from Saudi Arabia than to pump it from the ground," Brinkley said.

Brinkley's description of bad economic news was a message that didn't sit well in Alaska, the only state declared a "distressed area" in its entirety by the federal government.

Governor Egan, the state's congressional delegation, and the Alaska Chamber of Commerce protested the portrayal. Senator Bartlett called it "disjointed, prejudiced, pretty wicked, distressing in fact," while Egan said it was "grossly unfair."

Alaskans asked NBC to provide equal time for a program approved by the chamber of commerce to discuss Alaska's attractions and its potential. "I am sorry you did not like our program on Alaska," Brinkley wrote to one Lower 48 viewer who complained that the 49th state had been maligned. "Our purpose was to report both the good and the bad and that is what we did."

The TV newsman said that most of the information on the show about Alaska's economic troubles came from state officials and pointed out that other news media, such as the *Wall Street Journal*, also had reported the state's tenuous economy and its heavy dependence on the military.

Opposite: Alaska tourism received a boost with creation of the Alaska Marine Highway System and the launching of three ferries, including the *Malaspina*. Governor Egan meets Captain Reuben Jacobsen, skipper of the *Malaspina*, on the bridge of the new ferry on January 23, 1963. With the addition of more ferries the system grew to serve isolated communities on the coastline from Ketchikan to Dutch Harbor and provide regular service between Alaska and Washington state.

Above: Air service improved soon after statehood when Pan American World Airways and Northwest Airlines began offering jet service to Fairbanks and Anchorage. Regional carriers soon followed. A large crowd gathered on September 16, 1968 when Wien Consolidated inaugurated service to Barrow with a Boeing 737. The airline was founded by aviation pioneer Noel Wien in 1927 and was operated under at least seven names that include the word "Wien" until its demise in 1984.

The "air crossroads" had many dusty streets that had yet to be paved and most of those who lived along them had arrived after 1945. Anchorage had six percent of the population in 1939. Two decades later, nearly four out of ten Alaskans called it home. E. J. Kahn Jr., visiting Alaska during the infancy of statehood, wrote a profile of Alaska for the *New Yorker* headlined "The Ethnocentrics," reporting "by and large, the people who live in Anchorage are delighted with their town."

"Anchorage has television," another visitor wrote. "When it comes to listing all the conveniences of American life, young wives who grew up in the states say their new home is not the same. But for sheer atmosphere, where else is there a Garden of Eatin' restaurant in a Quonset hut?"

The physical isolation of Alaska meant higher costs for transportation and communications, both of which fostered a culture that remained apart in some ways from the American mainstream. Making a phone call to the Lower 48 was not attempted without good reason. A three-minute call from Fairbanks to New York cost $9 in 1959, the equivalent of $65 in 2008 dollars. But progress was coming. That year, for the first time, callers in Anchorage and Fairbanks could connect with the Lower 48 by using just one long-distance operator instead of two. The new equipment installed that year sliced the connection time to seconds, according to the Army-owned Alaska Communications System.

The National Geographic Society suggested that states far removed from Alaska should be referred to as the "contiguous 48 states," but the simpler term Lower 48 caught on instead. The federal General Services Administration offered "Aaa" as an abbreviation for Alaska, but that would sound, the *Washington Post* said, "like the death cry of a mountain goat." The U.S. Post Office told people not to abbreviate Alaska, as the potential for confusion with Alabama was too great in a time before zip codes had been introduced.

Trying to describe this vast landscape, Vide Bartlett, wife of Senator Bartlett, said it was a land attracting people who thought only of progress and the future. "Alaska is the last frontier where airplanes have replaced the dog team and children learn to fly before they learn to drive," she said.

A national advertising agency sent a delegation north to investigate conditions in Alaska. The ad men returned to headquarters with word that Anchorage was about the same size as Reno in 1959, but would be as important as Denver by 1978, with a population of 725,000.

Mayor George Byer, who would make headlines with an attempt to force recalcitrant Anchorage City Council members to wear suits and ties to meetings, had played a key role in winning "All-America City" honors from

Look magazine. "I picked up *Look* magazine and saw pictures of the All-America Cities. I said Anchorage could have that. So I tried to get the clubs and organizations interested. And they said Anchorage could never become that. So I took it on myself."

In the All-America City, when workers cleared the site for construction of the sixteen-story Westward Hotel, they found a secret subterranean concrete room, the hiding place for illegal booze stored behind George Valaer's bathhouse during prohibition. Dozens of empty jugs in the cache gave off an aroma of old liquor. Elsewhere, Anchorage boasted a new traffic light system downtown, making it theoretically possible to go twenty-four miles per hour and stay in the green from Third to Ninth Avenue. "Anchorage is more like Los Angeles than a typical Alaskan town," writer Herb Hilscher said. "Born in 1914, it is the product of planned parenthood. Its wide streets and rectangular blocks were all laid out on a federal drawing board before a town lot was sold or a false-front building erected."

The oil discovery on the Kenai Peninsula in 1957 accelerated the development of Anchorage as a commercial center. With its first wildcat well, the Richfield Oil Company tapped into an oil reservoir that produced 900 barrels a day. A second well drilled with Standard Oil of California proved to be a commercial find as well, prompting residents of the village of Kenai to erect a sign proclaiming Kenai to be "the oil capital of Alaska."

With the emergence of Anchorage as the commercial center of the state, a controversy took shape about the official capital and where it ought to be. Bob Atwood, publisher of the *Anchorage Times*, began pushing to move the capital from Juneau to Southcentral Alaska. Atwood argued for moving the capital "closer to the people" in a relentless campaign that he continued for the rest of his life. A new capital, he believed, would move the state off "dead center" and provide the sense of vitality that he saw missing in Juneau.

Atwood blamed "Juneau's trickery" for thwarting the capital move, but others said that Atwood was showing little regard for an entire region of the state. In 1982, two years before his death, former Gov. Bill Egan wrote an angry letter to the editor that the *Anchorage Times* did not print. He criticized Atwood for spending decades trying to destroy Juneau, having perfected the "big lie" technique and ignoring the "human misery" that moving the capital would cause there.

Over the decades Alaskans voted ten times on capital-move measures, with mixed results. After two defeats, voters approved a proposal in 1974

Fairbanks Daily News-Miner

As economic and political power slowly shifted from Southeast to Southcentral Alaska after World War II, tensions developed between the two regions in part due to unrelenting editorial campaigns by *Anchorage Times* publisher Bob Atwood, who fought unsuccessfully to move the capital from Juneau, above. In 1982, two years before his death, former Governor Egan wrote an angry letter to the editor that the *Times* did not print. In it, Egan accused Atwood of perfecting the "big lie" technique in his capital-move campaigns.

to move the capital, with a restriction that it could not be within thirty miles of Fairbanks or Anchorage. Yet, in the years that followed voters rejected measures to pay for a capital move, as arguments continued about the cost.

Time and again, Alaska voters thought the issue had been decided once and for all, but bills to move the Legislature or the capital continue to be introduced, beginning the divisive debate once more.

Over the past five decades, two of the most significant changes regarding life in Alaska have been improvements in transportation and communication. If together they have not yet led to the "death of distance" in Alaska, then they have managed to make the nation's largest state seem smaller than it once was. Alaskans watch the same twenty-four-hour news and entertainment channels as their Lower 48 cousins and they no longer dread picking up the phone for a long-distance phone call or worry about talking for more than three minutes.

In 1983, the four time zones in Alaska were reconfigured so that every major settlement in the state was placed in the same time zone. While some argued that this was like synchronizing clocks in Boston and Denver, most Alaskans appreciated the notion of being an hour closer to the rest of the country. That the sun reaches its highest point in Anchorage at about 2 p.m. on summer days is largely unnoticed. The consolidation of time zones was aimed at uniting the state.

Regional divisions remain, inflamed at times by political battles, but the process of government is closer to the people than ever before—thanks to the electronic revolution. Though many Americans in the Lower 48 still think of Alaska as a distant land of perpetual ice and snow, residents of the 49th state see themselves as less isolated than ever. Alaska may not be part of the mainstream of American life perhaps, but it's just on the border.

Fairbanks Daily News-Miner

Despite a decline in post-war spending, the military continued to be a mainstay in the Alaska economy during its first half-century of statehood. A B-52 bomber, above, arrives at Eielson Air Force Base for a training exercise in 1987.

CHAPTER 4
Military's shifting defense strategy

P ERHAPS THE MOST dangerous moment during Alaska's first half-century of statehood, though it received little public attention at the time, occurred on October 26, 1962 during the Cuban Missile Crisis. An off-course U-2 flight from Alaska may have come close to triggering World War III.

The United States monitored Soviet aboveground nuclear tests by collecting air samples on high-altitude U-2 flights in the Arctic. Six of forty-two missions flown from Eielson Air Force Base that month picked up traces of radioactive material.

Air Force Captain Charles Maultsby left Eielson on a midnight flight to the North Pole following a new route that required celestial navigation, according to various reports of the incident. The northern lights burned bright that night and the pilot made inaccurate measurements of his location. He veered far off course northwest of Alaska and flew into Soviet air space. This could have escalated into an armed encounter at any time during the Cold War. That it happened during the tense showdown between President Kennedy and Soviet leader Nikita Khrushchev over Soviet missiles installed in Cuba increased the chance of a worldwide catastrophe.

Maultsby, an Air Force pilot for eleven years, had been shot down over Korea and spent nearly two years in a Chinese prison. He later flew with the Thunderbirds, the Air Force acrobatic team, for two years. After eight hours in the air on the U-2 flight, he figured out that he must be over the

Soviet Union when he picked up a radio station that sounded like Russian folk music.

The Russians dispatched MiG fighters to shoot down the U-2, orders that the National Security Agency intercepted. Because of the hair-trigger atmosphere created by the showdown half a world away, Alaska forces stood at Defense Condition, or DEFCON 3, a heightened state of alert. The Soviets could have assumed that B-52 bombers with nuclear weapons would follow the U-2 over Siberia.

When word of the wayward U-2 reached the Pentagon, General David Burchinal recalled that Defense Secretary Robert McNamara yelled, "This means war with the Soviet Union!" McNamara later denied the accuracy of that account, according to historians familiar with the Cuban Missile Crisis. Still, the threat of firing a deadly first shot had been real on both sides.

Two F-102A jets based at Galena on the Yukon River had taken off to find the U-2 and escort it back to safety and to keep the MiGs out of U.S. air space, according to researchers. Because of the standoff in Cuba, the U.S. jets at Galena had been armed with nuclear air-to-air missiles. Had the fighters from Galena encountered the MiGs, the individual pilots in the single-seat aircraft would have had to decide whether to use their nuclear weapons. "The critical decision about whether to use a nuclear weapon was now effectively in the hands of a pilot flying over Alaska," Scott Sagan wrote in his 1993 study, "The Limits of Safety: Organizations, Accidents, and Nuclear Weapons."

Lucky for the world, the U.S. and Soviet fighters did not clash in the skies over the Bering Strait that day.

Maultsby, who wrote an unpublished memoir before his death in 1998, declared an emergency and shut down his single engine with about twelve minutes of fuel remaining. The U-2 could glide as far as 200 miles and Maultsby tried to make the most of that capability, historian Michael Dobbs wrote.

He was at 70,000 feet and the loss of power meant that his pressure suit inflated like a balloon and almost filled the cockpit. Condensation on the inside of his faceplate made it hard to see his instrument panel.

The U-2 managed to glide back to Alaska and Maultsby landed safely at Kotzebue in northwest Alaska. He was picked up by the Air Force, flown to Eielson and then to the Strategic Air Command (SAC) headquarters in Omaha.

"One asks, Mr. President," Khrushchev wrote to Kennedy soon afterwards, "how should we regard this? What is it? A provocation? Your aircraft violates our frontier and at times as anxious as those which we are now experiencing when everything has been placed in a state of combat readiness. For an intruding American aircraft can easily be taken for a bomber with nuclear weapons and this could push us toward a fatal step—all the more so because both the United States government and Pentagon have long been saying that bombers with atomic bombs are constantly on duty in your country."

Kennedy responded that the U-2 from Eielson made a "serious navigational error" when it turned south. "I regret this incident and will see to it that every precaution is taken to prevent recurrence," Kennedy said on October 29. Commenting on the close call to his advisers, Kennedy was reported to have asked, "Why is there always some son of a bitch who doesn't get the word?" The problem, as Sagan wrote, was that no word had been given to stop the flights in the midst of the crisis.

In one sense, the incident grew out of the central role Alaska played in military affairs during the Cold War. In 1935, in one of the most quoted maxims about Alaska, Brigadier General Billy Mitchell had described it as the "most important strategic place in the world." The northern territory had become a bastion of defense because of its central location on world air routes. After the defeat of the Japanese in World War II, military spending during the Cold War touched off a construction boom that propelled the Alaska economy to new heights in the 1950s. But as Alaska entered statehood, the nature of that military effort was changing in ways that would mean reductions in the number of soldiers and airmen, which in turn would affect the civilian population that depended upon military spending for jobs.

First and foremost, the definition of the threat to be dealt with in Alaska was subject to continual revision, based on changes in technology and world politics. When the Soviets launched Sputnik in 1957, the 184-pound beeping satellite effectively destroyed assumptions about American science and national defense. Major news magazines carried advertising from Lockheed Corporation and other defense contractors in which they played up the danger of Soviet attack. The Douglas Aircraft Company, which billed itself as "the nation's partner in defense," ran ads featuring Distant Early Warning (DEW Line) radar stations in the Arctic and touting the company's role in "perfecting the system of defense needed against tomorrow's aggressors."

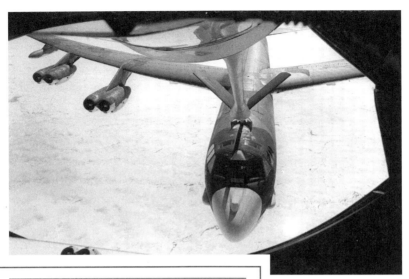

Some military historians believe an off-course surveillance flight by an Alaska-based U-2 aerial spy aircraft, similar to the one at left, may have come close to escalating the Cuban Missile Crisis into all-out war with the Soviet Union in 1962. Above, an Air Force tanker aircraft refuels a B-52 long-range bomber.

One of the regular sections of *Newsweek* magazine, "Space and the Atom," took note of how the national mood at the start of 1959 was brighter than it had been a year earlier, when a sense of panic had followed the success of Sputnik and repeated failures in the American rocket program. Three weeks before Alaska became a state, the first communications satellite was launched, carrying thirty-five-pound tape recorders that repeated a short message from President Eisenhower. "This is the President of the United States speaking. Through the marvels of scientific advance, my voice is coming to you from a satellite traveling in outer space. My message is a simple one," Ike said. "Through this unique means I convey to you and to all mankind America's wish for peace on earth and good will toward men everywhere."

The "wish for peace on earth" energized the race to space and brought with it a new role for Alaska in monitoring Russian military activities. The $600 million DEW Line across Alaska and northern Canada had been constructed to provide three or four hours of advance warning in case Russian bombers attacked from the north. That was the threat perceived in the 1950s, before missiles were added to the equation. In case the radar picked up bombers, cities could be evacuated and American jets could be directed to intercept the invaders, military planners said.

A 1957 book about the DEW Line imagined what might transpire: "Interception might come at any moment and when it does, the result will be terrifying. Imagine a bombing force of any imaginable number, loaded with every type of destructive nuclear weapon, trying to get by hundreds of jet fighters with equally destructive rocket weapons. The clash would be unbelievable in its fury."

The Russians first had detonated a hydrogen bomb 500 miles northwest of Alaska in 1954. The northern section of the DEW Line, one of the most difficult and expensive defense facilities built by the military up to that time, was declared operational on July 31, 1957, followed by the Aleutian segment in 1959.

By the end of that year, Nike surface-to-air missiles, designed to shoot down bombers, guarded the country's major cities. Missiles outside Anchorage and Fairbanks were intended to safeguard the military installations as well as cities from bomber attacks.

The Army built missile installations near Anchorage at Point Campbell, Goose Bay, and Site Summit in the Chugach Mountains. The missiles were thirty-two inches wide, twenty-seven feet long and could be equipped with nuclear weapons.

At various times during the Cold War, from 1956 to 1985, the Air Force operated more than thirty-five White Alice Communications System (WACS) sites, including this one at Cold Bay, to support Air Force operations. The system provided long-distance, high-technology defense communications. As a side benefit to Alaska, WACS brought modern communications to dozens of remote villages for the first time.

"Nike has been accepted as a permanent resident of the American neighborhood," the *Anchorage Times* declared. "People have come to know that all safety measures are used to insure the security of the public as well as that of the Nike site." In case of an enemy attack, an account in the Fairbanks newspaper said, nuclear warheads in the Nike missiles would be exploded far enough above ground that "the effect of blast, heat, and radiation on the ground would be negligible"—a false claim that went unchallenged.

By the time Alaska became a state, Pentagon planners had become far more worried about a missile attack launched with the rocket power that had propelled Sputnik into orbit. The DEW Line could detect aircraft a few hundred miles off, but it was of no use tracking missiles launched thousands of miles away. In response, the Eisenhower administration began work on the Ballistic Missile Early Warning System, which included a massive tracking station at Clear about seventy-five miles southwest of Fairbanks. "In theory," *Newsweek* said, "a Red ICBM (inter-continental ballistic missile) could be detected ten minutes after launching should the Kremlin push-button the world into a nuclear-showdown war."

In March 1959, *Time* magazine said BMEWS, pronounced "bemuse," would be a "welcome new weapon for the missile gap until more advanced systems of early warning and missile defense become available." The radar at Clear, supplemented by similar tracking facilities in Greenland and England, would scan the skies for 3,000 miles. *Time* said the "wild blue yonder" possibilities included tracking launches from space satellites and "death rays" that could make "sections of the sky impassable to missiles by the 1970s-1980s, much as they have in space fiction for years."

The tracking station at Clear, with three huge radar screens each the size of a football field and weighing more than two million pounds, would send news of a Russian attack to the North American Air Defense headquarters in Colorado Springs. The fifteen-minute warning wouldn't allow enough time to evacuate anyone in the United States, but it might be sufficient to launch a counterattack and begin an all-out war, sending hundreds or thousands of missiles and bombers on their way. This was the so-called MAD theory of "mutually assured destruction." The President, faced with news of catastrophe, would have five minutes to decide what to do. The human element was the most uncertain—no one would ever know just how the President would be able to seal the fate of the world when faced with the ultimate deadline pressure. "There are optimists in the Pentagon who argue that true missile defense, as well as brute retaliation, is possible,"

In 1959, the Air Force was building three Ballistic Missile Early Warning System (BMEWS) sites, including this one in Clear, Alaska. The system was designed to give the United States a long-range warning in the event of an incoming ballistic missile barrage launched by the Soviet Union over the polar regions.

Newsweek reported. They placed their hopes on an "anti-missile missile" (AMM) that would meet the enemy ICBM head-on and destroy it in outer space. The system was estimated to cost $6 billion.

A half-century later, Pentagon optimists remain. The Pentagon had planned to close Fort Greely, but early in the presidency of George W. Bush, the facility near Delta Junction became the major launch site for the Ballistic Missile Defense System, featuring the latest incarnation of an anti-missile missile. Promoted heavily by Alaska's Congressional delegation and the Defense Department, the system included as many as forty underground missiles that would be launched in response to a missile attack from North Korea or elsewhere.

Pentagon planners long denied that the system was intended to counter the Russians or the Chinese because those nations could overwhelm the system with a barrage of missiles. Opponents questioned the logic and cost. The Ballistic Missile Defense System remained a priority for Bush, though critics complained that it hadn't been put to rigorous tests and wouldn't work against an enemy that used simple decoys to fool the tracking equipment. Unlike earlier systems envisioned in 1959, the rockets at Greely don't contain warheads. The goal instead was to use the brute force of a direct collision in space to knock down incoming missiles, described by opponents as "hitting a bullet with a bullet."

In its first half-century of statehood, Alaska's position in military planning changed repeatedly because of the pace of technological change and the influence of Alaska's congressional delegation. What was built one day would be rebuilt the next as strategy evolved to deal with new interpretations of threats facing the United States. The construction of the BMEWS system drew praise in the Alaska press, but it was a warning system that did nothing to defend Alaska, which prompted harsh newspaper attacks, including one in the *Anchorage Times* published in 1959 under a scare headline:

OPEN TO ATTACK

The Eisenhower administration made a tentative decision to base ICBMs in the Anchorage area in 1958-59, with military planners believing that the Chugach Range provided some natural protection from a direct Soviet hit, given the difficulty of missile targeting at the time. The missiles, each with a force of up to 500 kilotons, could reach the four main Soviet bases. "There is no better place in the world to have missiles than in Alaska," the *Times* declared with enthusiasm. "It is known that the Russians have missiles on the Kamchatka Peninsula, virtually opposite Alaska. A member of Congress said that two installations have the missiles zeroed in on Alaska."

However, the Eisenhower administration was looking for ways to economize on military spending and rejected the Alaska missile plan, preferring instead to focus on a "Fortress America" concept with missiles based in the Lower 48. The Air Force eventually decided to send the missiles proposed for Alaska to NATO, the North Atlantic Treaty Organization comprised of America's World War II allies, contending that Air Force bombers could protect Alaska. One of the most outspoken critics of that idea was Air Force Lieutenant General Frank Armstrong, who warned that Alaska would be defenseless against a Soviet attack. He offered a nightmare scenario: "With the Russians in the Fairbanks and Anchorage areas, President Eisenhower would have to decide quickly whether to bomb Alaska to save Chicago or leave the country open to close range attack."

Armstrong envisioned a scenario in which two bombers could wipe out military installations at Anchorage and Fairbanks. "If these attacks were followed up with paratroop landings, Alaska itself would be lost," Armstrong claimed. The choice, if you can call it that, was between bombing Alaska and killing 50,000 to 60,000 people or allowing the Russians to bomb Chicago and killing two million. Alaska military boosters said the United States could avoid having to make that choice by putting short-range offensive nuclear missiles in Alaska to keep the Russians at bay.

Without those weapons, Armstrong believed, the American government might one day find itself having to drop nuclear bombs on Alaska to dislodge the Russians. The *Anchorage Times* took up the issue, portraying Alaska as the one place from which the United States could control the world with missiles capable of striking all the major targets in the Communist world. Echoing old arguments about the military neglect that preceded World War II, Armstrong said that the United States was moving to place missiles in the Lower 48 for political reasons. Sen. Bartlett said it was shocking to hear Armstrong's view that Alaska had a "paper defense."

Armstrong, as the chief military officer in Alaska, took a risk in opposing the Pentagon position on missiles, but he was a much-decorated war hero from World War II who had led a heavy bomber raid over Germany, dramatized in the book and movie, *Twelve O'clock High*. The political and business establishment in Alaska rose to his defense. "As he no doubt expected before making those remarks, he caught hell for it," Governor Egan said at a retirement dinner for Armstrong in 1961, "and we loved him for it."

"I recall that after reading what he had said I sent a wire to General Armstrong thanking him for his candor and his courage and assuring him that Alaskans were in his corner," Egan said. Armstrong's reply was along the lines of, "I appreciate your great interest. I may need all the help I can get."

The Joint Chiefs of Staff rejected Armstrong's views and advised him to keep quiet. The Pentagon preferred to emphasize Alaska's role as an early-warning site and to keep offensive missiles in the Lower 48. The notion that the Russians had covetous eyes on Alaska had more or less been a constant since the end of World War II, though there is no evidence that the Soviets intended to invade. The Alaskans who eagerly embraced Armstrong's claims did not consider the possibility that placing offensive missiles in the state might make Alaska a more likely Soviet target.

In the spring of 1960, the Air Force announced it would deactivate an interceptor squadron at Ladd Air Force Base, now Fort Wainwright, a move that created anxiety not only among those worried about the Soviet Union, but also among Fairbanks leaders concerned that it would cripple the local economy. Governor Egan said it was "foolhardy, if not irresponsible" to pull back one of the two fighter squadrons defending the state. The twenty-five F-89 fighters at Ladd carried missiles armed with nuclear warheads, Hanson Baldwin reported in the *New York Times* in 1962, and their removal left Alaska defended by thirty-three F-102 fighters at Elmendorf Air Force Base in Anchorage.

The fighters at Ladd could identify unknown aircraft, an essential task in Alaska given the proximity of Russia and the large number of commercial airliners and bush aircraft. Continuing on the "defenseless" argument, the *Times* said that Alaska had no fighters capable of reaching Russian bases and returning. Baldwin's report said that one advantage of increasing offensive capability in Alaska was that it would "have a strategic diversionary effect upon Soviet plans; some of the atomic 'lightning' would be attracted away from our shores by the Alaskan 'lightning rod.'"

The notion that Alaska would be a lightning rod and a more attractive Soviet target drew some attention in Alaska, but business and political leaders focused not on whether this would put the lives of every Alaskan at greater risk, but on its desirability because it would help the economy and protect the Lower 48 states. The Air Force had justified the shutdown

Worried about the possibility of Soviet long-range bomber attacks, the United States installed Nike surface-to-air missiles throughout the country, including Alaska, to defend cities and military installations. A Nike-Hercules missile, left, is test-fired at a simulated target near Eielson Air Force Base in February, 1970 while a missile sits ready for firing above.

of Ladd on grounds that improvements in missile technology were changing the nature of the Cold War. It said that four long-range Minuteman missiles in the Lower 48 could be deployed for what it cost to have one shorter-range intermediate missile in Alaska.

The *Fairbanks Daily News-Miner* said sardonically on the last day of June, 1960 that the news that the Air Force would "rub out" air defenses in Interior Alaska was "being viewed with satisfaction in Moscow." This was the second anniversary of the Senate passage of the statehood bill and the pullback would be catastrophic for the local economy, though the public comments about the opposition focused on the military implications for the nation.

The Nome Chamber of Commerce claimed the Bering Sea had become a "Russian lake" and that the U.S. government was abandoning the defense of its most remote territory. The Pentagon had concluded that the main military mission in Alaska was to provide warning of a Soviet attack. With BMEWS and the DEW Line, the Alaska radar sites were superb, the *New York Times* reported, "but the Alaskan command has no offensive capability whatsoever and no reconnaissance capability. And its defensive capabilities are badly in need of modernization."

Baldwin, the *Times* reporter, had made this argument several times over the years and also played up the idea that Anchorage and Fairbanks were the only two military targets in the state, which he compared to "stationary aircraft carriers in a sea of tundra." The only bombers in the state were the B-47s rotated through Eielson Air Force and Elmendorf Air Force Base. "These areas, and these only, will be defended," Baldwin reported. "All the rest of the military apparatus in Alaska exists for two other fundamental purposes: to provide early warning of enemy attack to the United States and to provide one 14,600-foot runway at Eielson and the necessary support for SAC's" bombers.

The Alaska Congressional delegation reacted with horror to claims that the rest of Alaska outside of the two cities would not be defended and following publication of Baldwin's article, it managed to get the secretary of defense to say U.S. forces would "defend every community, great and small, in every state." Baldwin responded in a follow-up article that most of Alaska was "physically indefensible," as the political leaders knew.

The Russians continued to fly near Alaska skies and on one occasion, flew over a corner of Southwest Alaska. This 1963 incident was followed soon after by Air Force deployment of longer-range fighters that could intercept the Soviet bombers.

Calculations about Alaska's strategic place in the world are invariably subjective. They have been influenced over the years by Senator Stevens, who served as Alaska's senior senator in Washington, D.C. for four decades. Before his career as a lawyer and Alaska politician, he flew missions for the Flying Tigers during World War II and in the Army Air Corps. Stevens once was described as being more like an ambassador than an ordinary senator. From his position on the Senate Appropriations Committee he had a greater say on the host of issues facing Alaska than any other person in history.

"No other senator fills so central a place in his state's public and economic life as Ted Stevens of Alaska," the *Almanac of American Politics* said about his place in Alaska politics. "Quite possibly, no other senator ever has."

Reporter Hedrick Smith, who covered Washington, D.C. for the *New York Times,* wrote in 1988 about a technique Stevens used to great effect many times during his decades in the Senate. The story deals with how a light infantry division ended up in Alaska in the early 1980s. The Army had decided to place one of these mobile divisions in Fort Drum, New York. "But the Army did not reckon properly on Ted Stevens, then chairman of the Senate Defense Appropriations Subcommittee, and, as a Pentagon power-game player, probably the Senate's most influential voice on military spending," Smith reported.

Stevens wanted a light infantry division for Alaska and pressed the case with Defense Secretary Caspar Weinberger in a "Dear Cap" letter. "When you examine the enclosed and realize that Alaska's votes in Congress have been consistently pro-defense, the request for consideration of Alaska as the place to deploy the light division just doesn't seem unreasonable," Stevens wrote. "Hope to see you soon."

"Within no time," Smith reported, "the Army brass was talking about the need to provide for 'theater defense,' or regional protection, of Alaska and the Aleutian chain. Somehow the Alaskan trouble spot had been omitted from the Army's original rationale for its light division."

Smith quoted Assistant Defense Secretary Larry Korb as saying, "Cap and the Army realized they couldn't tell Stevens, 'Well, you lost.' So they gave the other division to him.'"

"The whole light division thing is hilarious," Korb said, "training for hot-weather action at cold-weather bases."

The light division was deactivated in 1994. Over the years Stevens has used his clout to capture many other military prizes. When a 1995 National Intelligence Estimate on potential missile threats to the U.S. excluded Alaska and Hawaii, Stevens launched a counter-offensive about the potential for Alaska being targeted by North Korean missiles. In the end, Alaska was the only place on U.S. soil that could provide coverage to all fifty states and the missile defense complex went to Fort Greely.

From his position in the Senate, Stevens helped direct billions to his home state. While per-capita military spending in Alaska in 2008 was less than half of what it was in the 1960s, defense spending still accounted for about one out of every three federal dollars spent in Alaska. The Pentagon was spending $3 billion a year in Alaska on construction and wages for military and civilian personnel.

Alaska's strategic location and its vast training areas generally are cited as the main justifications for new or expanded military projects. Those arguments proved to be a key factor in removing Eielson Air Force Base from a base-closure list in 2006 and helped Stevens persuade the Air Force to station its most advanced fighter jets at Elmendorf Air Force Base. By the end of 2009, forty of the F-22 Raptor fighters, with a price including development costs of more than $300 million each, were expected to be based in Alaska.

During the Cold War, fighter jets based in Alaska frequently intercepted Russian bombers off the Alaska coast, but those incidents ended after the fall of the Soviet Union. In 2007, however, the Russians resumed unannounced flights in international airspace, with American fighter jets scrambling more than once a month to investigate. It was a reminder to some of the tensions from the era when the military presence in Alaska was largely a response to the Soviets.

"The issue involved today is not a Cold War issue," General Howie Chandler, commander of the Pacific Air Forces, said in 2008. "But in this day and time, you simply can't allow unidentified aircraft to run around in your airspace. So when the Russians do fly where they fly in the Arctic, without filing flight plans and without prior notice, then we have to go see what those aircraft are."

Fairbanks Daily News-Miner

A span of the remote Miles Glacier Bridge near Cordova collapsed into the Copper River after the March 27, 1964 earthquake. A temporary ramp was installed to carry traffic over the damaged span but permanent repairs were not undertaken until 2004.

CHAPTER 5
The 1964 Good Friday earthquake

K ENNETH T. PORTER of Anchorage, a surgery patient on the fifth floor of Providence Hospital, had just finished dinner when the room began to shake at 5:36 p.m. It was March 27, 1964. Porter felt a gentle roll, followed by severe jolts.

Within seconds after rising from his bed, Porter found it impossible to remain standing. The shaking seemed strong enough to tear apart the Anchorage hospital. For some reason, the words of Winston Churchill about what to do in the face of a bomb attack popped into his mind: "When your knees knock, kneel on them." In the midst of the chaos, Porter and others found reassurance from an unexpected source as plaster cracked, lights fell, and walls trembled. "Then came the cool, crisp comforting voice over the public-address system, assuring us that Providence would stand and asking all to remain calm," Porter wrote a year after the quake. "I shall always remember the effect which that unknown voice brought to us. Some would call it 'verbal sedation.'"

Outside the trembling hospital walls on that Good Friday, nothing was sedate. One of the world's strongest earthquakes struck with fury, bringing with it the worst natural disaster in the state's history. The quake registered 8.6 on the Richter scale in 1964 and later was revised upward to 9.2 by the U.S. Geological Survey (USGS).

Scientists estimated that the energy released during the quake might have been double that of the catastrophic 1906 San Francisco earthquake,

In downtown Anchorage, left, a car was crushed by heavy slabs of concrete siding that fell from the new J.C. Penney department store while a block away, above, a large section of Fourth Avenue and street-front businesses collapsed into the sinking ground. The Seward Highway at Portage, above, was one of many roads and highways left with serious damage.

perhaps equal to ten million times the force of the first atomic bomb. The shaking continued for three to four minutes in most places with a violence that knocked people to the ground, as terra firma rose and fell likes waves on a stormy sea. In downtown Anchorage, Bert Londerville remembered thinking the Westward Hotel might collapse. "I will probably always remember the screams of the people on the top floors of the hotel. It seemed as though the ground was moving in all directions—sideways, in circles, and up and down," he said.

The quake raised or lowered the earth six feet or more across an area the size of Oregon, triggering landslides and deadly tsunamis while smashing houses, twisting railroad tracks, crumbling roads, snapping trees, and tossing cars like toys. The entire planet "vibrated like a tuning fork," the USGS said. Water levels in an artesian well in Georgia rose three and a half feet. A man in Delaware reported waves in his indoor swimming pool, and the manager of the Space Needle Restaurant in Seattle felt the structure sway as if pushed by a powerful wind. G. Ray Bane, a teacher in Wainwright on Alaska's north coast, observed cracks up to two inches wide in the ground and residents in almost every community in Alaska, from Petersburg to Kotzebue, felt the ground move or saw objects swaying.

The earthquake killed 115 people in Alaska, nine of them in Anchorage, while sixteen others died from tsunamis that slammed into the Oregon and California coasts. The bodies of eighty-two victims in Alaska never were recovered. No doubt the death toll would have been much higher had the quake occurred at a different time on a different day. Most of the earth's fury was expended in unpopulated areas. It was daylight, the temperatures were not severe, few fires were started, school was out, it was not fishing season, and the canneries were not operating. Most people had their shoes on and were wearing warm clothing, allowing them to move to safety more easily.

"Had it struck at the same time of day three weeks earlier, it would have been dark, and no one without a flashlight would have been able to see to rescue children, avoid falling objects, escape from breaking and falling structures, or avoid the numerous crevasses which were opening and grinding closed in the earth," said Dr. Martha Wilson of the Alaska Native Service Hospital.

In downtown Anchorage, nearly 700 children were watching a Disney film at the Fourth Avenue Theater when the screen went black. Emergency lights went on in a minute or so. Theater manager Joe Marboe said he thought the children might have been more scared of him than of the earthquake because of the stern way he ordered them to remain seated. Geologist William Binkley was on the twelfth floor in the L Street Apartment Building when disaster struck. "The motion was so violent that I was thrown to the floor and was unable to regain my feet until it stopped." He figured that the building swayed back and forth about eight to ten feet horizontally and two feet vertically during the worst of it.

Blanche Clark had just left the new J.C. Penney in downtown Anchorage, and gotten into her car beside the north wall of the store on Fifth Avenue. She started her 1963 Chevy and was waiting for a traffic light to change so she could pull away from the curb when the car began to pitch back and forth. "I figured something had gone wrong with the mechanism of the car," she recalled. As the ground rose and fell around her, she considered driving away from the building. Within seconds, however, several tons of concrete and other debris smashed onto her car, compressing it into a pile of rubble three feet high. After the ground became still, she heard a woman say, "I wonder if there's anyone in there." Clark suffered a broken neck, arm, ribs, and punctured lung, but she was conscious and called out for help. Bystanders rounded up three wreckers, bumper jacks, and a blowtorch. It took a half-hour to free her.

Genie Chance was driving north on C Street near Ninth Avenue and thought at first she had a blowout or that a strong wind was blowing in from Cook Inlet. "Boy, it's some wind," said her thirteen-year-old son Winston, sitting next to her in the front seat. All about them, cars bounced like rubber balls.

Outside West High School, principal Les Wells, his wife Edith, and son Scott watched as the school shook "like a tablecloth after Sunday dinner." The ground moved in waves like you'd see at an ocean beach and windows popped out as if they had been hit by rifle shots.

The quake shook loose the bluff at Turnagain Heights, the first modern suburb of Anchorage, unleashing a landslide of millions of cubic yards that destroyed seventy-five homes, one of five major slides in Anchorage. Bob Atwood, who had completed one lesson on his new trumpet, had just started to practice when the chandelier in his Turnagain home began to swing and the walls swayed. The *Anchorage Times* publisher ran outside and turned back to watch as his house disappeared into huge cracks that opened in the earth all around him. He fell into a ditch, still clinging to the trumpet, and the ground began to close around him. "I remember how

In Valdez, thirty-one children and adults perished. The Alaska Hotel, left, was destroyed and U.S. Army soldiers stood guard over what was left of the devastated town. When the ground under Valdez was found to be unstable, a new townsite, above, was developed a few miles to the west by the U.S. Army Corps of Engineers. Cost of a lot: $400. Over the next four years, more than sixty buildings were moved to the new site.

reluctantly I relaxed my three fingers in the loops of the horn and withdrew my arm, leaving the horn to eternity somewhere in the Bootlegger Cove mud," he recalled later.

Outside Anchorage, the worst damage was caused by water. In Seward, about twenty minutes after the quake, a wave estimated at thirty to forty feet high engulfed the city, pushing houses, boats, and railroad cars along like pebbles in a stream. Oil storage tanks along the waterfront burst into flame. In no other town were there so many close calls.

"Residents in low-lying areas at the head of Resurrection Bay, unable to reach high ground, survived the earthquake-generated waves by climbing trees or onto rooftops seconds ahead of surging water that swept through and in many cases demolished their homes," the National Academy of Sciences wrote five years later in a landmark report on the disaster. "Families sped ahead of the waves in their cars as far as they could go, then fled on foot." The force of the rushing water wrenched a fishing boat from its moorings in the small-boat harbor and heaved it over the seawall, with two men and a woman still aboard. The water pushed the boat up onto the road, and the three ran for safety.

In Valdez, the S.S. Chena had docked and was unloading its cargo, including Easter lilies. Scientists determined later that the violent quake touched off an underwater slide in which about ninety-eight million cubic yards of material collapsed into the ocean. It was as if a massive bomb had exploded next to the ship, destroying the dock and raising the 400-foot ship above the warehouses. All but two of the seventy boats in the harbor were destroyed, but no one was aboard any of the boats. However, all twenty-eight people on the dock that afternoon died when it collapsed, including Fairbanks teacher Jim Growden, who had brought his two young boys down to the waterfront to see the freighter being unloaded. Two workers inside the Chena died when the ship rolled and the cargo shifted, crushing them.

Meanwhile, the captain of the Chena, M.D. Stewart, ran from the dining room up three decks to the bridge as soon as the tumult began. The ship rose thirty feet on a wave and smashed down where the dock had existed a moment before. "I saw people running—with no place to run to. It was just ghastly. They were just engulfed by buildings, water, mud, and everything.

The Chena dropped where the people had been. That is what has kept me awake for days," he said shortly after the disaster. As the ship continued to be tossed about, briefly touching the floor of the harbor with no water beneath it, Stewart gave orders to start the engine. The ship made it out into the bay and escaped destruction.

The force of the water propelled by the massive underwater landslide, the equivalent of forty percent of the excavation work on the Panama Canal, created waves rolling out from Valdez that splintered spruce trees with trunks two feet in diameter near Shoup Bay, 101 feet above sea level.

In Kodiak, waves washed away buildings and deposited a 131-ton crab boat about five blocks in from the waterfront. In Chenega, a village in Prince William Sound, fifty miles northeast of Seward, a seventy-foot wave killed twenty-three people. The school, which had been built ninety feet up a hillside behind the village, was about all that remained of the fishing village.

Arriving at the scene in the days following the quake, *National Geographic* writer William P. E. Graves said it was hard to see that a village once existed. "All the homes had been swept away. When the wave caught Chenega, it simply plucked it forever from sight. There are no miraculously comforting figures to Chenega's death toll. Of eighty Aleut villagers, twenty-three were lost, thirteen of them children," Graves wrote in the magazine in July 1964.

Among the survivors in Chenega and throughout Southcentral Alaska, there was grief, shock, and a resolute spirit. Tony's Bar in Kodiak told customers that "we took a little trip up the street, but we'll be back" while in Anchorage the sign outside Mac's Photo proclaimed that the store had been "closed due to early breakup." Many Alaskans displayed a generosity of spirit. Chuck Dart of Manley Hot Springs said it would be unrealistic to expect the federal government to pay for the entire recovery. "We who did not suffer should rightly expect to contribute more and expect less from the state," he said. "The Legislature will have to increase taxes and curtail less necessary expenditures. We will tighten our belts and work harder. Can we do less?"

Joseph Mraz of Fairbanks wrote to Governor Egan after the earthquake to return his $122.61 state income-tax refund. "With the recent misfortunes that have befallen the state we cannot accept this check," he said. The family had planned to remodel its home, Mraz told the governor, but the needs elsewhere in Alaska were more pressing.

In addition to unprecedented aid from the federal government, private agencies ranging from the Red Cross to the Teamsters Union, the International Brotherhood of Electrical Workers, and the employees of

Alaska Earthquake Archives/Rasmuson Library, UA Fairbanks

U.S. Geological Survey

U.S. Geological Survey

Outside of Anchorage, many communities were damaged by massive waves, fires, and ground motion. In Kodiak, left, incoming waves pushed these two fishing boats several blocks in from the harbor, leaving them high and dry. In Seward, above, a wall of water believed to be more than thirty feet high engulfed the city, scattering railroad tank cars like toys along the waterfront.

THE CHENA RIVER FLOOD

Gov. Wally Hickel encounters state Sen. John Butrovich during his inspection of flood damage.

Three years after the Good Friday Earthquake devastated Southcentral Alaska, Fairbanks had to cope with its own natural disaster—a summer flood that claimed seven lives, forced thousands to flee their homes, and caused $180 million in damages.

The culprit was an unusual series of storms that dumped several inches of rain across thousands of square miles. The remnants of Typhoon Hope left downtown Fairbanks with flood waters up to five feet deep.

Rebuilding the community was a challenge, aided by low-interest federal loans and other assistance.

The August 1967 disaster had a galvanizing effect on a community fund drive to build Fairbanks Memorial Hospital to replace Saint Joseph's Hospital, heavily damaged in the flood.

"Here's a community that's been pretty well devastated and I can't help but think that if it hadn't been for that flood, I just wonder whether that subscription drive would have been so successful," recalled Jim Meckel, who worked for the U.S. Geological Survey. "An event like that tends to put all sorts of trivial matters in their place."

Congress appropriated funds so that the Army Corps of Engineers could build a $250 million flood-control project between North Pole and Eielson. The dam and levee system is designed to protect Fairbanks from a repeat of the catastrophic flood, with four 30-ton floodgates that periodically are closed to impound water and keep it out of the city center during the times of high water.

Army engineers estimate that the flood damage prevented over the years has exceeded the money spent on the project.

International Telephone & Telegraph sent help to the state. Perhaps the smallest contribution, but one that earned a mention in the Congressional Record, came from John Loeb Beaty, a seven-year-old from Port Jefferson, New York. "I wanted to send my Easter Basket, but my daddy said the eggs would not last. I am sending you $1 instead," he wrote.

To those who worried that Alaska might not recover, Morris Reese of Anchorage wrote the newspaper to say that Alaska's resources would provide an economy for the future. "The fish are still in our oceans, the oil is still in our soil, the farm crops are still on our farms, and our wildlife is still in our forests," he noted. "Let it be said of us that we were a solid people in this, our hour of decision."

Senator Bartlett said he was distressed to hear one Alaskan—who was not from Anchorage—say that Seward and Valdez should be abandoned and the money be used to benefit his own community. "I reject that without qualification," Bartlett said. "I propose to dedicate myself to the rebuilding of Valdez and Seward and Kodiak and Anchorage and assist every other community damaged. We are citizens of one state, one Alaska."

On the night that it occurred, and for a long while afterwards, no one thought of the earthquake this way, but within a year, Senator Gruening would suggest that perhaps the disaster was a blessing in disguise. After the victims were mourned, the rubble was removed, railroad tracks were repaired, and roads rebuilt, Gruening said there would be "a better Anchorage, a more prosperous Kodiak, and a new and better located Valdez."

The reconstruction effort began almost immediately, spurred by unprecedented assistance from the federal government, which spent $326 million, a figure that came close to the sum of all damages. "There is little equity in natural disaster," the National Academy of Sciences said in its report. "In the aggregate, however, Alaskans bore little in the way of losses. Inflows of federal funds exceeded some of the loss estimates."

Almost no one had earthquake insurance. Local insurance agents had written $4,811 worth of earthquake coverage in 1963 in Anchorage, compared to $5 million worth of fire coverage.

The Alaska economy depended on the federal government before the quake, when a large portion of its infrastructure was in operating condition, so it was not hard to understand why the state might become even more dependent afterward. The Alaska Railroad, major highways in the region, port facilities, utilities, airports, water and sewer systems, electrical lines, and other essentials needed prompt attention to avoid further calamity.

"It is true that never before has a disaster had such a terrific impact on so much of a state's economy," said Bartlett. "Never before has the productive capacity of a state been so impaired by the violence of nature."

President Lyndon Johnson declared Southcentral Alaska a disaster area and immediately set up a system for a coordinated federal response, with the Army, Air Force, and National Guard working closely with civilian authorities. Writing in 2006 about failures of the federal response to Hurricane Katrina, the administrator who had coordinated the earthquake response in 1964 said the Alaska approach was a model that should have been followed in New Orleans.

Dwight Ink, an official with the Atomic Energy Commission, directed the federal response in Alaska, which was made urgent by the fear that unless much of the damage was repaired during the summer of 1964, tens of thousands of Alaskans would leave the state, further crippling an economy that already was weak. Johnson assigned most of his cabinet members to work with Ink on a commission chaired by New Mexico Sen. Clinton Anderson.

Ink said that because of the short construction season in Alaska, the response in 1964 had to be fast. It was the most complex federal response to a U.S. disaster in the years between the 1906 San Francisco earthquake and the devastation caused by Hurricane Katrina in 2005. "Had we been required to follow existing agency processes, we could not have completed our mission in time to save the viability of pre-oil Alaska or avoid half the population abandoning the state," Ink said.

The government moved Valdez to a new townsite four miles from the old town, rebuilt Alaska Railroad facilities in Seward and elsewhere along the system, repaired roads, replaced bridges, and instituted some post-earthquake planning. Fishermen and homeowners qualified for low-interest loans.

The work continued through the winter of 1964-65 and for the first time, contractors began to see that using Visqueen to shelter a construction site from the elements, there was no reason to shut down construction in October. The extension of the northern construction season might be one of the foremost benefits of the reconstruction effort, a 1966 study by the Office of Civil Defense concluded.

Murray Morgan, a Seattle historian and journalist, visited Anchorage a year after the quake. He observed that while from the air the broken and

Fairbanks Daily News-Miner

Senators Ernest Gruening, left, and Bob Bartlett, center, inspected earthquake damage with Edward McDermott, federal director of emergency planning from Washington, D.C. The federal government spent $326 million in a massive reconstruction effort. It was an unspeakable thought in March, 1964, given the extensive loss of life and heavy property damage, but within a year, Gruening would suggest that perhaps the disaster was a blessing in disguise.

twisted heaps of earth from the Turnagain slide remained in plain sight, other signs of the catastrophe were less visible because everyone was rebuilding. "What can there be but praise for the spirit of a community which, shaken by the most severe earthquake in modern times, has not only picked itself up but carries on as if nothing unusual has happened?" Morgan wrote in the *Seattle Post-Intelligencer*.

In the rush to restore Anchorage to the way it was before the earthquake, there was considerable controversy over proposed new rules on rebuilding that were intended to lessen hazards from future quakes. Property owners, business leaders, and politicians resisted following the advice of geologists to designate a large area in Anchorage as "high risk," arguing that only land that actually had been damaged should carry that damning label. New office buildings and other structures complied with the building codes required by the city, but as one analyst put it, "It doesn't matter how well you engineered a building. If the soil gives way underneath it, there is going to be a problem."

A review taken nearly two decades after the earthquake showed that most of the recommendations for "hazards mitigation" were not followed in Anchorage. Over the decades some forty buildings were built on what the geologists said were potentially hazardous sites.

When Wally Hickel announced plans to build the Captain Cook Hotel downtown, he disregarded the advice of some geologists. He said Anchorage was in the same position that San Francisco had been in 1906 after the earthquake and fire. "We are going to build back right where we are. All it will take is some soil analysis and some intelligent engineering," he said. A study on urban planning in Anchorage in 1970 concluded that architects had proposed plans for the central business district of the city to take quake risks into account, but "private interest often prevailed over the public interest and sound planning considerations. The long-range economic effect that had been evaluated in the preparation of the plans was ignored in favor of the immediate expediency of reconstruction using old and outmoded methods."

Alaska is one of the most seismically active places in the world. There is no question, scientists say, that other serious quakes will occur. But no one knows when. The geologists and seismologists who look at earthquake hazards see the risk differently than the developers who stand to profit by developing projects and who say they are following building codes and that the risk is minimal.

In 1967, Anchorage established Earthquake Park when the jagged chunks of what had been an exclusive neighborhood were vivid evidence of the power unleashed during those frightening few minutes in 1964. With the passage of time, the edges of the debris have lost their sharpness and the evidence of the unbelievable destruction that occurred that day no longer is in clear focus, just as the sharpest memories of one of the world's great earthquakes have faded.

In the fall of 1970, Interior Secretary Wally Hickel met with leaders of the Alaska Native land claims movement at his office in Washington, D.C. The land claims fight was one of the issues dominating Alaska politics. Clockwise, from left, are Hickel; Tim Wallis, president of the Fairbanks Native Association; Charles (Etok) Edwardsen, executive director of the Arctic Slope Native Association; former state Sen. Eben Hopson, Barrow; Emil Notti; attorney Barry Jackson (standing); state Sen. Willie Hensley, Kotzebue; Alfred Ketzler, Nenana; Barbara Trigg, Nome; unknown; Delois Ketzler; Harvey Samuelson, Dillingham; George Miller, Kenai; unknown; state Sen. Ray Christensen, Bethel (far right); Frank Degnan, Unalakleet; Moses Paukan; Morris Thompson; and John Borbridge (back to camera)

CHAPTER 6
Statehood lands in question

I F THE PROPONENTS and opponents of Alaska statehood in the 1950s agreed on anything, it was that the land was the key to whether the state would become a viable entity. They differed on just how much land was enough, however.

Alaskans always have predicted a brighter tomorrow and assumed that oil, gold, other minerals, farmland, timber, and other resources would be more than enough to create a strong economy. But no one knew exactly how much land was enough. Opponents of statehood, by raising the specter of financial ruin, helped create a political climate that allowed a far more generous land settlement from Congress than might have been the case a decade earlier or a decade later.

The statehood land grant was a reflection of prevailing attitudes during the late 1950s. It was fortunate that statehood was not delayed another decade. It's impossible to imagine the state getting anywhere close to 104 million acres of land in the political environment of the 1970s, when the drive to keep land off limits to development gained a national following. By the mid 1970s, the environmental movement had reached the point where Interior Secretary Cecil Andrus would say, "In Alaska, we must not fumble away our last chance to do it right the first time."

The final version of the Alaska Statehood Act provided a land grant larger than the size of the state of California. To select its land on a consistent basis, Alaska would have had to select an area larger than Rhode Island every ten weeks for a quarter-century. This was an enormous task requiring much study and analysis of the available "vacant, unappropriated, and unreserved" lands to determine which ought to be left in federal hands. The federal Bureau of Land Management surveyed only 2.8 million acres a year in the entire country in the 1950s, but Alaska alone would require four million acres a year to finish the job in twenty-five years.

A *New York Times* reporter offered this hypothetical job description for the ideal land boss to oversee one of the biggest real-estate transactions in history:

WANTED: A CRYSTAL BALL GAZER.
Twenty-five years steady employment
guaranteed for right man. His application must be
accompanied by evidence of near-perfect record.

The state land transfers that were supposed to take a quarter-century will take more than a half-century, largely due to the complexities of surveying and the jurisdictional arguments that have dominated politics in Alaska. The statehood act led to a freeze of federal land, halting major land transactions for more than five years. That led to the forty-four-million-acre Alaska Native Land Claims Settlement Act in 1971, which in turn led to the 104-million-acre Alaska National Interest Lands Conservation Act (ANILCA) of 1980.

Given the slow pace of land transfers and an announcement by the BLM in 2001 that the process would continue until 2020, Congress approved the ironically named "Alaska Land Transfer Acceleration Act" in 2004, with the goal of completing the carving up of Alaska in time for the fiftieth anniversary of statehood in 2009.

However, as BLM puts it, the "acceleration act" did not relieve the agency of the need to conduct "time consuming and expensive surveys," so it would not be finished in 2009. The goal is to convey 94 percent of the Native lands and 96 percent of state lands by the start of 2010.

This process began with one of the first bills approved by the first Alaska Legislature, a measure establishing a Department of Natural Resources to handle land matters. The state selected its first land on Sitkalidak Island, near Kodiak. State officials charged with making the decisions wanted land that would produce money for the state as soon as possible. "We don't want mountains and glaciers and the available land is greatly limited in other respects," Phil Holdsworth, the first commissioner of natural resources, said in 1959.

The *Anchorage Times* asserted that much of the land in Alaska was worthless, suggesting that with twenty-five years to complete selections, there was no need to rush.

Meanwhile, there was a growing consciousness among Alaska Natives about their unresolved land rights, which had been recognized in federal law for nearly a century, but never defined. For Alaska Natives, the twenty-five-year deadline for state land selections loomed as a threat to their heritage. The prospect that lands they traditionally had used for subsistence purposes soon might be taken away inspired a Native-rights movement that led to the formation of the Alaska Federation of Natives in 1966, a statewide group that symbolized the emergence of a new force in Alaska politics.

In a paper about Native land rights he wrote for a college class at the University of Alaska, Willie Hensley of Kotzebue, studying under Justice Jay Rabinowitz of the Alaska Supreme Court, wrote that "a controversy of immense proportions is rapidly coming to a head in Alaska." Native organizations were part of the organized resistance to a pair of mega-projects that they foresaw as cultural and ecological disasters—the proposed Rampart Dam on the Yukon River and Project Chariot, a scheme to use nuclear explosions to blast a new harbor near Cape Thompson on the northwest coast.

Alaska's newspapers and the political and business establishments supported both the Rampart Dam and the atomic harbor as economic-development projects, but those who valued Alaska's wild places above all else and a growing number of Native leaders raised questions about safety, economics, and a myriad of threats to wildlife and humans. Both proposals joined the long list of Alaska projects that never reached the construction stage.

Edward Teller, the "father of the hydrogen bomb," was among the chief pitchmen for Project Chariot. "In retrospect, given the steadily increasing public hysteria over radiation, we should have given up without beginning," Teller wrote in his memoirs. The truth was that biologists didn't know much about the long-term effects of low-level radiation and it was not hysteria, but reasonable doubt that defeated Chariot.

Teller claimed the underground nuclear explosions posed no risk and would be an economical means of excavation for large-scale construction projects around the world. Critics said the Atomic Energy Commission simply was looking for a new place to test atomic weapons, that the supposed

State Senator Willie Hensley of Kotzebue, shown in this 1972 photograph taken in the Senate chambers, was studying constitutional law under Chief Justice Jay Rabinowitz of the Alaska Supreme Court when he wrote a paper analyzing the Native land claims issue and offering background that Native leaders needed to press the claims.

economic benefits never would be realized, and that the risks had not been evaluated.

In the post-Sputnik era, Teller won over pro-business audiences in Alaska with the alluring prospect that nearly $4 million would be spent in Alaska for nuclear excavation. He claimed, in an address in Fairbanks, that nuclear blasts could be so well controlled that the scientists could "dig a harbor in the shape of a polar bear, if desired."

"The Alaskan press threw itself into enthusiastic support of Chariot as a lucrative federal project which would put the new state on the world map," critics Paul Brooks and Joseph Foote wrote in a detailed account that explained the project to a national audience. They revealed deficiencies of the Chariot plan and contradictory statements of its proponents in a devastating April 1962 article published under the headline "The disturbing story of Project Chariot," in *Harper's Magazine*.

Opponents of the plan included several key government officials, a few members of the science faculty at the University of Alaska, and a handful of citizens.

One of the handful was Fairbanks resident Ginny Hill Wood, who compared the physicists and engineers hyping the atomic harbor to small boys with chemistry sets who were merely interested in testing their concoctions. "No one, least of all the Atomic Energy Commission, knows for certain what the results, both harmful and beneficial, will be," she said.

Opposition also came from Native villagers, who gathered in November 1961 at a conference in Barrow and concluded that the nuclear blast was a bad idea. "We the Inupiat have come together for the first time ever in all the years of our history," they said. "We had to come together in meeting from our far villages from Lower Kuskokwim to Point Barrow. We had to come from so far together for this reason. We always thought our Inupiat Paitot (homeland) was safe to be passed down to our future generations as our fathers passed down to us."

Teller's dream that underground nuclear blasts, far larger than the Hiroshima bomb, would be used like dynamite to excavate civil engineering projects never led to the building of a second Panama Canal or a first harbor at Point Thompson. Reporting on the subsequent demise of Project Chariot later in 1962, *Harper's* editor John Fischer summed up the case by saying that the project to build a "worthless harbor" would "do nobody any good, and would do harm to nearby Eskimos, Alaskan wildlife, and American taxpayers."

Opposition to enormous development projects such as Project Chariot and Rampart Dam stirred a political awakening among Alaska's Native people in the early years after statehood. Rampart Canyon, opposite page, was proposed as the site for a hydroelectric dam likened to Grand Coulee Dam in Washington state. Ardently supported by Senator Gruening, the proposed 520-foot-high dam would have created a reservoir the size of New Jersey and forced relocation of several Native villages. Gruening hoped the dam's relative low-cost power would attract industry and create new jobs. A study group, above, visited Rampart Camp near the proposed dam site while, opposite page, Army engineers explained the Rampart proposal to elders in the village of Grayling.

An unexpected legacy of Project Chariot was the Native land-rights movement that it helped to inspire.

In some ways, the battle over the Rampart Dam featured a similar combination of conflicting visions. Senator Gruening, who mentioned the Rampart Dam proposal every time he had an audience, viewed it as the future economic foundation for most of Alaska. The lowest-cost power in North America would attract industry, starting with aluminum, and mean jobs instead of joblessness for generations, he said. He saw it as a way to bring new hope to Natives who were among the most impoverished people in the United States. They could work cutting timber from the area to be flooded or on the dam construction.

Over a twenty-year period the lake behind the 530-foot dam would fill, creating a reservoir larger than the state of New Jersey. Native people would then find jobs "in the guiding, boating and fishing on the lake," Gruening said. They would have better homes, villages that would be safe from the threat of flooding, a chance to provide a better life for their children, and a way to escape from poverty.

At least twenty Native villages had moved voluntarily in the past to better locations, so it was not unreasonable to move Fort Yukon and six other villages that would be covered by the world's biggest artificial lake, Gruening believed. He said the swamps of the Yukon Flats were "one of the few really ugly areas in a land prodigal with sensational beauty," adding that from the standpoint of human habitability, the region was "about as worthless and useless an area as can be found in the path of any hydroelectric development."

Supporters said the Rampart Dam would do for Alaska what the Grand Coulee Dam did for the Northwest—help create prosperity and allow people to have better housing and living conditions. Governor Egan said the "hard realities of the coming energy gap must be faced and the problems resolved." Other dam projects were proposed for Bradley Lake on the Kenai Peninsula and the Susitna River north of Anchorage, but it would be inexcusable if Alaska had to "limp along on an insufficient supply of power because of the inability of others to make up their minds," Egan said.

The main arguments against Rampart were that the power wasn't needed, damage to wildlife would be great, and it would be a waste of federal money. The *New York Times* referred to Rampart as the "world's biggest boondoggle." Representative John Saylor, R-Pennsylvania, said it was out of the question because of the cost. "The Rampart project was announced under what could have been the spell of the aurora borealis," Saylor said.

"It would be too expensive even if it had the capacity to generate a competing display of northern lights."

Fred Stickman Sr., Alaska's most prodigious writer of letters to newspapers in the 1960s and 1970s, worried that the Rampart Dam would ruin the Yukon River. "What's the cheap electricity going to do for us? It's only going to ruin our health. We'll get heat without cutting wood. That might be good for whites, but not for us," Stickman wrote. The real issue about Rampart, in the eyes of Fairbanksan Charlie Purvis, was land ownership and Native rights. "Many Natives are only now learning what they should have been taught in school over forty years ago in preparation for U.S. citizenship," Purvis said. "This whole question of aboriginal land rights should have been settled at least two generations ago."

A 1965 *Atlantic Monthly* article critical of the project was headlined:

THE PLOT TO DROWN ALASKA

Senator Gruening responded with an article headlined:

THE PLOT TO STRANGLE ALASKA

Like Project Chariot, the ultimate rejection of the Rampart Dam was a sign of the increasing concerns about environmental consequences of development, the rights of Alaska's first residents and a growing awareness about the value of preserving wild spaces. The Alaska Conservation Society, the first statewide conservation organization, was formed in 1960 to push for creation of the Arctic National Wildlife Range, later the Arctic National Wildlife Refuge. The society fought the Rampart Dam, Project Chariot and other proposals. Ginny Wood, one of the conservation society's founders, wrote in 1957 that "Outside commercial interests are welcomed as 'developers' of the Territory," while conservationists were attacked as "intruders." An Alaska conservation group "might get further because of this," she wrote.

Just as the conservation society provided a voice for the growing environmental movement, the *Tundra Times*, published in Fairbanks and edited by Eskimo artist Howard Rock with the help at first of newspaperman Tom Snapp, grew into a powerful statewide voice for Native issues. In the first issue, Rock wrote of the pressure facing Alaska's Natives to adapt to life in the 20th Century because white men were showing great interest in

From left: Howard Rock, editor of the weekly *Tundra Times*; newspaperman Tom Snapp, and photographer Theodore Hetzel, a prominent Indian-rights activist, examine type for an issue of the *Times* at a print shop in Fairbanks. The newspaper grew into a powerful statewide voice for Native issues, including the Native claims.

Among the Native leaders who emerged in the 1960s were Joe Upicksoun, left, and Eben Hopson. Upicksoun was an outspoken leader of the Arctic Slope Native Association, which opposed the Alaska Native Claims Settlement Act of 1971. Upicksoun and other Inupiat Eskimos believed the federal settlement did not allocate enough land to allow their people to support themselves in their traditional manner. Hopson was elected to the Alaska Territorial Legislature in 1956, and then was elected to the first state Senate. He later helped found the North Slope Borough, bringing home local-government powers and taxing authority in a vast area that included the North Slope oilfields.

lands the Natives regarded as their own. "Since civilization has swept into their lives in tide-like earnestness, it has left the Eskimo, Indian, and Aleut in a bewildering state of indecision and insecurity between the seeming need for assimilation and, especially in the Eskimo areas, the desire to retain some of their cultural and traditional way of life," Rock wrote.

Nothing was more traditional than the land, which is why gaining legal title to areas that had been used over the centuries for hunting and fishing became a rallying cry. "Land that has been kind to one's ancestors and the same land that is kind to their descendants today is hard to leave, let alone give up," the *Tundra Times* declared in 1963. "We Natives should realize that we will not be able to compete fully with big business for a long time yet. Since we cannot do that now, we should try to hold on to our lands because that is the greatest insurance we can have for the well being of Native children that will come after us. Without land we can become the poorest people in the world."

There were other signs of encroaching bureaucracy that sparked Native resistance, most noticeably with acts of civil disobedience that took place in Barrow in 1961. When federal authorities began enforcing for the first time a decades-old treaty against spring duck hunting, the two arrests they made in Barrow prompted 138 villagers to show up with illegal ducks asking to be charged. The government backed down in what was known as the "Duck In."

In essence, the burgeoning Native land-rights movement collided head-on with the interests of the state government that followed the prescription of the statehood act in carving up Alaska. One of the first conflicts happened in Minto after villagers learned of plans to create a state recreational area. Villagers saw this as a threat to their way of life. "Claims were laid by the state on what the Minto people basically thought were their aboriginal hunting and fishing areas," said Morris Thompson, a Native leader who later served as president of Doyon Limited, one of the corporations set up as part of the land claims settlement. "This was the first real kind of conflict between the state of Alaska and the people of Minto and the Native community in general."

Ted Stevens, who had returned to Alaska from a job with the Interior Department in Washington, D.C., provided free legal advice to the Minto villagers. The pattern was repeated over and over in the years that followed. The Native groups described the lands they wanted and filed paperwork that found its way to the Interior Department in Washington, D.C. There, a sympathetic special assistant to the assistant secretary of the interior postponed action on them. The official, Newton Edwards, did this because he knew that if the claims were acted upon, the results would be contrary to the Natives' wishes, Don Mitchell, a leading historian of the land-claims movement, has written.

The attitude of many Native people was expressed in comments made in a 1968 hearing by Andrew Isaac, the traditional chief of Tanacross: "I saw my first white man in 1904. He was a preacher. During the course of the years I saw more white men. In the early 1940s, a highway was built near Tanacross, and white men have come on to our land more and more . . . We made our claim in 1963 because the state came in and selected our land—everything, even our village and graveyard. This is not fair. We own our land—the white man does not . . ."

By 1965, applications from Natives seeking 3.25 million acres had been placed in a "seemingly perpetual purgatory" by Newton Edwards of the Interior Department, Mitchell wrote. In what Mitchell described as an "unheralded contribution" by an "obscure career bureaucrat" to the Native claims effort, Edwards stalled the paperwork because Congress had not defined Native rights.

Two years later, overlapping Native claims had grown to cover 380 million acres, which was greater than the entire area of the state. Interior Secretary Stewart Udall put an informal freeze on state land transfers in 1966 and made it formal in 1968, saying at one point that it was necessary to hold people's "feet to the fire, or perhaps I should say to the ice," to force a resolution of the Native claims. This brought the state land-selection process to a halt. The impasse finally would be broken with discovery of oil on the North Slope.

The oil companies proposed building a pipeline across Alaska to carry oil to Valdez, where it would be loaded on tankers and delivered to refineries. But the trans-Alaska pipeline would have to cross Native lands that remained in dispute and it became clear that it never would be built until the Native land claims were settled. This created a sense of urgency that allowed the settlement dispute to receive far more attention from Congress and the President. With this dynamic added to the political mix, the question became one of national importance and in 1971 produced the most generous land settlement with Native Americans in U.S. history.

The Alaska Native Claims Settlement Act provided a land grant of forty-four million acres and payments totaling $1 billion. Just as the statehood land grant was designed to provide an economic foundation for the state, the

Native land grants were envisioned as a way to allow Natives to gain economically and to retain hunting and fishing grounds.

Addressing the AFN convention in 1980, Willie Hensley said the campaign for the land-claims settlement was a matter of survival. "I'm talking about our original goal of the survival of our tribal spirit, our languages, our culture, and our self-respect," he said.

"People can quibble about the settlement," he said in an interview eight years later. "But we actually got about as much land as we went after. We always knew Congress would have preferred to pay us a few dollars and not convey the land, but we refused to accept that."

As Senator Stevens put it during a 2003 speech to the Alaska Federation of Natives, $1 billion in 1971 would translate into more than $4 billion that year and with forty-four million acres, Alaska Natives were the largest land owners in the state, holding more land than the combined acreage of Delaware, Connecticut, Rhode Island, New Jersey, New Hampshire, Hawaii, Vermont, Maryland, and Massachusetts.

The idea that the land would go to state-chartered corporations had come from Fairbanks attorney Barry Jackson, Mitchell writes in *Take My Land, Take My Life*. The plan was to set up a flexible system that allowed Alaska Natives to escape the control of the Bureau of Indian Affairs and to gain as much freedom as possible.

The law established a dozen regional corporations within the state to manage the land and money, while a thirteenth corporation provided for Natives in the Lower 48. About 180 village corporations are active in the state. Some of the corporations have been wildly successful in the decades following approval of the Alaska Native Land Claims Settlement Act with ventures in construction, oil, tourism, mining, and defense contracting. Some have expanded far beyond the borders of Alaska in a multitude of enterprises, aided by contracting rules that Senator Stevens inserted into federal law that give Alaska Native firms advantages in bidding for government contracts not enjoyed by other minority contractors.

Stevens also inserted a provision into federal tax law that allowed many Native corporations to turn early financial losses into gains. Until the authority was repealed in 1988, the change allowed Native corporations to "sell" a loss to a profitable company. There were buyers for these losses because the profitable company used the loss to lower the amount of taxes it paid to the federal government.

The regional corporations turned the losses into about $445 million in cash, according to one estimate. The "transactions were instrumental in recapitalizing many Native corporations," Anchorage attorney James Linxwiler wrote in a paper analyzing the first thirty-five years of the settlement act.

A survey of the regional corporations and about thirty village corporations in 2006 showed total employment of 12,536 people, about one-quarter of them Alaska Native. The Native corporations created by ANCSA became a major economic force in Alaska, with 103,000 shareholders and assets of about $3.5 billion in 2008. Seven of the top ten Alaska-owned corporations are Native corporations.

"By any measure, ANCSA's business success is overwhelming," Linxwiler wrote.

Much of this success occurred in the 1990s and in the first years of this century. Two of the most successful areas were oilfield service work and in the sole-source government contracts championed by Stevens. The dollar value of these contracts with Native corporations jumped from $265 million in 2000 to $1.1 billion four years later.

Alaska Natives make up about twenty percent of the state population and while Natives have made great strides in business, the rates of alcohol abuse, suicide, imprisonment and the number of high school dropouts, remain much higher than for the population at large.

ANCSA did not bring prosperity to all Alaska Natives, but it created opportunities that otherwise would not have existed. Reflecting in 1991 on the pros and cons of the landmark settlement, Morris Thompson of Doyon, one of the regional Native corporations, said that securing title to Native land helped encourage Natives to take pride in their heritage. Thompson, the first Native American to head the Bureau of Indian Affairs, was a key leader in many aspects of life in Alaska until his death in 2000 in an airplane crash.

"The economic clout of the regional and village corporations is very helpful to us on the state and national scene," Thompson said. "When you stop and think how we were created—becoming instant businesses overnight—we didn't have a growth curve, didn't have a learning curve. I think we have a real good record."

Fairbanks Daily News-Miner

In 1969, Alaska's future as a major player in the oil industry seemed assured when the state took in a jaw-dropping $900 million in bids from oil companies for leases to explore on newly acquired state land at Prudhoe Bay. By comparison, the state's operating budget in 1968 was $112 million.

CHAPTER 7
Realizing a financial dream

D OZENS OF EXECUTIVES from ten oil companies secretly traveled aboard the "Blue Sky Special" on one of the strangest train trips of the 20th Century. It took place in the five days preceding the 1969 oil lease sale in Alaska that would signal a turning point in the state's history.

The sixty-some rail passengers covered a lot of territory on those September days, repeatedly traveling back and forth between Calgary and Edmonton, but their attention was focused not on the Alberta countryside, but on the North Slope of Alaska. They were competing for a piece of one of the greatest oil discoveries in history.

The train, leased for $10,000 a day, served as a hideout for oil executives who had taken extreme measures not to be disturbed or observed. A domed car served as a conference room to discuss strategy for the lease sale, but only on the properties for which the companies would submit a joint bid. For anything having to do with bids by individual companies, the oilmen kept to their own compartments on the fourteen-car train.

"Meals were served at staggered times to separate bidding groups; certain groups had to be isolated from one another because all ten companies were not bidding together on every lease block," wrote oil historian Jack Roderick. When an Edmonton radio station carried news of the train crisscrossing a swath of Alberta and speculation about its connection to the planned September 10 lease sale in Anchorage, the Canadian National Railway refused to talk.

Native rights activist Charlie Edwardsen organized a demonstration in front of the auditorium where the 1969 oil lease sale was held, calling attention to the unresolved Alaska Native Lands claims.

The secrecy surrounding the oil bids was extraordinary, but understandable. The largest oil field ever found in North America had been discovered on Alaska's North Slope in 1968, and each company conducted its own research and analysis of the worth of acreage that had yet to be leased. "We thought it was as secure a place for our meetings as we could get," Paul Marshall, vice president of Hamilton Brothers Oil Company, said of the oil train in interviews with reporters in Calgary.

Hamilton had a drill rig in operation north of the Prudhoe Bay discovery well, Roderick wrote. Information from the well was relayed in a secret code from an airplane circling overhead on the North Slope and transmitted to Canada where it was delivered to the men on the train.

Roderick, who provides the most authoritative account of the mystery train in his book, *Crude Dreams: A Personal History of Oil & Politics in Alaska*, said that three weeks before the sale the twenty-nine men at the drill rig were given the chance either to remain locked in at the site or go home, collecting a $1,000 bonus if they stayed. All but three of the men opted for the bonus. The rig had been covered in canvas, which cloaked its operations from companies that might be tempted to use helicopters for aerial reconnaissance, seeking clues that would reveal the subsurface geology.

The drill rig gave the Hamilton Brothers group a strategic edge, but it was not foolproof. Having made their best analysis, the oilmen left the train in Calgary. At 3 a.m. on September 10, about twenty of the executives boarded two planes at the Calgary airport and flew to Anchorage. The Hamilton Brothers jet and the Ashland Oil jet both carried duplicates of checks prepared for bids in the bonus lease sale, Roderick said, a precaution in case one of the planes didn't make it to Anchorage on time. The group bid $100 million on fifteen tracts and won ten of them at a cost of $73 million, Roderick said. Their largest bet was on land that would produce no oil, but nine were successful, justifying the bizarre chartered train.

When the jets reached Anchorage International Airport that day, it was almost as if the center of the oil world had moved to Alaska. One writer said the corporate jets at the airport outnumbered the city's taxi population. Oil-industry people filled every hotel room. The Anchorage Telephone Utility and the Alaska Communications System asked Anchorage residents to avoid calling anyone in the Lower 48 that day unless it was an emergency. Between the oil companies and the world press, thirty operators were assigned to handle the calls from twenty-eight phone lines and three pay phones.

In the late 1960s, having begun an exploration program on the North Slope following small oil-lease sales in 1964-65, the industry began having doubts after drilling numerous costly wildcat wells without finding oil in commercial quantities. Then, in 1968, Atlantic Richfield Company discovered the largest oil reserve ever found in North America. The rush was on. The discovery well, opposite page, flowed at a rate of 2,400 barrels per day. Above, roughnecks wrestle with drilling pipe at a North Slope well.

The Anchorage Petroleum Club, atop the Anchorage Westward Hotel, never had been busier. The walls featured photographs of oilrigs and the menu featured such delicacies as a Platform Sandwich (corned beef on rye) and the Wildcatter (top sirloin). During the club's early years, some joked that membership was open to those who could smell the difference between oil and alcohol. The membership rolls listed 575 names in 1969. There was only one limitation on guests—women were not allowed before 1 p.m.

The modern era of the oil industry, celebrated at the Petroleum Club and elsewhere in Anchorage, began with the Swanson River discovery in 1957 on the Kenai Peninsula. The find unleashed waves of speculation and an aggressive leasing program that helped keep the state from going bankrupt. "We'd be in a hell of a fix if it weren't for the oil excitement," pilot Bob Reeve, owner of Reeve Aleutian Airways told a reporter in 1963. "How long can we count on it bailing us out?"

That question, still asked in Alaska, seemed irrelevant during the 1969 oil frenzy. About 165 reporters, photographers, and cameramen representing eighty-one news organizations converged on Anchorage to cover the sale, with NBC anchorman David Brinkley the biggest star in the bunch. Gov. Keith Miller had gone on TV the night before to tell Alaskans, "Tomorrow we reach out to claim our birthright; we will rendezvous with our dreams."

An Oklahoma company used the occasion to announce plans for the most ambitious residential dream in Alaska history, one that dwarfed any of the repeated attempts to move the capital from Southeast to the Railbelt. "Seward's Success," it was to be called, an $800 million effort to create the first and only town in the world with a controlled climate, a "21st Century city."

Tandy Industries of Tulsa said the domed city would be made possible by Alaska's newly found oil riches and would take shape across Knik Arm northwest of Anchorage. Upwards of 10,000 people would call it home within five years, traveling to and from Anchorage in gondolas on an aerial tramway. The key building at the heart of the new city would be the twenty-story "Alaskan Petroleum Center," the boosters said. Coats and boots would not be needed, unless one wanted to travel to Anchorage, because it would always be sixty-eight degrees inside the dome.

The dream never materialized, but it symbolized new assumptions about how the lease sale money would create conditions, as one writer put it, for a "future untroubled by financial worries. There was no more

Gov. Keith Miller, above, was one of the first political leaders to propose putting aside a portion of the state's oil wealth. In a statewide TV address the day before the 1969 lease sale, Miller promised to push for an amendment to the state constitution establishing a "permanent fund" to invest a portion of future oil revenue. Miller was not immediately successful, but others took up the cause and an amendment to establish the fund was approved by voters in 1976.

enthusiastic advocate for the benefits of development than former Gov. Wally Hickel, who by then was serving his tumultuous term as interior secretary under President Richard Nixon.

Hickel had achieved national notoriety for comments such as "a tree looking at a tree doesn't do anything, but a person looking at a tree does something" and that he didn't believe in "conservation for conservation's sake." It was Hickel who had said that the North Slope's address should be "Number One Wall Street for Alaska's Future."

The Wall Street in Manhattan certainly paid attention to the lease sale, as did residents of Anchorage who watched it on TV. Elementary-school classes tuned in to see history in the making, though the young students may not have understood the fine points of the bidding process. In that age before electronic banking, the state had contracted with the Bank of America to handle investment of the receipts from the bids, which some expected to top $1 billion. The bank leased a DC-8 from United Airlines and two Alaska State Troopers were to be on board when it took off with the checks that night, aiming to reach New York before banking hours began the next day so that the money could start to collect interest.

When the doors to the Sydney Laurence Auditorium opened at 7 a.m., a long line of men holding briefcases filed inside. The oilmen and journalists walked past a demonstration organized by Native rights activist Charlie Edwardsen blasting the sale as a $2 billion robbery of Native lands. He held a sign that said "ESKIMOS OWN NORTH SLOPE." The night before the sale he had recruited young people to help him picket and he built the protest single-handedly. The demonstration, a public relations coup for Edwardsen that garnered worldwide attention, helped dramatize the point that Native land claims had yet to be settled by Congress and the state.

Inside, the bids were placed in double envelopes to preserve confidentiality. The oil executives marched in with their bids, hoping to have outguessed or outsmarted their competitors. The stage contained a large map of the North Slope marking the 179 tracts on which the world's leading oil companies would wager millions on a gamble for a big payoff.

There were excited comments and cheers at some of the high bids, topped by $72 million for four square miles. A consortium led by the Hunt Brothers outbid Phillips, Mobil, and Chevron by a paltry $164,000 for the highest-priced tract, offering $72.3 million, compared to $72.1 million. Roderick said that most oil men "still suspect that something fishy went on" because it was hard to believe the bids could come in that close. The losing bidders investigated, he said, but never proved anything improper had happened.

When the sale ended, the DC-8 took off for New York at 7:05 p.m. with a cargo of oil-company checks and assorted paperwork. The state began earning about $45,000 a day in interest beginning the next day—an amount that increased to more than $200,000 two weeks later when the balance of the winning bids reached the banks. It was the most money ever offered at a U.S. lease sale, topping the previous record by nearly fifty percent.

To preserve a competitive edge, the key companies with holdings on the North Slope had released few details about what they had found, but after the 1969 sale, they began to talk a bit. British Petroleum (BP) estimated its reserves at 4.8 billion barrels. The *Anchorage Times* declared, "It appears that all of our golden dreams will become realities and that production royalties in the years ahead will make the $900 million in lease revenues seem insignificant." The state's take was more than nine times greater than the total amount bid on all Alaska lease sales in the decade since statehood.

Some went so far as to suggest that the global balance of oil politics would shift and that the Mideast no longer would have the dominance it once did. "For the industry, it means that oil's center of gravity has shifted northward from Venezuela, Texas, and Kuwait toward the Arctic Circle," the *Washington Post* reported.

While Charlie Edwardsen protested outside the lease sale, saying that Native land rights had been trampled, officials of the Alaska Federation of Natives took a more positive outlook. "The sale portrays the true value of the land that represents the basis of the Native claims," said AFN leader Don Wright. "It is a dramatic comparison as to the reasonableness of the Natives' demand in Congress. Natives are pleased with the results of the sale and want to help the state go forward in its development."

AFN vice-president John Borbridge agreed that the dollar figures "clearly demonstrate that the demands of the Natives are not out of line."

"It also places the state in a very difficult position. It can no longer continue to minimize the substantive rights of the Natives," Borbridge told the *Tundra Times*.

The oil industry had been in Alaska in a major way since before statehood, going back to the development of the Swanson River oil field on the Kenai Peninsula and other petroleum deposits in Cook Inlet, but the massive discovery on the North Slope was unmatched in North America. And almost immediately the rhetoric about state taxation and regulation fell into a pattern that would, like the Alberta mystery train, cover the same tracks over and over: "Whether this is the last of the big-time oil spending sprees in Alaska or one of several may well depend on the action of the state lawmakers," the *Oil and Gas Journal* said. "They face a decision in tax deliberations at their next session between 'soaking the rich oil companies' for a quick cash-in or encouraging a stable long-term development of a great natural resource. Forcing the decision are proposals to increase sharply the state severance tax and jack up the royalty on future leases."

The $900 million was enough to run the state government at 1968 levels for more than four years, but nothing stayed at 1968 levels. Alaska had some catching up to do, with inadequate facilities and services and a steady chorus of demands for new services. The proceeds of the sale were so large that some feared the $900 million would be used to justify a reduction in federal funding to the state, a prospect that has been raised many times over the decades. "I have already been confronted with the comment in the Capitol that Alaska has more funds to put into its own projects now and has less need of federal support," Senator Stevens said on September 12, 1969, when he had yet to serve a full year in the Senate. "Realistically, it may complicate efforts to procure federal funds for transportation or satellite communication or any other burgeoning needs."

In the decades that followed, Stevens would become a master at securing federal funds for Alaska, often arguing that Alaska hadn't been a state long and its towns were so far apart and the cost of living was so high that it was a federal responsibility to do more, instead of less. He effectively countered the notion that Alaskans could and should pay more by using the strongest weapon at his disposal and the only weapon available to the state with the smallest delegation in Congress—the seniority system of the U.S. Senate.

As it was, Alaskans had no shortage of ideas about what to do with the $900 million, which for a moment or two seemed so large as to be inexhaustible. While some wanted to reduce property taxes, others came forth with such ideas as a monorail to the North Slope, a new capitol in front of the Mendenhall Glacier, and a repeal of the state income tax.

Flush with cash and ideas, the state budget doubled and doubled again and again in the years that followed. By the mid-1970s, "What happened to the $900 million?" became a rallying cry for grandstanding politicians who had trouble answering their own question. About two-thirds of the money went into expanding education, but that didn't stop many from making the claim that the money was wasted. There had been discussions from the start that the money should be invested and the state should try to live off the interest. This was the origin of a movement that led to the creation of the Alaska Permanent Fund in 1976.

One of the advocates of this idea—and there would be many over the years claiming a share of the credit—was Gov. Keith Miller, who told Alaskans in a televised address on the day before the 1969 lease sale that "I shall seek to amend the state constitution to establish a permanent fund for some of the proceeds from tomorrow's sale and all future sales of non-renewable petroleum and mineral resources." The amendment did not pass the Legislature, however, as the consensus in Alaska was that the need to invest in better schools, roads, and improved public services was a higher priority.

In 1976, with a state work force that had more than doubled in seven years, and the state on the verge of receiving substantial annual revenues as soon as the pipeline was completed a year later, the voters gave overwhelming approval to establishing an investment account that could not be spent on day-to-day government operations. The debate in 1976 was founded on the notion that some of the oil money from the North Slope should be put away and held in reserve to benefit Alaska after the oil was gone.

That the state found itself in the unusual position of dealing with wealth instead of poverty during most of the first half-century of statehood was more than anything else a matter of timing and good luck. The fortunate series of events began with a unique set of geological formations that allowed oil to collect in large quantities and to remain trapped at Prudhoe Bay for millions of years. "The field resulted," petroleum geologist Gill Mull once wrote, "from a one-in-a-million chance of a fortuitous combination of geological factors that took at least 360 million years to form. Similar combinations of favorable factors are not likely to occur elsewhere in northern Alaska or the offshore Beaufort Sea, but smaller individual fields are likely to be present in the area."

That the land containing the largest oil field on the continent was under state control was the result of a fortuitous combination of political factors that took several years to form. Selecting that land was perhaps the most important decision ever made by Alaska's state government. And strictly speaking, the justification given for selecting the land was to solve a bureaucratic problem, not to encourage oil exploration.

The state chose 1.4 million acres on January 13, 1964 along the coast, announcing that it would "remedy future serious title problems" on the

PRESERVING SOMETHING FOR THE FUTURE

With the memory fresh in mind of the $900 million that had been collected in the 1969 lease sale—and spent in short order—the Alaska Permanent Fund came into existence in 1976 when voters approved a constitutional amendment with the thought of saving some of the oil wealth for the future.

The simple amendment required deposit of at least twenty-five percent of the value of oil royalties received by the state.

Alaskans approved the amendment about eight months before oil began flowing in the trans-Alaska pipeline. Most agree that the fund, with a value of nearly $36 billion in 2008, succeeded in holding down government spending by reducing the amount of money available for appropriation by the Legislature.

What has yet to occur in Alaska, however, is a discussion about how the fund's assets will fit into the future economy of Alaska and whether its purpose will go beyond the payment of annual dividends.

A year before the amendment, the Legislature approved a bill to create a permanent fund, but Governor Jay Hammond vetoed it. Attorney General Avrum Gross argued that the bill violated the ban in the state constitution against "dedicated" funds. The drafters of Alaska's constitution inserted a provision against restricted funds because they worried that so much money could become tied up that the Legislature would not have the flexibility to control state finances. Still, there was strong support by Hammond and others for preserving some of the expected oil windfall.

The constitutional amendment won approval on a vote of 75,588 to 38,518. The measure contained a simple guideline about what to do with the money. The deposits would be placed in "income-producing investments," as defined by the Legislature. Regarding the earnings, it said, "All income from the permanent fund shall be deposited in the general fund unless otherwise provided by law."

That means, as Hammond explained in a newspaper column just before the 1976 vote that it is up to the Legislature to decide what happens with the earnings.

"The income from the permanent fund will be available for general appropriation by the Legislature, but the principal of the fund may not be touched," Hammond wrote.

So far, lawmakers have chosen to spend about half the earnings on the Permanent Fund Dividend program, which paid qualifying residents annual dividends topping $2,000 in the highest year. The rest of the earnings have been returned to the fund.

At first, as envisioned by Hammond, the size of each person's dividend would be determined on length of residency. But the U.S. Supreme Court agreed with attorneys Ron and Penny Zobel of Anchorage that Hammond's plan was unconstitutional.

Instead, the state adopted a plan to give the same annual payment to all residents. A one-year residency requirement was adopted in 1989.

coast. Lands director Roscoe Bell said by selecting the tidelands, the state avoided the thorny question of determining where the boundary was for surveying purposes. Under the Alaska Statehood Act, the state was given title to all lands within three miles of shore, but the coastline changed with every major storm, so federal land managers were more than happy to get rid of the legal headache of deciding where the three-mile boundary began on the North Slope. It would have taken one hundred years to do the survey work with the limited funds dedicated to the task each year.

Tom Marshall, a petroleum geologist with the Division of Mines and Minerals, had studied geological reports about the North Slope and what had been published about the Navy's exploration in the National Petroleum Reserve. He believed the land had oil potential, but state land managers concluded the best way to avoid a political fight with their federal counterparts would be to focus on the surveying nightmare presented by the shifting coastline. "We used that as a real reason to draw, precipitate the selection in the area that looked more favorable and it turned out that was a fairly good selection," Bell once said, one of the great understatements of all time.

Governor Egan's land managers sold the concept in such a way that it overcame the governor's reluctance to run afoul of those who wanted the land to remain in federal hands. Had Egan not selected the lands, Roderick says, the federal government would have offered the land in noncompetitive oil leases, which means that many individuals, some in Alaska, could have become billionaires. Noncompetitive leasing was like playing the lottery as individuals became middlemen with lease rights who hoped the oil companies would buy them out. Instead, the state retained ownership of the largest oil field found in North America and the lease rights were sold to the highest bidders, setting the stage for what Wally Hickel would call the "owner state."

"Made solely to solve an immediate bureaucratic land-title problem, Egan's decision would be the most important ever made by a public official in the history of Alaska," Roderick wrote in his book. "Soon Alaska would become the number one oil state in the nation." Two weeks after the land selection, Egan told the Legislature that Alaska's greatest problem was unemployment, but the state had just finished a "milestone year in the advancement of Alaska's petroleum industry."

The first refinery had opened, Cook Inlet had been the site of a major oil discovery, and exploration on the North Slope looked promising. "Many in the industry believe the potential of the North Slope is as great as any presently known oil-bearing province in the world," Egan said in 1964.

The preceding fall the governor had told the Alaska State Chamber of Commerce, during a "salute to the Alaska oil industry" that the state and the oil business started at about the same time in Alaska. "Have no doubt about it, you are welcome here. It is correct to say that the Alaska petroleum industry and the state of Alaska were born almost simultaneously. There is no reason why we shouldn't remain members of a close and happy family."

The state half of the happy family held North Slope lease sales in 1964 and 1965 that brought in $12 million and placed much of Prudhoe Bay under lease, with BP, Atlantic-Richfield, and Humble—the company that later would be known as Exxon—emerging as the major industry players.

Ted Armstrong, the West Coast editor of the *Oil and Gas Journal*, reflected the Alaska philosophy about oil in 1966 when he said that yesterday was tough and today was a bit better. "But tomorrow? Tomorrow, Alaska is going to be a great oil state. Within fifteen years it conceivably could be passing Kansas and Oklahoma and heading for a spot among the top three producing states," he wrote.

The industry grew with the speed of a giant cabbage in a Matanuska-Susitna Valley summer, touched off by the 1957 Richfield discovery on the Kenai Peninsula with wells tapping into oil more than two miles below the surface. That was at a time when the oil and gas potential in Cook Inlet was deemed to be the state's best hope for a secure financial future, while the promise of the North Slope remained elusive. "The North Slope, despite its lack of excitement so far, is generally expected to hold tremendous reserves," Armstrong said in 1966.

The difficulty on the North Slope was the lack of access, which meant that it was expensive to bring in drilling equipment and move to the most likely drill sites. After a half-dozen wildcat wells had failed to produce commercial quantities of oil, many in the industry began to have doubts. Oilmen believed that petroleum could be found on the North Slope, but they didn't know where. "The potential is there," one industry official said. "It's a huge basin and the dry holes to date are merely pinpricks on a vast expanse. You can't write it off."

If oil were found, the difficulty of getting it to market would be enormous. But the explorers figured they would worry about transporting oil after they discovered it. The problems of a heated and buried pipeline melting permafrost and the risks of elevating the line above ground were obvious, according to the *Oil & Gas Journal*'s 1966 report. The thinking then was that a discovery of from 200 million to 500 million barrels would be needed at a

Fairbanks Daily News-Miner

On February 10, 1969, three oil companies with oil reserves at Prudhoe Bay, seen at left in this 1970 photograph, announced plans to build a $900 million, forty-eight-inch pipeline to carry oil south to the port of Valdez. A boom mentality soon gripped Alaska as C-130 Hercules cargo planes, above, carried construction supplies twenty-four hours a day to Prudhoe Bay. The oil companies said oil would begin flowing through the pipeline by 1972. But it was not to be.

minimum to consider starting the difficult and expensive work to get it to market. "Even then," the *Journal* predicted, "producing it and moving it to market will test the ingenuity of the American petroleum industry."

In January 1966, an entire drill rig was airlifted to the North Slope from Cold Bay, requiring seventy-two flights over three weeks on a C-130 Hercules that moved 1,500 tons. The aircraft leased by Alaska Airlines made as many as four flights a day. After drilling what turned out to be a disappointing dry hole called the Susie well about sixty miles south of Prudhoe Bay, the rig was moved north for one last attempt. The optimism that had built up over the decades about the North Slope had become a jinx, with industry officials growing increasingly wary about risking more money.

"If the Prudhoe well had been dry, we were going home. It was our last shot," said Robert Anderson, chairman of Atlantic-Richfield. Drilling began in April 1967 on Prudhoe Bay State Number One. One of its early visitors was Gov. Wally Hickel, the Anchorage hotel man who had beaten Egan in the governor's race the preceding fall.

Hickel went to the North Slope on May 2 with an entourage of oil people, state officials, and two reporters. Pilot Neil Bergt of Interior Airways flew the DC-3, chartered by ARCO, around the abandoned Susie well where ARCO had spent several million on an empty hole more than two miles deep. "I don't know why everyone's so interested in that dry hole," ARCO executive Harry Jamison said. "I'm trying to forget it."

Reporter Lael Morgan wrote that as Bergt flew close to the Prudhoe Bay well, the sight of the drill rig above the tundra was enough to prompt the passengers to change the subject. She said everyone on the plane was optimistic that this would be the well that would strike oil. "There'll be oil for Christmas," predicted a man from Humble. "Or how about by the time the Legislature starts," said Hickel. He had campaigned on the idea of "opening up Alaska" and wanted to build a railroad and a road to the North Slope.

While visiting the muddy drill site that day, where the temperature was thirty-six degrees, Hickel toured the operation and ate steak, French fries and salad for lunch, following it up with a piece of cake, and a game of shuffleboard with the off-duty rig crew. He reminisced about working for fifty cents an hour on a well back in Kansas and how the men would dip their coveralls into water so they would freeze and become windproof. The governor, who had said he wanted everyone in his cabinet to be a salesman, believed in positive thinking. He predicted the North Slope drilling operation would hit oil. "I'll be back when the well comes in," he said. "And there was

Fairbanks Daily News-Miner

Gov. Wally Hickel and his wife, Ermalee, greet President Richard Nixon and the First Lady, Pat, at the Hickels' home in Anchorage on September 27, 1971. Nixon and Hickel were all smiles although less than a year before, Nixon had fired Hickel as his interior secretary after Hickel wrote the President a letter critical of Nixon's Vietnam War policy.

a general feeling that trip might be made in the near future," Morgan added in her report.

It was on his return flight aboard the DC-3 that Hickel proclaimed the North Slope had forty billion barrels of oil, a bombastic remark that would have struck most people as outlandish, given the history of exploration failures. But when cold weather returned that fall and drilling resumed after the summer break, the rig struck natural gas and oil right about Christmas, the first solid evidence of an improbable discovery that later would make Hickel's outrageous prediction sound almost conservative.

Gill Mull of Exxon said the natural-gas fireball that lit up the long winter night "sounded like the roar of a nearby jet plane." As Hickel had wished, there was oil by the time the 1968 Legislature gathered in Juneau. The first public pronouncements were cautious, but as Senator Bartlett put it in March, "My information is that the oil men who are informed, conservative as they are, look upon this as one of the great North American strikes." A confirmation well drilled seven miles away that spring and summer established the richness of the prospect, the largest oil field ever found in North America and the 18th largest in the world.

A boom psychology gripped Alaska in 1968-1969, especially in Fairbanks, where the airport was far busier than it ever had been and C-130 Hercules cargo planes flew round-the-clock with tons of freight for the North Slope. "We have enough contracts and requests on hand to keep five Hercules flying twenty-four hours a day, all winter long," said Burton Atwood of Alaska Airlines, which had five cargo planes flying. Interior Airways had six Hercules flying 45,000-pound loads up to six times a day.

Interior Airways, which later was forced to reorganize under the bankruptcy laws when the boom collapsed, grew from a force of nine pilots in 1967 to seventy-six in 1969. The Fairbanks airport handled 1,000 tons of cargo in May 1968 and 17,000 tons in May 1969.

On February 10, 1969, BP, ARCO, and Exxon announced plans to build a $900 million, forty-eight-inch pipeline to Valdez. The oil companies formed the Trans-Alaska Pipeline System, a consortium later replaced by the Alyeska Pipeline Service Company. The oil would be flowing south by 1972, the companies announced.

Other proposals for shipping the oil attracted public attention, such as the idea of General Dynamics to construct a fleet of 900-foot-long submarines to carry 1.2 million barrels of oil under the Arctic Ocean ice, or the plan to use ice-breaking tankers in the Northwest Passage, or the talk of flying the oil out in giant twelve-engine jets. But the pipeline across Alaska was the industry choice, as opposed to a pipeline route through Canada that would have offered less expensive transportation by avoiding having to move the oil in tankers.

On the day in 1969 when the lease sale netted $900 million for the state, a ship carrying the first load of imported pipe from Japan neared the port of Valdez. Construction was expected to begin at any time.

However, environmental objections and the long-delayed issue of Alaska Native land claims stopped the project cold. It would be five years before pipeline construction began.

Fairbanks Daily News-Miner

Caribou wander under an above-ground section of the trans-Alaska Pipeline. Initially, the oil companies planned to build the line almost completely under ground in what some critics characterized as a "build it now, fix it later" approach. However, after federal intervention and additional engineering studies, it was decided to build approximately half of the pipeline above ground to avoid problems related to permafrost and unstable soil.

CHAPTER 8
The trans-Alaska pipeline

S ENATOR ALAN CRANSTON, a California Democrat, was a late arrival
on the floor of the U.S. Senate on July 17, 1973. In his absence, an
amendment sponsored by Alaska Sen. Mike Gravel to limit court challenges
to the proposed trans-Alaska pipeline had scraped through on a 49-48 vote.
But Cranston joined the anti-Gravel forces and tried to keep the vote from
becoming binding, resulting in a 49-49 tie.

As the tally took place, Vice President Spiro Agnew moved into the
president's chair in the Senate chambers and at its conclusion, he announced,
"The vice president votes yeah." The tie-breaking vote, only his second as
vice president, came less than three months before Agnew resigned in
disgrace over charges of tax evasion and taking illegal kickbacks. Agnew's
vote helped clear the way for construction of the trans-Alaska pipeline
beginning in 1974.

During the more than four years that followed the 1969 announcement
of plans to build the pipeline from Prudhoe Bay to Valdez, opponents raised
a series of legal and political obstacles that kept 800 miles of Japanese pipe
stockpiled in Valdez, Fairbanks, and Prudhoe Bay. The appointment of Wally
Hickel as interior secretary by Nixon did not lead to the immediate action
on the pipeline that many of his supporters in Alaska had hoped.

Bill Egan, elected for a third time as governor in 1970, blamed Hickel for
not allowing the pipeline to proceed, as did many business leaders in Alaska
who witnessed the oil boom collapse that followed the exuberance of the

Fairbanks Daily News-Miner

After several years of delay, during which Congress settled Alaska's Native land claims, construction of the pipeline began in 1974. Sen. Mike Gravel, opposite page, later posed triumphantly on a section of pipe north of Fairbanks. Not everyone was so enthusiastic. In Fairbanks, a student, above, examines a display of 48-inch pipe, on which someone had spray-painted "sellout." Some worried that the pipeline would harm the environment and alter the traditional independent Alaska lifestyle.

$900 million oil lease sale and the inflated expectations in towns across the state. Unemployment and business losses took a heavy toll in Alaska. "His failure to act at a critical time precipitated the greatest crisis in our business life—bankruptcy," said Jim Magoffin, founder of Interior Airways, the Fairbanks company that flew thousands of tons of freight to the North Slope before everything came to a halt.

Hickel, who served as interior secretary for twenty-two months before Nixon fired him, found himself trying to balance the demands of environmentalists with those who wanted immediate action. He said repeatedly he would not allow the project to go ahead until he was sure it could be done without harm to the environment. He was relying in part on the advice of government scientists who said that the oil companies were slow to adapt their plans to the realities of building on permafrost.

"They're talking about burying a pipeline carrying 180-degree oil in permafrost and you can't be sure of the safety of a thing like that," Bill Pecora, director of the U.S. Geological Survey, said in 1970. "When you melt ice you have ten percent shrinkage, a compaction. You simply can't bury the pipeline in those conditions. It would shift and sag and very probably break."

Pecora and other federal officials balked at what some saw as a "build it now, fix it later" attitude. They said that the oil companies had ordered the pipe and decided on a plan for a buried pipeline before applying for a permit to cross federal lands. "They didn't do anything inherently improper, just backwards," Pecora said.

The federal intervention and the call for more investigation did lead the oil companies to see the problems with burying the pipeline in permafrost. In later years, everyone involved agreed that it made sense to elevate about half of the pipeline over unstable soil, a precaution against sagging and breaking. The oil companies would contend that the first design of the pipeline would have been revised without government intervention as the engineers delved into the problems and refined the pipeline plan. Critics doubted that reasoning.

After Nixon sent Hickel packing in 1970, the next interior secretary predicted more delays. "We are going to do everything we can to protect the environment, and I'm a long way from deciding that this pipeline is the way to do it," Interior Secretary Rogers C. B. Morton told Congress on February 19, 1971.

Two newspaper advertisements from that time reveal the gulf that separated the oil companies and the growing environmental movement. "Will a pipeline ruin their arctic?" a 1971 Alyeska ad asked in the *Wall Street Journal*. It featured a photo of two caribou. The answer was "no."

"On this you have our pledge: The environmental disturbances will be avoided where possible, held to a minimum where unavoidable, and restored to the fullest practicable extent. And we can assure you that the pipeline will be the most carefully engineered and constructed crude oil pipeline in the world."

The Friends of the Earth, headed by David Brower, published a full-page ad in the *New York Times* on February 17, 1971 saying that Prudhoe Bay oil should be left in the ground until the country really needed it. "Rest assured," the group said, "if oil is pumped out at Prudhoe Bay and then shipped down the West Coast, we will, eventually, have an oil spill leading to the greatest kill of living things in history."

Meanwhile, many Alaskans blamed environmentalists and Lower 48 politicians for the pipeline postponement. This gave rise to bumper stickers that said, "Let the Bastards Freeze in the Dark," "We don't give a damn how they do it Outside," and "Sierra Go Home." Later, when the pipeline was well underway, a new one appeared—"Happiness is 10,000 Okies Going South with a Texan under Each Arm."

As State Sen. Bob Blodgett, known as the "Heller from Teller," declared in 1970, "In Canada, you don't find conservationists messing with economic development. I'm sick of hearing from people in the United States who've made garbage cans of their own states. All those do-gooders and bug-hunters and bird-watchers can mind their own damn business."

The Native land claims debate, environmental lawsuits, and the long federal regulatory process kept the project on ice until the fall of 1973. Nixon signed the authorization act just as the Arab oil embargo that grew out of the Yom Kippur war with Israel led to long gas lines across the nation.

As he signed the bill, Nixon said it was the first step to making the United States self-sufficient for its energy supplies by 1980. He gave the four pens he used to sign the bill to Stevens, Gravel, Alaska Rep. Don Young, and the widow of Bill Pecora.

Some called the battle over the project an environmental holy war. Supporters of the pipeline agreed with Bill Egan, who echoed an oil company analogy that the ramifications were no greater than "taking a pencil and

At its peak, the pipeline construction project employed 28,000 workers, mostly non-residents, many of whom worked twelve-hour shifts, seven days a week. On the opposite page, crews bury pipe on a hillside just north of Fairbanks. The pipeline crosses the Tazlina River, above, 113 miles north of Valdez, on a cable suspension bridge.

drawing a line over a large land." The conservationists responded that a pencil line across the face of the Mona Lisa was more like it.

In the end, the economic and political pressure brought to bear by the oil industry, the state, the federal government, and those in Alaska who saw the project as the opportunity of a lifetime overcame appeals for preservation of the wilderness.

That winter, even before the federal government issued the right-of-way permit on January 23, 1974, the oil companies were moving as fast as they could, announcing that oil would flow in 1977. In the three-and-a-half years that followed, wartime allusions became common metaphors for what was unfolding across the 800-mile swath of Alaska.

"This thing has to be viewed almost like the Normandy invasion," Ed Patton, president of Alyeska, told author Robert Douglas Mead. "There was a whole lot more materiel than they needed. You knew you had to get those guys there and you knew that once you'd committed yourself to that invasion, you had to go whole hog—to save as many lives as you could. You had to get your foothold and you had to expand this foothold, and then you had to go into a mature operation of winding up the war."

The invading army appeared in a vast fleet of yellow trucks, the color of choice for every Alyeska vehicle. When it became clear that the new vehicles were too obvious, the pipeline company ordered replacements in any color except yellow. Anyone who lived through the pipeline "war" remembers that claims of waste and inefficiency soon seeped into the public consciousness. Tales of workers who spent days on buses playing cards became legendary.

Some Alyeska officials were more inclined to blame workers for the problems. An ARCO official wrote that he was shocked and dismayed "that never have so many done so little for so much." Another ARCO executive said it was not fair to blame the unions.

"Many of the abuses that have been charged to the unions, such as too many men on the job and doing nothing, or sitting in buses playing cards, or not working because of weather, buses delaying to get to camps or work sites, or stopping at bars before reaching the camp site, or performing work in a sloppy manner, or the large number of welds that are rejected without remedial action taken, are principally the result of the contractors' failure to exercise their managerial supervision and enforcing the necessary contract positions with the workers," said V.R. D'Alessandro of ARCO.

Frank Moolin, the no-nonsense pipeline construction boss, said the project was like an assembly line in reverse, but it was difficult to get every

The 800-mile pipeline crossed more than 800 rivers and streams and three mountain passes. A finished section of pipe is seen in the approach to the south fork of the Koyukuk River.

part moving at the right speed. "If one thing is missing, that whole crew sits on its ass and you go out there and you see hundreds of guys sprawled around," he said.

The North Slope haul road, later named for Jim Dalton, who had worked for decades to develop the petroleum potential of northern Alaska, was built over six months in 1974. A year later, when the estimated pipeline cost had risen to $6.4 billion, workers began installing the pipe. As thousands of construction workers flooded union halls in Alaska looking for work, the words "pipeline impact" entered the lexicon of Alaskans. The term and the staggering statistics, with a peak employment of more than 28,000, didn't begin to convey the real consequences of the biggest boom in the state's history.

While the United States endured its worst recession since World War II in the mid-1970s, Alaska enjoyed more prosperity than many people could handle. With the delay in the project, Alaska's cities hadn't done much to prepare, yet realistically it wouldn't have made sense to make major expenditures to deal with a massive and short-term influx of transient workers.

It became almost impossible to get a dial tone in Fairbanks, the electric utilities worried about brownouts, crime was out of control, and the streets were jammed. About 50,000 people lived in the city and every service was near the breaking point. A two-bedroom Fairbanks rooming house where as many as forty-five people lived, most of them awaiting work on the pipeline, was an extreme example of how bad the rental shortage had become. "I enjoyed the company of some interesting people while bunking with five other human sardines in that ex-living room," said Len Will, who left his cramped quarters for a job on the North Slope.

Alyeska spent millions of dollars a day, but in a big organization, smaller amounts sometimes proved more troublesome. Such was the case on August 26, 1974 when C's Motel in Delta evicted twenty workers because Alyeska hadn't paid its bills. Other Richardson Highway motels were threatening to do the same, so Frank Moolin asked his superiors to send someone directly to businesses who could write checks on the spot for up to $5,000. *All-Alaska Weekly* editor Tom Snapp, one of the state's most flamboyant journalists, captured one aspect of the era in a memorable headline:

FAIRBANKS BECOMES WILD CITY,
Prostitution Up 5,000 Per Cent

The world's oldest profession became so visible on the streets of Fairbanks and Anchorage that a move to legalize prostitution gathered momentum in Anchorage and in the Legislature. An Anchorage commission said it should be legalized and regulated, while the Fairbanks City Council took a different route, approving a measure for a mandatory sixty-day jail term for anyone convicted of the crime. Passage of this ordinance reportedly prompted twenty-five prostitutes to leave Fairbanks and join the 200 or so working in the state's largest city.

Fairbanks journalist Ben Harding, writing in 1976, said that although the community had been split over the desirability of a pipeline, most people were wholeheartedly in favor of the money it would bring. "Even so, local businessmen could be, in private, as disdainful of the quality of the pipeline effort as the most vehement environmentalist," he said. "And the first thing that supporters of a trans-Alaska natural gas pipeline have to assure the Fairbanks public is that a gas line would be different from the oil line."

The pipeline was such a massive endeavor of people, money, machinery, and bureaucracy that it disrupted every facet of life. "It seems that Alaska is not so much in a state of transition as trauma," Gov. Jay Hammond said in 1975. "No matter what aspect of the state one considers, something of major or even catastrophic significance seems imminent. Alaska isn't transitioning, it is transcending from its rather slumberous past and literally leaping into a national and international maelstrom of change that encircles our globe today."

Hammond, who always seemed as if he'd rather be flying his bush plane or hunting, beat Egan in a close 1974 election. Hammond supporters saw him as an advocate of "slow growth," but his opponents derided him as a "no-growther" who specialized in gloom and doom. When Hickel, who lost to Hammond in 1974 and 1978, declared himself to be a "practical environmentalist," Hammond claimed the mantle of "practical developer." The *Anchorage Times* dismissed Hammond as a mediocre legislator who wrote poetry and was charming, but had no leadership qualities and filled his administration with do-nothing dreamers.

Along with *Anchorage Times* publisher Bob Atwood, one of Hammond's most strident opponents was Jesse Carr, head of Teamsters Union Local 959, who commanded an empire that some said made him the most powerful man in Alaska. Carr said talking about development with Hammond was "like discussing chastity in a house of ill-repute—purely academic."

Fairbanks Daily News-Miner

In the 1974 gubernatorial election, amid the pipeline construction boom, Alaskans may have been attracted by the reputation of Jay Hammond, opposite page, as an advocate of "slow growth." The relatively unknown Hammond, a bush pilot and guide elected to the state Senate from southwest Alaska, beat Bill Egan in a close election. One of Hammond's major detractors was Jesse Carr, above, head of the Teamsters Union Local 959. Another was *Anchorage Times* publisher Bob Atwood, at right, who characterized Hammond as a charming but mediocre legislator who wrote poetry.

Fairbanks Daily News-Miner

Carr, whose empire collapsed after completion of the pipeline, often called Governor Hammond a "son of a bitch," prompting Hammond to write in a newspaper column that while both he and Carr had served in the Marines, the governor didn't know he had anything else in common with the Teamster boss.

The misgivings that some people held about the future of Alaska as envisioned by Atwood and Carr played a key role in Hammond's election. Bearded and burly, with a booming voice like an Old Testament prophet, Hammond found a ready audience among those who thought Alaska was accelerating out of control. He did well on television, and his 1974 campaign included an ad in which he was out chopping wood on his homestead, every bit the backwoods politician for the electronic age.

He spoke endlessly about "healthy versus malignant" growth, a term from the extensive lexicon of "Hammondese," as his colorful way of speaking was called by friends and foes alike, and he stressed the need to preserve "one-time-only oil dollars." He said the likes of Atwood, Carr, and Hickel never met a development project they didn't like. Hammond also won allies with his sense of humor and self-deprecating style. After a tour of the pipeline in 1975, Hammond said he last had been to the North Slope in 1952 when he had seen several thousand caribou. "This time I saw eleven moose, seventeen caribou, one fox, three ducks, one beer can, and one drunken Texan," he said. He said morale seemed OK, but then again, "It's hard to get too down in the dumps with the food they're eating and the salaries they are drawing."

Many of the North Slope workers made considerably more than the $50,000 the governor earned, mainly because they worked seventy to eighty-four hours a week and earned time-and-a-half pay for everything over forty hours. *Money* magazine featured the dilemma of a Teamster, twenty-four, who said "sudden and unexpected wealth has left me somewhat dazed." The magazine said it had trouble finding financial advisers to help the young Teamster because so many Alaskans regarded pipeline workers as carpetbaggers. The magazine's experts advised the young man to try to save $300 a week, the equivalent of more than $1,000 in 2008 dollars.

Carpetbagger or not, he was one of tens of thousands of people who had a chance to save or spend extra money during the pipeline boom. Employment on the project peaked at 28,072 in 1975 and dropped off rapidly a year later. Welders completed the last joint on the 100,000-plus pieces of pipe, clearing the way for oil to flow across Alaska in the summer of 1977, three years and two months after construction began. The final construction cost was $8 billion, though if you add the cost of borrowed money, the figure would be closer to $10 billion. In 2008 dollars, that would be about $35 billion.

An economic slowdown was expected after the pipeline began pumping oil to Valdez, but it was widely assumed that a second pipeline soon would be built, transporting natural gas from the North Slope either to Valdez or to the Midwest. Along with the vast oil reserves, the Prudhoe Bay and other North Slope fields contained trillions of cubic feet of natural gas. Building a natural gas pipeline to Fairbanks and then along the Alaska Highway to Canada was still in the talking stage more than thirty years after startup of the oil pipeline. If built, it is expected to cost tens of billions of dollars and become the largest private construction project in North America.

As of 2008, the second pipeline has yet to be built.

Advertised as the best option for the state and nation, the trans-Alaska oil pipeline won the support of every pro-development group in Alaska and the oil industry in the 1970s. Alaska's political and business leaders dismissed the idea of an oil pipeline through Canada as longer and more costly. However, the cost of shipping oil by tanker from Valdez to the West Coast and through the Panama Canal to other regions never was factored into the discussion of the "all-Alaska pipeline."

"If there has ever been a greater waste of energy economic potential than what Alaska and the nation paid for the all-Alaska pipeline route, I don't know what it might be," Hammond wrote years later. "It has already cost uncounted billions of dollars and has been a major contributor to the nation's enormous trade deficit."

The tanker route proved especially costly on the night of March 23, 1989 when the helmsman and the third mate in the wheelhouse of the *Exxon Valdez* failed to turn the three-year-old supertanker and it ran aground on Bligh Reef, ripping open eight of its eleven cargo tanks.

"We've fetched up hard aground north of Goose Island off Bligh Reef and, evidently, leaking some oil," Captain Joseph Hazelwood radioed the Coast Guard in Valdez.

The oil gushed out from the tanker and the smell was described by one of the state officials who responded as being like putting your nose down to the gas tank of your car.

Hazelwood, who had been drinking, was charged with operating a vessel while under the influence of alcohol. He was acquitted of that charge and convicted of negligent discharge of oil. He was fined $50,000 and performed 1,000 hours of community service in Alaska.

THE OTHER PIPELINE

A few hundred business and political leaders gathered at a Fairbanks hotel in 1977 to applaud the latest news about the proposed natural-gas pipeline from the North Slope.

Buoyed by what they heard, 300 people left the Travelers Inn expecting construction of a gas pipeline to begin within two years and be completed by the mid-1980s.

Three decades later, the pipeline still had not been built.

The much-discussed natural-gas pipeline became the longest-running story in Alaska, a testament to the high cost of construction, low natural gas prices in the Lower 48, the complexity of world energy markets, and the mysteries of internal oil-company strategies.

In the 1970s, three projects were proposed.

One plan, backed by major oil and gas companies, was to build a pipeline that would have been routed east from Prudhoe Bay to Canada and then south.

A second proposal was the trans-Alaska route that would have gone south to tidewater, where tankers would transport liquefied natural gas to the West Coast.

A third proposal, championed by John McMillian, was to build a pipeline that would parallel the oil pipeline to Delta and follow the Alaska Highway into Canada, and then connect to the Lower 48.

McMillian, described by *Forbes* Magazine as a "one-time West Texas roughneck-turned-oil-promoter," won the support of the Carter administration, but never won favor with those who would have had to risk billions of dollars to finance the pipeline.

"McMillian proved unabashedly opportunistic," *Time* magazine said. "When he heard, for example, that influential congressional staffers favored a route south from Prudhoe to Fairbanks, he seized on it. His approach inspired a Washington insider's joke: 'McMillian would ship the gas south in cellophane bags if we asked him to.'"

In 2008, a new round of proposals to ship the trillions of cubic feet of natural gas to the Lower 48 envisioned a pipeline that could be in operation by 2020. The 48-inch pipeline would run about 1,700 miles from the North Slope to Alberta at a cost of tens of billions of dollars.

The Alaska Legislature granted a license to a Canadian firm, TransCanada, to try and put a project together, approving a deal that Gov. Sarah Palin has made the centerpiece of her administration. At the same time, a competing proposal, a joint venture backed by BP and ConocoPhillips, had also started with a goal of developing North Slope gas.

"Today, with the affirmative vote of both chambers of the Alaska State Legislature, we now begin a lifelong partnership with a company that has shown its true commitment to Alaska's future," Palin said on August 1, 2008.

No one believes that two separate pipelines will be built, which is why the two sponsoring organizations are expected to try and seek common ground in what may be a complex series of negotiations.

Bud Ehler/National Oceanic and Atmospheric Administration

Alaska Department of Environmental Conservation

Alaska Department of Environmental Conservation

Soon after taking on a cargo of oil on March 23, 1989, the *Exxon Valdez,* left, ran aground on Bligh Reef, spilling what was officially estimated at eleven million gallons of oil. The spill killed hundreds of thousands of seabirds, as many as 5,000 otters, 300 harbor seals, 250 bald eagles, and 22 Orca whales while polluting 1,300 miles of coastline. An oily seal, on the opposite page, sits on a buoy while workers, above, attempt to clean a beach with high-pressure hoses. Exxon is believed to have spent in excess of $2 billion on the cleanup effort.

About eleven million gallons spilled from the crippled tanker, while about forty million gallons remained on board and were pumped onto four other Exxon tankers dispatched to the site. The spilled oil spread throughout Prince William Sound and into the Gulf of Alaska, polluting about 1,300 miles of shoreline. Researchers estimated that the oil killed from 375,000 to 435,000 birds and upwards of 5,000 otters.

The sense of complacency that had developed after nearly a dozen years of safe tanker traffic from Valdez and transportation of billions of barrels of oil carried a great price for Alaska and its wildlife, not to mention for Exxon and other oil companies.

"Industry's insistence on regulating the Valdez tanker trade its own way, and government's incremental accession to industry pressure, had produced a disastrous failure of the system," the Alaska Oil Spill Commission found.

One of the towns hardest hit by the spill was Cordova, a fishing town with a population of about 3,000. After the spill the salmon fishery and other species recovered, but the herring fishery never rebounded and the town is still feeling the effects of the loss. Since the spill, herring fishing has been banned during most years. Exxon disputes the research, but some scientists say that residual oil contributed to the unprecedented collapse of the herring fishery in 1993.

The *Exxon Valdez* was repaired and renamed the *Sea River Mediterranean.* Congress banned the infamous tanker from Prince William Sound under a law that prohibited any ship that had spilled more than one million gallons of oil from entering those waters.

Exxon sold the tanker in 2008 to a Hong Kong firm that renamed it the "Dong Fang Ocean" and planned to convert it for use hauling bulk ore.

In addition to questions about recovery of herring and other species, the spill led to years of court battles and endless debate about what should have been done to prevent the second Good Friday disaster in Alaska. But unlike the 1964 earthquake, the spill was not a natural disaster.

"A lingering effect of the Exxon oil spill is the loss of innocence. Many Alaskans believed the oil industry's promises, to use the utmost care to protect our environment. We've learned to our sorrow that oil promises are good only if they don't interfere with profits," Alaska environmental leader Celia Hunter said in a radio interview a decade after the spill.

After nearly two decades of court battles over just how much Exxon should pay in punitive damages, the U.S. Supreme Court settled the case in 2008. The court reduced a punitive damage award from $2.5 billion to $507.5

million. The initial jury verdict in 1996 called for damages of $5 billion, but the 9th U.S. Circuit Court of Appeals had reduced that.

Exxon paid $507 million to about 33,000 fishermen, workers, and landowners to compensate for actual damages caused by the spill. In its 2008 decision, the Supreme Court ruled 5-3 that punitive damages to be paid to that group, assessed against Exxon as punishment, should be no greater than the actual damages. "The punitive damages award against Exxon was excessive as a matter of maritime common law," wrote Justice David Souter.

In another action, the company reached a $900 million civil settlement with the state and federal governments in 1991 for the damage to natural resources. That was not the subject of the Supreme Court challenge.

For the spill cleanup, a massive job that Exxon said cost more than $2 billion, Exxon hired VECO International, the company headed by Bill Allen of Anchorage, as a lead contractor. Allen, the central figure in the Alaska political corruption scandal that erupted in 2006, used earnings from the cleanup to help expand his operations in Alaska.

"At its peak, the cleanup effort included approximately 10,000 workers, 1,000 boats, and roughly one hundred aircraft known as Exxon's 'army, navy, and air force.' However, many believe that wave action from winter storms did more to clean the beaches than all of the human effort involved," the Exxon Valdez Oil Spill Trustee Council notes on its Web site.

In its first three decades, the trans-Alaska pipeline has transported more than fifteen billion barrels of oil to Valdez, surpassing early estimates about how long the pipeline and oil would last. By 2008, the daily oil flow had declined to about 700,000 barrels per day, down from more than two million barrels in 1988. Of the eleven pump stations that were built, five remained in operation with one as a standby. Every month more than two dozen tankers loaded up in Valdez.

In the five decades since the Swanson River oil discovery and the four decades since the Prudhoe Bay discovery, the oil industry became part of everyday life in Alaska. The invisible river of oil that flowed south at about five miles per hour became the economic lifeblood of Alaska. However, the quantity of oil flowing began to decline each year, representing a future economic threat to the state.

Wien Collection/Anchorage Museum at Rasmuson Center

Fifty years after statehood, the complex and often emotional subsistence rights issue remained unresolved due to a legal conflict. Federal law gives rural residents priority for access to fish and game on federal lands while state courts have ruled that under the Alaska constitution, it is illegal to discriminate against people based on where they live. In this photo, believed to have been taken in the 1960s, a subsistence fisherman removes salmon from a fish wheel in the Yukon drainage.

CHAPTER 9
The final division of Alaska

O N THE MORNING of December 2, 1980, less than a month after he had lost his bid for re-election to Ronald Reagan, President Jimmy Carter signed the third landmark federal law that divided the lands of Alaska. The Alaska National Interest Lands Conservation Act, ANILCA, set aside 104 million acres of Alaska in parks and refuges.

No other law dealing with Alaska had caused such deep division within the state and Congress. The idea was to preserve for "present and future generations certain lands and waters in the State of Alaska that contain nationally significant natural, scenic, historic, archeological, geological, scientific, wilderness, cultural, recreational, and wildlife values," according to the opening line of the legislation. But opponents derided the result as a move to "lock up Alaska."

One of those in attendance in the East Room was Rep. Morris Udall, an Arizona Democrat who had joined Carter in championing the cause of placing much of Alaska off-limits to future development.

Udall touched on the intense negative reaction the prolonged lands debate had sparked in Alaska, where many people thought the bill was a federal betrayal of the promises of statehood. It was an era in which Alaskans protested claims that they wanted to bulldoze the "crown jewels" of Alaska. Udall mentioned the booth at a summer fair in Fairbanks where the organizers had gathered 2,000 empty beer bottles as ammunition.

Fairbanks Daily News-Miner

Fairbanks Daily News-Miner

President Jimmy Carter was unpopular among some Alaskans because of his efforts to set aside vast amounts of federal land. On December 11, 1978, demonstrators in Fairbanks burned Carter in effigy, left, and later picketed in front of the U.S. Post Office, above. The protesters opposed Carter's use of the 1906 Antiquities Act to create seventeen national monuments totaling 56 million acres, removing the land from development and many other uses.

"They had four pictures on the wall that you could pay a quarter and throw a beer bottle at—Jimmy Carter, Cecil Andrus, Mo Udall, and the Ayatollah," said Udall, who in those years was thought by some pro-development Alaskans to be as radical as the revolutionary leader of Iran.

Carter, who had been burned in effigy outside the Fairbanks post office during one protest, knew what Udall was talking about. They both thought of the lands act as one of the greatest conservation measures of the 20th Century. A quarter-century later, on a visit to Anchorage, Carter went a step further, saying; "It was the most important environmental legislation in the history of the entire world."

The bill classified about fifty-six million acres as wilderness, created ten new national parks, nine new national wildlife refuges, two new national conservation units, two new national monuments, designated twenty-six Wild and Scenic rivers and expanded Denali National Park.

The Alaska lands act had come about because of a provision in the second of the two major land measures—the Alaska Native Claims Settlement Act of 1971. A short portion, known as Section 17(d)2 had authorized the interior secretary to withdraw up to eighty million acres for possible inclusion in parks and other conservation areas. Years of legislative in-fighting led to the 1980 compromise.

Senator Stevens had voted against the bill and worked to modify the parts that many Alaskans found the most objectionable, but he attended the signing ceremony. He said the bill was not balanced. "Over half of the federal lands that will remain under the control of the Department of Interior will be in Alaska after the passage of this bill. Over half of the hydrocarbon resources of the United States are in Alaska's lands. We know that the time will come when those resources will be demanded by other Americans. And we seek to protect our freedoms, to try to prevent us from becoming a 'permit society' where we have to have a permit to do everything," Stevens said.

Alaska's other senator, Mike Gravel, also opposed the bill, but he was not in attendance. This was understandable given the ferocious opposition Gravel had mounted to the legislation and the bitter relationship between the two Alaska senators. In the late 1970s, Stevens told reporters in Fairbanks that to him the letters "g-r-a-v-e-l" meant nothing but road-building material. When Stevens urged Alaskans to take a unified approach, Gravel responded, "There is a great unity in lemmings as they march over the cliffs into the sea."

They both had come to Alaska and had success in politics and business— Stevens in the law and Gravel in real estate, but otherwise had little in common and came to intensely dislike each other. According to one account in 1979, Stevens had tried to settle their differences soon after they joined the Senate, but Gravel said he would not be Stevens's friend. "I wanted nothing to do with him socially," Gravel told a reporter.

While Stevens advanced in the Senate as a Washington insider, working with others to get things done, Gravel reveled in being an unpredictable free agent. "In the Senate, Gravel is unpopular, partly because mavericks always are, partly because he can be a very annoying man," *Washington Post* reporter Nicholas Lemann wrote in a lengthy account of the Stevens-Gravel relationship in 1979, headlined:

THE GREAT ALASKA FEUD

Gravel "lets others do the detail work while he makes speeches and goes on trips," Lemann wrote.

Stevens said on one occasion Gravel broke his word to him. He called Gravel an "international playboy" who needed psychiatric help. Gravel responded by campaigning against Stevens in 1978, signing political ads that said Alaskans should send Stevens a message, "Toughen up or we'll get rid of you."

Their predecessors in the Senate, Bob Bartlett and Ernest Gruening, didn't get along either. Bartlett occasionally referred to Gruening as "Your Worship" and "His Honor" in private correspondence and said one of his goals was to "serve in public office at a more advanced age and for more years than a certain someone." As historian Claus Naske wrote of the events of 1968, the year of Alaska's greatest political transition, "Virtually at the same time, death ended Bartlett's career and political defeat ended Gruening's."

Stevens first ran for the Senate in 1962 when he was thirty-eight and Gruening was seventy-five. "I believe Alaska has suffered for almost four years because Ernest Gruening was elected in 1958. He is a cantankerous old man. He has delayed many programs for his own selfish objects. He has embittered his own colleague, Alaska's senior Sen. Bob Bartlett, by his back-biting techniques and absolutely insatiable appeals for personal publicity," Stevens said as he opened his 1962 campaign.

Anchorage journalist Michael Carey notes that Gruening paid little attention to Stevens in that race, though Gruening supporters dismissed the Anchorage lawyer as "Teddy Bear."

Stevens lost the Senate race that year and, after serving two terms in the state House of Representatives, he lost again in 1968 when fellow

Mike Gravel, right, had reason to smile as he greeted Sen. Ernest Gruening, whom he had defeated in the 1968 Democratic primary election for nomination to the U.S. Senate. Although Gruening, eighty-one, took a swim in the Arctic Ocean in an effort to demonstrate that he was in good shape, age appeared to have been a factor in the election.

Republican Elmer Rasmuson won the GOP primary for the U.S. Senate. He told reporters, "This is not my swan song."

The 1968 upheaval began when Gravel beat Gruening, then eighty-one, whose physical exploits of swimming in the Arctic Ocean were not enough to overcome questions about his age. Gravel positioned himself as being "on the sunshine side of forty." As the year neared an end, Bartlett was gone from the Senate, too, dead at sixty-four due to heart trouble.

Two hours before Bartlett died, President Nixon nominated Wally Hickel as interior secretary. Before taking the federal job, Governor Hickel appointed Stevens to replace Bartlett. Because he was sworn in ten days before Gravel, Stevens become the senior senator from Alaska. In time, with benefit of decades of seniority, he emerged as the most influential political leader in Alaska's history.

The relationship between Gruening and Bartlett may have been strained in their final years, but it was more of a family feud than the civil war that existed between Stevens and Gravel. The two differed on every major bill dealing with Alaska in the 1970s, including the 200-mile limit, the trans-Alaska pipeline, and the Native Land claims settlement.

Among the most painful and poignant comments Stevens ever made in public took place on February 6, 1979 in a hearing before Udall's committee. Two months earlier, on December 4, 1978, Stevens and his wife Ann were among the passengers on a Learjet flying to Anchorage, where Stevens was to appear at a fund-raising event to support lobbying efforts against the lands bill. The jet crashed in crosswinds at Anchorage International Airport, killing Ann Stevens and four others. The only survivors were Ted Stevens and Tony Motley, who headed the pro-development lobbying group Citizens for the Management of Alaska Lands (CMAL).

The fund-raiser was needed because Gravel had killed a lands bill compromise in 1978, which was what Stevens was referring to when he told Udall's committee, "I don't want to get personal about it, but I think if that bill had passed, I might have a wife sitting at home when I get home tonight." Stevens said years later he was not blaming Gravel for his wife's death, he was just stating a fact, as they would not have been on that plane to raise money for CMAL had Gravel not killed the compromise.

Where Stevens was a party loyalist accustomed to working behind the scenes, Gravel enjoyed the spotlight, gaining national attention for reading the Pentagon Papers into the *Congressional Record* and having himself

Fairbanks Daily News-Miner

Ted Stevens, above, campaigned for the Republican nomination to the U.S. Senate in the spring of 1968, traveling around the state in this bus. From left are the Stevens children, Beth, Susan, Walter, Terry Jr., Ben and, partially obscured, Stevens' wife, Ann. Stevens lost the election to Anchorage banker Elmer Rasmuson. Four months later, after the death of Sen. Bob Bartlett, Stevens was appointed to the U.S. Senate by Gov. Walter Hickel. Ann Stevens was killed in an Anchorage airplane crash that Stevens survived in 1978. Stevens and second wife, Catherine, opposite page, were photographed with Lily, their five-month-old daughter, in 1981.

THE PRESIDENT AND THE POPE

When President Ronald Reagan visited Fairbanks on May 2, 1984 to meet Pope John Paul II, he made no earth-shattering entries in his diary, but he did mention how he had left China, crossed the International Date Line, and arrived in Alaska at 3:20 a.m.—five hours earlier than he left on the same day. The President wrote:

> *Believe me that can confuse you. We drove to a new home belonging to Sen. & Mrs. Murkowski who haven't lived in it yet & went to bed until about 11 a.m., but it was still May 1 & still Tuesday.*

The visit to Fairbanks and the Murkowski home is mentioned in "The Reagan Diaries," a compilation featuring the private thoughts he recorded for eight years as President. More than 220 Secret Service agents converged on Fairbanks for the occasion.

> *We had juice & coffee & headed for the U. of Alaska for a welcoming ceremony—about 3,000 people. The Sen. introduced me & I made a short speech. Some children presented us with gifts—Native handcraft.*

> *Then to the William Wood student center for lunch & more remarks. Back to the Murkowski home at 2:30 p.m. & into pajamas. We saw the midnight sun—it was still up at 11 p.m. We finally got to sleep, but it was strange getting away from China time."*

The following day, Reagan went to Fairbanks International Airport where a crowd of 10,000 gathered to greet the Pope, whose plane was making a refueling stop during the pontiff's journey to South Korea.

Fairbanks Daily News-Miner

Pope John Paul II and President Ronald Reagan.

We both spoke briefly to the crowd then went into the airport for a meeting. I briefed him on our China trip. He is anxious to enter into talks with the P.R.C. (Peoples Republic of China). They haven't established diplomatic relations because the Vatican has relations with Taiwan.

The two world leaders met for two and a half hours at the airport, then went their separate ways.

nominated as a vice presidential candidate at the 1972 Democratic National Convention.

In part because of the hostility between him and Stevens, Gravel had lost a primary bid for re-election in 1980, which ended Gravel's political career. Long after leaving Alaska, he resurfaced early in the 2008 presidential campaign, using outlandish tactics to attract publicity, just as much of a contrarian as he had been during the twelve years he spent in the Senate fighting with Stevens.

The fallout from the Stevens-Gravel feud never entirely disappeared. Some pro-development forces argue that had Gravel succeeded in stopping the lands bill in 1980, the next version would have been less restrictive. The political landscape shifted to the pro-development side with the election of Ronald Reagan and the U.S. Senate took a distinct slant to the conservative side in the early 1980s.

Stevens maintained that Gravel's grandstanding harmed the state's case, but because environmental leaders in Congress concluded that they would lose ground under Reagan, they accepted a lands bill that they believed was far from ideal shortly before Carter left office.

Stevens and Gravel split over tactics, but they agreed that interior secretary Cecil Andrus's claim that he sought to save Alaska from the "rape, ruin, and run boys" was an exaggeration. They attacked the Carter administration and Udall for what they portrayed as a federal land grab that would stifle the rights of Alaskans and lock up the state forever.

While the law set the rules for future development, it did not settle a crucial question that was still being argued in 2008—whether oil drilling would be allowed on the coastal plain of the Arctic National Wildlife Refuge (ANWR) to the east of Prudhoe Bay. The 1980 legislation had doubled the size of the refuge and provided for a study of oil potential on the coastal plain, which made up less than ten percent of the total acreage.

A battle over the future of the coastal plain has continued almost without interruption. No Alaska environmental issue since the battle over the oil pipeline has been so intense, with the possible exception of the on-again, off-again furor that erupts whenever the state of Alaska proposes to shoot wolves so that more moose and caribou will be available for hunting.

When oil prices rose, the pressure to open ANWR increased, leading to a polarized debate in which the land is either "America's Serengeti" that should not be defiled or a "God-forsaken expanse" of worthless territory, very little of which would be disturbed by oil development. The coastal plain is a symbol of wilderness to some, while others see it as an acceptable location to extend oil drilling and help the U.S. or the Alaska economy.

Stevens stopped short of ever saying that Gravel might have been right about ANILCA, but he expressed misgivings in later years that accepting the lands bill had been the right strategy. "It's not something I would tilt a glass of champagne for," he said in 2000. He also said that he was promised by Senators Henry Jackson and Paul Tsongas that ANWR would be open to oil development if an environmental-impact statement showed it could be done safely. But Jackson and Tsongas are dead and that promise never was spelled out in the bill.

A second unsettled question concerned the battle over subsistence rights. One section of ANILCA provided that rural residents receive priority for access to fish and game, but there is a conflict between the federal law and the state constitution. The courts have ruled that under the Alaska Constitution, it is illegal to discriminate against people based on where they live. However, federal law requires a subsistence priority for those who live in rural areas. The contradiction remains unresolved, a source of continual tension between groups competing for scarce fish and game resources.

Most Alaskans have lost count of the special legislative sessions, summit meetings, and blue-ribbon committees that have tackled this issue in an attempt to resolve the dispute in a way that would satisfy hunters who live in the city and those who live in small villages. So far, the efforts have failed.

Both the state and the federal governments have a role in subsistence decisions, featuring so many layers and levels that historian Frank Norris said it resembles a "tyranny of democracy." The repeated changes in law and court decisions on subsistence over the years have shown that "turbulence is the norm rather than the exception, and it should come as little surprise if further dramatic changes occur within the next few years," he wrote in a history of subsistence in the national parks.

Sterling hunter Les Palmer, writing in the *Peninsula Clarion*, said that most Alaskans have no clue about what followed the court decision on equal access.

"The court said the state couldn't discriminate against people because of where they live. The feds, on the other hand, can and do discriminate in

During his early years in the U.S. Senate, Republican Ted Stevens worked closely on many issues of mutual interest with Sen. Henry Jackson, a Democrat from the state of Washington.

this manner on federal lands, and a fair amount of case law supports their legal right to do so," he said.

As a result, the federal government manages subsistence on federal lands and waters, granting a preference to rural residents, while the state manages subsistence on its lands, with all Alaskans eligible for the same preference.

"The present situation of 'dual management' poses significant threats to vulnerable fish stocks and wildlife populations. Because the subsistence preference has the potential of closing all other uses except subsistence, it threatens sport, personal-use and commercial fisheries, as well as hunting," Palmer said. "Worst of all, it makes a mockery of the whole idea of subsistence, and erodes what dwindling support remains among those of us who once thought it seemed like a fine and noble idea."

For better or worse, the Alaska National Interest Lands Conservation Act that Carter signed in 1980 was the final part of a trilogy of Congressional actions dividing and apportioning Alaska's vast territory, a drama that unfolded during the first twenty years of statehood and was still being played out after half a century.

Along with the Alaska Statehood Act and the Alaska Native Claims Settlement Act, ANILCA set the terms for Alaska's participation in the Union, some of the details of which are still the source of debate. Together, the three bills established the ownership and policies that would determine the future control and planning for more than 250 million acres, a Texas-sized chunk of the continent.

Eric Muehling/Fairbanks Daily News-Miner

Some of Alaska's statehood founders, including many members of the Alaska Constitutional Convention, were honored at the University of Alaska Fairbanks in January 1984. From left, bottom row, were Rolland Armstrong, Robert Atwood, Dorothy Awes Haaland, Seaborn Buckalew, Jack Coghill, George Cooper, James Doogan, William Egan; middle row: Herb Hilscher, Helen Fischer, Jack Hinckel, James Hurley, Yule Kilcher, Eldor Lee, Maynard Londborg; top row: Leslie Nerland, Katherine Nordale, Peter Reader, Burke Riley, George Sundborg, Dora Sweeney, and Ada Wien.

CHAPTER 10
Re-examining statehood

B ARELY TWO DECADES after joining the Union, Alaskans went to the polls in 1980 and approved a measure calling for re-examination of statehood. Voters were asked, "Shall the Alaska Statehood Commission be convened to study the status of the people of Alaska within the United States and to consider and recommend appropriate changes in the relationship of Alaska to the United States?"

By a margin of just 1,600 votes, Alaskans said yes. It was the first time since the Civil War that any state had raised this question.

Three weeks after the vote, Governor Hammond addressed visiting newspaper publishers in Juneau's Baranof Hotel about what he called the "latest American bombshell," namely what had been portrayed widely as a vote in support of secession from the Union. "I've emitted thousands of words on the subject, not so much to defuse that projectile, as to point out that it's a dud," said Hammond. "Certainly some Alaskans would like to secede from the Union; just as some claim to have traveled intergalactically on UFOs, assert that they commune with spirits, or support Pogo Possum for President."

Creating the Alaska Statehood Commission was not a call to separate the 49th state from the Union, though a Fairbanks gold miner and land developer named Joe Vogler had founded the Alaska Independence Party to pursue just such a course. It was no surprise that the commission reported back two years later that Alaska could support legal independence as long as it was wealthy, but the commission could find no reason to advocate secession. "The Civil War answered the question of secession once and for all," the commission said in its report to Alaskans. Still, the report said, the federal government had reneged on land-conveyance obligations, and there was talk about states in other parts of the country using their political muscle to limit Alaska's taxation powers on oil—a worrisome prospect.

In its final report, the commission recommended that Alaska and other states "resist the federal drive toward supremacy." It recommended a host of steps to fight what it portrayed as a federal grab for power that came at state expense.

Alaska should seek to overturn the ban on the export of Alaska oil, the commission said, and try to get the Jones Act amended. The Jones Act is the federal law that required that shipments between American ports be made on ships made and crewed by Americans. Prohibiting the use of foreign-flagged vessels manned by foreign crews, with their lower costs, was a penalty on Alaskans designed to bolster the fortunes of U.S. shipbuilders, owners and the shipping unions.

Despite the commission's recommendation, Alaskan political leaders never have made a concerted effort to battle the Jones Act, reflecting the political influence mustered by the shipping industry in Congress.

Congress banned Alaska oil exports as a condition of the right-of-way for the trans-Alaska oil pipeline, reflecting the political consensus that Alaska oil should go to the Lower 48 and not to Japan. For Alaska, the ban meant that its oil was worth less because of the higher transportation costs for shipping oil to the South and Midwest by way of a pipeline in Panama. The ban was eventually overturned in 1995, but by then the oil flow from Prudhoe Bay had dropped off so much that little oil was exported. By 2008, the national opposition to exporting Alaska oil was stronger than ever because of U.S. dependence on foreign oil.

The creation of the Alaska Statehood Commission and its work reflected long-standing frustrations with the way the federal government treated Alaska. Many Alaskans didn't care much to hear Arizona Representative Mo Udall, the champion of the drive to put as much of Alaska land into parks as possible, say that Alaskans had no reason to complain. "We have been fair to the state of Alaska—far, far fairer than to any other state in the Union. There is no basis whatsoever for any feeling of obligation or 'states' rights' to this most favored state."

Had the commission continued its existence into the 21st Century, it would have had new elements to consider. Any evaluation would include the pivotal role of the man whose name is on the international airport at Anchorage, Ted Stevens. His involvement in Alaska's development spans the entire half-century of statehood. In the edition of the Juneau newspaper that announced the presidential statehood proclamation in 1959, a front-page story appeared under the headline, "Theodore Stevens gets promotion," referring to a new job he took in the Interior Department. He later returned to Alaska and served in the state legislature before going to the U.S. Senate, becoming the most enduring, if not endearing, political leader in Alaska history. In 2000, an Anchorage group dubbed him "Alaskan of the Century."

In the decades since Stevens entered the Senate, he has used the power of Senate seniority to increase the federal presence in Alaska to the tune of billions of dollars—the exact number is one that people are hesitant to calculate for fear of drawing unwanted attention to it. He also used his position on the Senate Appropriations Committee to create new programs such as the Denali Commission to help find ways to meet basic needs in rural areas.

For decades, the names of the Alaskans in Congress have been Stevens, Young, and Murkowski. Don Young won his first race for the U.S. House in 1973 and has served ever since. Frank Murkowski was elected to the U.S. Senate in 1980 and served until he appointed his daughter Lisa to follow him when he became governor in 2002.

The seniority of Stevens, along with Young and Sen. Frank Murkowski, led a Capitol Hill newspaper to report that by the early 1990s the tiny Alaska delegation had the "most extreme case of clout imbalance" of any state. At the time, Young chaired the House Resources Committee, while Murkowski ruled the Senate version. A decade later, the newspaper *Roll Call* said that on a "clout per member basis," Alaska had the most powerful delegation in the Congress.

That clout was apparent during the years that Stevens chaired the Senate Appropriations Committee, when Alaska earmarks added to the federal budget helped transform Alaska finances so that the state received about $2 in federal spending for every $1 its residents paid in federal income taxes.

"About a third of all jobs in Alaska can be traced to federal spending here and over the past decade the rapid increase in federal spending drove much of the economic growth. Federal spending in Alaska more than doubled between 1995 and 2005 and in 2006 it was $9.25 billion," University of Alaska Anchorage economist Scott Goldsmith wrote in July 2008.

The remark was in the context of a presentation on how vulnerable the state economy would be to a reduction in federal spending, which at last count was 71 percent higher, per capita, than the national average. Federal spending is likely to decrease in the years ahead, mainly because Stevens is no longer chairman of the appropriations committee, a position that gave him enormous influence over the federal budget.

A political corruption scandal that sent several former state lawmakers to jail changed the political climate in Alaska in the period 2006-2008 as this work neared publication. Nothing like it had occurred before in Alaska history, as the scope of the investigation far exceeded previous corruption controversies, such as the bribery conviction of former State Senator George Hohman in 1981 and the impeachment proceedings against former Governor Bill Sheffield in 1985. Sheffield had been accused of covering up his role in attempting to steer a $9.6 million state lease to a political ally in Fairbanks. The grand jury claimed Sheffield was "unfit" to hold office, but the Alaska Senate found insufficient evidence to impeach the Democratic governor.

The 2006 scandal led to the election of Sarah Palin as governor on a platform stressing ethics and openness in government. Palin, a former mayor of Wasilla and one-time TV journalist, became Alaska's first woman governor and its youngest at age forty-two. During her first two years in office, a protracted federal probe led to a federal indictment of Stevens making him vulnerable at the polls for the first time in forty years.

The Stevens indictment was not unexpected, given that the FBI had raided his home in 2007, but its timing—less than a month before the 2008 primary— was a stunning development.

Stevens was charged with failing to reveal gifts worth about $250,000 from Bill Allen, the oilfield services tycoon who built Veco into one of Alaska's most powerful companies. Allen pleaded guilty in 2007 to extortion, bribery, and fraud. His deal with the government was that if the prosecutors believe he is fully cooperative, his son or other family members won't be charged with any criminal offenses arising out of the case.

The gifts to Stevens were mostly in the form of labor and materials on his house in Girdwood, which was remodeled and expanded by Allen's company over six years, the government charged. Stevens said he paid every bill submitted to him, about $130,000, and declared his innocence.

"Every bill that was sent to us has been paid, personally, with our own money, and that's all there is to it. It's our own money," Stevens told reporters in 2007.

One of the other allegations was that Stevens did not disclose that in 1999 he traded a 1964 Mustang, worth less than $20,000, plus $5,000 in cash, for a new Land Rover purchased by Allen for $44,000.

"The impact of these charges on my family disturbs me greatly," Stevens said in a statement after the case was filed. "I am innocent of these charges and intend to prove that."

In the building of modern Alaska, there is room for debate about who is the second-most influential person in Alaska politics. A strong case could be made for Bill Egan, Jay Hammond, or Wally Hickel. But there is little question that Stevens leads the list due to his durability and the rules of the United States Senate that value longevity.

When Stevens controlled the appropriations process in the Senate, Alaskans began to think "ask and you shall receive" was the way to get almost anything funded.

Alaska journalist Michael Carey wrote of a breakfast interview he attempted to conduct with Stevens at an Anchorage hotel several years before the FBI began its investigation. They were continually interrupted by Alaskans asking Stevens to fund a "little project." This became such a common occurrence in Alaska that the phrase "Stevens-money" became part of the vocabulary of Alaskans.

"As a former chairman of the Senate Appropriations Committee (and later the ranking minority member), Stevens has delivered hundreds of millions of dollars to his constituents, sometimes through agency appropriations, sometimes through the now-vilified earmarks. In Alaska, the presence of so-called Stevens-money is as prevalent as the winter snow. Everywhere you look, Stevens has left his mark," Carey said. "Stevens' ability to deliver—and his invulnerability to electoral challenge because he could deliver—transformed him from an elected official into something of a frontier fertility god—worshiped, propitiated, feared. Stevens answered to no one."

No matter what happens with the federal investigation, it seems that Alaskans will have to get used to a reduced reliance on federal spending, in part because of the national furor over the "bridge to nowhere" and in part because when Stevens leaves the Senate, the ability to slip "little projects" into the federal budget will leave with him.

BOUNTY OF THE SEA

Much of what people around the world know of Alaska's fishing industry comes from watching "Deadliest Catch," the popular reality TV show about crab fishing boats in the Bering Sea.

While the series depicts the dangers the crews face, there are many facets to commercial fishing in Alaska, a multi-billion dollar industry with a total harvest of about half of the nation's seafood.

About 40,000 people on 18,000 fishing boats ply the waters off Alaska, while about 30,000 others work in canneries and cold storage facilities. "In many respects, fisheries are to Alaska what wheat is to North Dakota and coal is to West Virginia," writes Neal Gilbertsen, a longtime commercial fisherman in Alaska,

When Alaska became a state, one of the first steps taken by the new government was to ban fish traps. Fish traps were despised because they were owned by companies from outside Alaska.

That single action wasn't enough to save Alaska's salmon fisheries from overharvesting or reverse a long-term decline.

"Over time a system of managing fisheries was developed based on the concepts of 'harvestable surplus' and 'maximum sustainable yield,'" Terry Johnson, a University of Alaska fisheries professor wrote in "Ocean Treasure: Commercial Fishing in Alaska."

"State managers also took an aggressive approach to monitoring and regulating the fishery," Johnson said.

The goal was to limit the catch to levels that protected the resource. In addition to regulations on fishing gear and where fish could be taken, habitat enhancement and fish hatchery production, the main tool the state used to help fishing was to limit the number of fishermen.

In 1972, Alaska voters amended the state constitution to allow for limited entry on a permit system. The state issued more than 16,000 permits in 65 fisheries, according to the Alaska Commercial Fisheries Entry Commission. By the end of 2005, about 14,500 remained active, with 23 percent held by nonresidents. The permits can be given to family members or transferred by sale.

After fifty years of statehood, despite competition from fish farms, Alaska's commercial fishing industry employed about 40,000 people on 18,000 fishing boats working the waters off Alaska.

Fairbanks Daily News-Miner

In a 2006 presentation in Anchorage by Frank Homan, chairman of the entry commission, he said there are "severe" constitutional constraints on the program, but it has withstood court challenges. He said it has "protected Alaska's fisheries from an influx of new fishermen from West Coast fisheries where fishing opportunities have been severely reduced by court decisions and stock conditions."

During boom years, some permits sold for prices as high as $400,000, but for other fisheries, depending on market conditions, permits have sold for as little as $2,000, according to a state brochure.

The state regulates fishing up to three miles from shore, while the federal government has extended its authority to cover the region from three miles to 200 miles off the coast under the Magnuson-Stevens Act, first passed in 1976.

The act, named after the late Sen. Warren Magnuson of Washington and Sen. Ted Stevens of Alaska, has been amended and extended. Foreign fishing vessels had long been taking much of the catch offshore until Congress exerted authority over the waters now known as the Exclusive Economic Zone.

Johnson said commercial fishing is "an exciting yet troubled industry," in which key challenges include dealing with conflicts over resource allocation and reducing the catch of unwanted fish, called bycatch.

One of the other problems facing Alaska's fishing industry is the growth of farmed salmon and salmon trout, which made up two percent of world supply in 1980 and 65 percent of world supply in 2004. The competition from farmed salmon has pushed down the value of Alaska's wild salmon catch by $500 million in the last quarter-century, according to the Institute of Social and Economic Research at the University of Alaska Anchorage.

In the aftermath of Hurricane Katrina, the move by Stevens and Don Young to designate $223 million in federal highway money for a bridge in Ketchikan to Gravina Island, the mostly unpopulated home of the city airport, created a national flood of bad publicity. The bridge project, which was stopped, became the nation's leading symbol of waste in government.

The Stevens era redefined Alaska's relationship with the federal government in a way that would have surprised both proponents and opponents of Alaska statehood a half-century before.

Jay Hammond had been among those who opposed statehood on the grounds that Alaska could not afford to be a state. "At that time oil had not been discovered. We had almost no economic base on which to build. Moreover, I contended that with our tiny population virtually any idiot who aspired to public office might well be elected," he once said.

While some of his opponents saw Hammond as the realization of that latter fear, the Bush Rat governor, as he was called in the title of his autobiography, *Tales of Alaska's Bush Rat Governor*, said the Prudhoe Bay bonanza showed that Alaska was financially able to hold its own, at least for the short term. "However, for the long term, that question looms far larger," he said in 1980.

Before that decade was out, the oil boom stalled, triggering a severe recession. Oil was not the only industry in Alaska after the pipeline began operation, but it towered above everything else. Fishing had been the dominant industry before statehood and was one of the largest employers, providing the lifeblood of communities all along the coast, through seasons both good and bad. The timber industry remained a vital element in Southeast until the 1990s. When the mills closed, loggers lost their jobs and communities struggled. The industry was responsible for 3,500 direct jobs in 1990, but ninety percent of those disappeared by 2008.

For more than a century in Alaska, gold mining had its ups and downs depending upon the price of the precious metal and the availability of the resource. Since statehood, it has more often than not been the gyrations in the world oil market that have reinforced the boom-and-bust mentality of the 49th state. The strategy of the Organization of Petroleum Exporting Countries (OPEC), actions by Congress and the President, growing consumption of oil in the U.S. and lately, the surging demand of China and India, have produced repeated episodes of prosperity, interspersed with moments of gloom in the 49th state.

Soon after startup of the pipeline, the price of oil tripled because the Iranian revolution in 1979 disrupted world oil markets. With the sudden growth in state revenues, the state government went on a spending spree. "Things were so wild the Legislature actually voted money to build a harbor and airport on an uninhabited island," wrote brothers Mike and Tim Bradner, long-time Alaska reporters. "Legislators didn't even meet to deliberate capital projects. The appropriations were simply punched into the Legislature's central computer, which printed out what was to be the capital budget."

That all of the money wasn't spent is a tribute, of sorts, to Alaskans both inside and outside of government. In 1976, voters approved a seventy-five-word amendment to the state constitution creating the Alaska Permanent Fund. It was a unique effort to direct at least twenty-five percent of oil royalties into a fund so that they could not be spent, only invested. Only earnings from the investments could be spent. The words "income-producing investments" could have been construed to apply to almost any proposed boondoggle, but the state followed a course that lived up to the spirit of the amendment.

The state opted to establish a program to send a check with a share of the fund earnings every year to every resident. The so-called Permanent Fund Dividend, in the form eventually approved by the Legislature, provided for a payout of 50 percent of the fund's earnings each year. The idea was Hammond's, a variation of something he called "Alaska, Inc."

"We have gotten ourselves into a situation where almost everybody and every industry are being subsidized by oil wealth," Hammond said in 1977.

To avoid the pain of future budget cuts or tax increases, he wanted to "suppress unhealthy government growth" by sending annual checks to people, reducing the amount the government could spend. He wanted the state to "claw back" dollars from the people if they were needed and favored a spending limit, which he compared to an article of clothing.

"I believe we can structure a garment which won't totally strait-jacket government, but will certainly gird up the frayed, elasticized belt of legislative and administrative constraint, which with fat money about, finds it hard to resist the pull and tug of every special interest's desires. The hour is late, our trousers imperiled," he told a Fairbanks business group.

The elasticized belt snapped in the 1980s, so to speak.

Lawmakers approved the dividend and distributed billions to projects both large and small. The population boomed, with 75,000 people moving into the state to sample its prosperity. The state offered loan subsidies and incentives that overheated the economy. The real-estate market boomed, with strip malls, stores, and office buildings taking shape in record time, along with thousands of houses and condos. As with other speculative markets, the oil-induced mania prompted builders and buyers to step up the pace. "I don't do any market studies," one contractor told a banker in a moment of candor. "I just build 'em. Somebody will rent 'em."

Then, in 1985, Saudi Arabia increased its oil production to get a bigger share of the world market. Alaska had acted as if it controlled its economic future. It didn't. Oil prices collapsed, and the Alaska economy did likewise. Oil slipped back to $10 a barrel and the state's economy stalled, taking down half of Alaska's banks and savings institutions, as well as many of the new strip malls, businesses, and thousands of homeowners. More than 16,000 foreclosures on residential property were recorded in the latter half of the 1980s. By 1989, the Alaska Housing Finance Corporation (AHFC), which had lent money freely, owned more than 4,500 properties, ranging from condos to mobile homes.

Meanwhile, the rental market in Anchorage saw vacancy rates soar to as high as forty percent. Thousands of people walked away from homes they no longer could afford. Condo prices in Anchorage dropped fifty percent. In a speech in 1987 to his branch managers, Anchorage banker Elmer Rasmuson said the explosive growth in real estate in the early 1980s was a crash waiting to happen. "Too many people and institutions, many outside Alaska, deluded themselves in thinking that the rate of expansion would keep on forever," he said. "When the expansion stopped, the bubble burst."

By 1986, five years after the Legislature was spending so fast it didn't debate projects, Gov. Bill Sheffield observed, "Alaska is America's fastest-growing state with the fastest-shrinking budget." In 1983, Sheffield had suggested that the state should end the new practice of paying annual dividends to residents before it became an entitlement. "This may be our last chance," Sheffield said in 1983, "because next year is an election year and after that the dividends will be an institution."

He was right. In 2008, many Alaskans believed they had as much right to an annual dividend as to state support for the public schools. Hammond believed that the dividend was the best way to protect the Alaska Permanent Fund, but the most vocal constituency in Alaska exists not to preserve the fund, but the dividends it pays, which totaled $1.3 billion in 2008.

In any event, the fund has been one of the greatest success stories. It is not only an insurance policy against high taxes in the future, but also the most likely way to turn oil dollars into a renewable resource.

Past performance is no guarantee of future results, but in Alaska the tendency has long been to believe that the conditions existing on one day are bound to continue, despite the continued pattern of boom and bust. When oil prices fell to $9 per barrel in the late 1990s, huge layoffs hit the oil industry and some thought things would get worse before they got better. In most parts of the United States, cheap oil was cause for celebration and a reason to increase consumption and buy bigger cars and SUVs. In Alaska, people bought bigger cars and SUVs, too, but low oil prices threatened the state's treasury.

Legislators cut the budget, worried about predictions of hard times ahead and saw little hope for higher oil prices.

Since the early 1990s, the state had relied on a rainy-day account known as the Constitutional Budget Reserve to make ends meet as oil revenue declined along with production. The date at which the reserve fund would run out was considered to be the date on which Alaska would go over a financial cliff. In 2001, Gov. Tony Knowles asked the Legislature to agree that if the fund fell below $1.5 billion, new taxes would be enacted automatically. The Legislature balked and continued to resist proposals by Knowles' successor, Frank Murkowski, for higher taxes and budget cuts. Talk of how to handle the job losses and hardships of an impending $1 billion budget cut—or the institution of some taxes and use of some permanent fund earnings—dominated the headlines for years.

Economists predicted that the reserve fund would be tapped out by 2005 or 2006 and the state would go over the long-predicted cliff. However, world events intervened once more.

"What's our plan for increasing revenue? Well, ladies and gentlemen, the single word is oil," Republican Gov. Frank Murkowski told the Legislature during his first State of the State address in 2003. Murkowski predicted an increase in oil production. That didn't happen. In fact, the opposite occurred, yet the price of oil—and thus the amount of revenue to the state—rose due to events that had nothing to do with Alaska.

Due to international speculation, increased demand fueled by the war with Iraq, and rising demand from China and India, oil prices soared higher than anyone had expected, giving Alaska budget surpluses once again. The multi-billion-dollar surpluses of 2008 brought back memories of the early 1980s, when Hammond warned the situation was out of control—"The hour is late, our trousers imperiled."

With state revenues at record levels and nearly $36 billion socked away in Alaska Permanent Fund investments, lawmakers struggled with the problems of unexpected billions. At the same time, Alaskans had to cope with record prices for fuel in much of the state, creating pressure for more "share-the-wealth" programs.

Yet, there remained widespread concern over the latest spending spree because Alaska oil production has been declining by a few percentage points each year, down by nearly two-thirds from the peak in 1988. While the high prices made every barrel more valuable and temporarily quieted debate about bringing back a state income tax, the production decline was seen as the greatest threat to the state's economic future.

Oil may flow for decades in Alaska and the long-delayed natural gas pipeline may be built as well, but additional exploration and development will be needed to keep the industry healthy in Alaska. The benefit of higher oil prices is that fields that would be uneconomic at $25 a barrel could be highly profitable at $100 a barrel.

For nearly fifty years, Alaska's fortunes have risen and fallen on developments in the world of petroleum. Since the discovery of Prudhoe Bay, the financial worries that made statehood a questionable proposition have been all but done away with. The state has tens of billions in the bank and a small enough population so that an individual still can make a difference.

Alaska enters the second half of its first century facing new political and economic challenges. Holding a state together with more than half of its population residing in a relatively small portion of its territory almost guarantees continued regional divisions such as those that have inflamed the capital move issue, subsistence battles, and resource development questions.

As long as oil prices remain high, the state will avoid the prospect of budget cuts and new taxes, but the decline in oil production and the unpredictability of world events leaves room for doubt about the road ahead.

Meanwhile, the FBI wiretaps and Justice Department investigations revealed corrupt influences at work in the political system, eroding the confidence that many Alaskans had in their government. As this book went to press, it was not clear how long the investigations would go on or how many officials would be drawn into the scandal before it ends. Until then, Alaska politics would be in turmoil.

No one would have predicted this set of problems on the day Alaska entered the Union in 1959 when Egan declared that "we shall strive to maintain and enhance this moment's glorious radiance of America's 49th star."

THE GOVERNORS LOOK AHEAD

At forty-two, Sarah Palin became Alaska's youngest governor when she took the oath of office in 2006 in Fairbanks, holding the inauguration ceremony outside of Juneau for the first time since statehood.

Thousands of people came to the Carlson Center to hear Palin honor those who wrote the state's constitution fifty years earlier at the nearby University of Alaska. Palin pledged to uphold the constitution's guiding principles and protect the state's interests.

"I will unambiguously, steadfastly, and doggedly guard the interests of this great state as a mother naturally guards her own," she said. "Like a nanook defending her cub."

The other eight Alaskans who served as governor had many aspirations and visions for the state when they took over, all of them expressing optimism about Alaska.

Here is what other governors said at their inaugurations:

BILL EGAN

In January 1959, the forty-four-year-old Bill Egan declared that Alaskans were proud to "accept the proud challenge of statehood."

Re-elected in 1962, Egan said his second term would focus on creating more jobs and using the state's wealth to benefit its people. "Because the people of Alaska have returned me to office, the philosophy of responsible and progressive purpose that has guided the first state administration will continue."

Elected for the third time in 1970, Egan pledged to "harmonize and orchestrate our efforts in the common good" and said: "We cannot heed one set of goals while ignoring another. We share an obligation to treat this land wisely and sensitively."

WALLY HICKEL

Hickel, forty-seven, defeated Egan by 1,080 votes in the 1966 campaign. In his inaugural address in January 1967, Hickel sounded a theme that he touched on countless times over the decades.

"We must take stock of what we are today, our resources, our strengths, our weaknesses. We must have a vision of tomorrow, for all things of reality must first be an idea, a vision, and a dream. We will build a strong course of economic development and progress for all Alaskans, and in the course of that vision, many of the good things of life will come to us."

Hickel became secretary of interior in 1969, and Keith Miller, forty-three, moved up from the job now known as lieutenant governor to finish the term.

When Hickel, then seventy-one, returned to Juneau in 1990 for another term, he pledged a "new day for Alaska" and said that it ought to be fun. "True pioneers know wealth is not money," he said. "Wealth is a sense of purpose. It comes from inside."

JAY HAMMOND

Hammond, fifty-two, who edged Egan by 287 votes in 1974, made reference to his margin of victory, saying "I come before you upon this occasion not buoyed by a surging electoral groundswell, but rather bobbing, somewhat restively, upon a ripple—a wavelet of modest pomp and spare proportion."

"Heaven help us should we not remain aware that 'environment' is not an obscene, four-letter word. It has eleven letters, just as does the word 'development.'"

Re-elected in 1978, Hammond spoke of the danger of government excess in his ornate phrasing known as "Hammondese."

"Each lush, governmentally subsidized endeavor seems to impollinate itself to sprout up as yet another weed which must then, as well, be winnowed from our field of view. Too often such programs are conceived in hope only to abort later in dismay, leaving naught but windrows of sere huskings."

He said he believed the state had been "especially blessed" by the Almighty.

"Because of my self-acknowledged inadequacies, I was compelled more ardently to recognize the fact that there is an authority above us all, an authority which if called upon, collectively, can lead this state and this nation to our proper destiny despite the fumblings and deficiencies of those who might hold public office."

BILL SHEFFIELD

When he became governor in December 1982, Bill Sheffield, fifty-four, promised to help put people back to work, saying that Alaska's oil bonanza had not made everyone wealthy.

"We're not nearly as rich as most people think," Sheffield said. "If you have any doubt of that, just ask the people in Anchorage or Fairbanks who have neither job nor home; or ask the unemployed railroad worker in Skagway or the out-of-work logger in Wrangell. They are out of job or home because of events out of their control, whether it be hard economic times in the Lower 48 or a decision on the other side of the world by a foreign government. Despite our wealth, Alaska is not immune to world events."

STEVE COWPER

In a ten-minute speech in December 1986, Cowper, forty-eight, said the recent collapse in oil prices was something that Alaskans could survive.

"We can no longer afford to be the prisoners of events we cannot control, such as oil price agreements in the Middle East, or decisions made in our national capital based on shortsighted political consideration," he said.

"We have an obligation to govern ourselves wisely and well, because a short-sighted and profligate government is an intolerable burden on a people who aspire to be leaders," he said.

TONY KNOWLES

Referring to himself as "Landslide Knowles" after a 536-vote win in 1994, Tony Knowles, fifty-one, called for regional and racial unity.

"Our responsibility is to have the courage to unite," he said. "No longer can we afford to pit one group against another, region versus region, and urban versus rural."

After winning re-election by a comfortable margin in 1998, Knowles said that because of a steep drop in oil prices, the state had to focus on holding the state budget down and creating new jobs.

"Alaskans achieve greatness when we put aside our differences, unite behind Alaska goals and values, and move with a sense of purpose to take responsibility for our own destiny," he said.

FRANK MURKOWSKI

Murkowski, sixty-nine, said that Republican control in Juneau and Washington, D.C. was a good sign for the state when he became governor in 2002.

"For the first time in a long time there is unity in the House and Senate, not only in Juneau but in Washington as well," Murkowski said. "And never before have the stars been so in alignment."

SOURCE NOTES

INTRODUCTION

15.   "unbelieving crowds" : New York Times, July 1, 1958
15.   "Alaska is not so much": New York Times, January 4, 1959
16.   "Alaska's Ordeal": Wall Street Journal, March 16, 1960
17.   "North to the Future": Alaska Blue Book 1991-92 (Juneau: State of Alaska, 1991), 242.

CHAPTER 1

21.   "It was a little choppy": Seattle Post-Intelligencer, January 20, 1959
21.   "The next night": Fairbanks Daily News-Miner, January 25, 1959
22.   "He is desperately": Seattle Post-Intelligencer, January 21, 1959
22.   "a miniature of": Ibid.
22.   Egan read about three paragraphs: Juneau Independent, April 22, 1959
22.   "Once I recall": Fairbanks Daily News-Miner, April 18, 1959.
23.   "I urge all Alaskans": Ibid. January 20, 1959.
25.   I got ten cents an hour": Government Executive Magazine, Feburary 1974.
25.   He hitched a ride: Vic Fischer, Alaska's Constitutional Convention (Fairbanks: University of Alaska Press 1975), 29.
25.   "he had committed": Author's interview with Katie Hurley, June 2008.
25.   One of the secrets to his: Murray Morgan, Harper's Magazine, October 1965.
25.   "After many years": Fairbanks Daily News-Miner, April 25, 1959.
27.   "It never looked particularly": Salina Kansas Journal, December 2, 1962.
27.   "He started reading the Congressional": Ibid.
27.   "Be sure to make it 1959": New York Times, January 4, 1959.
28.   Some grumbled later: Anchorage Daily News, January 7, 1959.
28.   Eisenhower had been: Claus-M. Naske , Bob Bartlett of Alaska (Fairbanks: University of Alaska Press, 1979) 161.
28.   "But I was overruled": Fairbanks Daily News-Miner, January 5, 1959.
30.   "History had been made": Ibid.
30.   As he raised his other hand: Juneau Independent, January 8, 1959.
30.   Alaska's radio stations: Fairbanks Daily News-Miner, January 3, 1959.
30.   Dignitaries gathered outside: Juneau Empire, January 5, 1959.
31   "sat on the stage with": Jessen's Weekly, January 8, 1959.

31   "Saturday was the greatest": Ibid.
32.   "We Dood It": Juneau Empire, January 5, 1959.
32.   The bold, black letters: Anchorage Times, June 30, 1958.
32.   "Conga and Bunny Hop": Fairbanks Daily News-Miner, June 30, 1983.
34.   It was a matter of: Jessen's Weekly, February 2, 1959.
34.   When the chance to select: Bits and Pieces of Alaska History, Vol. 2 (Anchorage: Alaska Northwest Publishing Co., 1982), 14.
34.   "Few contests in Congress": New York Times, July 1, 1958.
34.   Johnson won the backing: Ketchikan Daily News, January 14, 1959.
35.   Because neither man: Naske, Bob Bartlett of Alaska, 171.
35.   "I'm sure the opponents": Fairbanks Daily News-Miner, January 5, 1959.
35.   "meaning of statehood": Tom Stewart, The Meaning of Statehood to Alaska, State Government, Autumn 1958.
35.   Egan made good on one: Seattle Post-Intelligencer, January 6, 1959.
38.   "Alaska's enemy number one": Fairbanks Daily News-Miner, June 30, 1958.
38.   "I can't begin to express": Fairbanks Daily News-Miner, April 14, 1959.

CHAPTER 2

43.   On the day Alaska: Ketchikan Daily News, January 8, January 9, 1959.
43.   "It is noted that mail": Ibid, January 8, 1959.
43.   Such was the state of: Fairbanks Daily News-Miner, January 25, 1959.
43.   A majority of the sixty: Ketchikan Daily News, February 11, 1959.
46.   "merely the power to persuade": Ernest Gruening, Many Battles: The Autobiography of Ernest Gruening (New York: Liveright, 1973), 287.
46.   The Territorial Legislature typically: Juneau Independent, March 4, 1959.
46.   "make a saber tooth": Harper's Magazine, October, 1965.
46.   As they gathered in Juneau: Ketchikan Daily News, January 13, 1959.
47.   "Yours is a role comparable": William Egan papers, University of Alaska Fairbanks Rasmuson Library, Box 70, Folder 9.
47.   minimum of words": Juneau Independent, January 26,1959.
47.   "This was a stupendous": Fairbanks Daily News-Miner, April 20, 1959.
51.   "Now boys, it's really outrageous": Juneau Independent, February 18, 1959.
51.   "Not one working man": Ketchikan Daily News, February 10, 1959.
51.   The legislative pay bill: Ketchikan Daily News, February 11, March 21, 1959.
52.   Lawmakers changed the age: Sessions Laws of Alaska, 1959,
52.   "Those were fantastic days": Anchorage Daily News, November 2, 1968.
53.   Floyd Guertin, forty-five: Fairbanks Daily News-Miner, April 4, 1959.
53.   For the most part": Lansing Michigan State Journal, August 15, 1960.
53.   "a sense of awe": Fairbanks Daily News-Miner, November 11, 1959.
53.   "loot the new state of Alaska": Ketchikan Daily News, February 7, 1959.
55.   The honeymoon is over": Wall Street Journal, March 16, 1960.
55.   "Alaska is beset": U.S. News & World Report, September 4, 1961.
55.   Yet, the trend in the early: Wall Street Journal, July 29, 1961.
55.   "an invalid ward": Saturday Evening Post, October 12, 1963.
56.   "Personally, I doubt": William Egan papers, University of Alaska Fairbanks Rasmuson library, Bob Bartlett letter to W.O. Smith, April 23, 1960.
56.   "Alaskan lumber mills": George W. Rogers, The Future of Alaska: Economic Consequences of Statehood (Baltimore: John Hopkins Press, 1960), 234.
56.   "Truly, a financial crisis": Anchorage Times, January 29, 1960.
57.   "If we do nothing": New York Times, August 2, 1960.
57.   "It is this type of backward": Anchorage Times, January 30, 1960.
57.   "The first fruit of statehood": London Observer, July 13, 1958.

CHAPTER 3

59.   "The city has a potential": Anchorage Daily News, February 4, 1959.
59.   "There's just enough": Saturday Evening Post, September 19, 1959.
59.   Where could he go: Walter J. Hickel, Who Owns America? (Englewood Cliffs, N.J.: Prentice-Hall, 1971) Chapter 2.
62.   "Alaska's number one young": Herb and Miriam Hilscher (Boston, Little, Brown & Co., 1959), 203.
62.   "In all of Alaska": Fairbanks Daily News-Miner, Februray 26, 1960.
64.   "When the Malaspina": Bern Keating (National Geographic Society, 1969), 64.
64.   In March of that year: Fairbanks Daily News-Miner, March 1, 1960.
68.   "by and large, the people": New Yorker, April 2, 1960.
68.   "Anchorage has television": New York Times, November 30, 1958.
68.   Making a phone call: Fairbanks Municipal Utilities System phone book 1959.
68.   The ad men returned: Hilscher, 36.
69.   Dozens of empty jugs: Anchorage Times, April 1, 1959.
69.   "big lie": William Egan papers, University of Alaska Fairbanks Rasmuson Library, Box 65, Folder 13.
71.   In 1983, the four time zones: Carl Benson, University of Alaska, Alaska Science Forum, March 25, 1983.

CHAPTER 4

73.   Air Force Captain Charles Maultsby: Michael Dobbs, One Minute to Midnight: Kennedy, Khrushchev and Castro on the Brink of Nuclear War (New York, Alfred A. Knopf, 2008) , 260.
74.   "The critical decision about whether": Scott Sagan, The Limits of Safety: Organizations, Accidents and Nuclear Weapons (Princeton University Press, 1993), 137.
75.   "One asks Mr. President": The Presidential Recordings, John F. Kennedy, The Great Crises, Vol. 3 (New York, W.W. Norton, The Miller Center of Public Affairs, 2001) 515.
75.   "serious navigational error": Ibid, 524.
75.   "most important strategic place": Melody Webb, Yukon: The Last Frontier, (UBC Press, 1993), 167.
77.   "This is the President": John Chapman, Atlas: The Story of a Missile, (New York: Harper, 1960), 165.
77.   "Interception might come": Richard Morenus, DEW Line: Distant Early Warning, The Miracle of America's First Line of Defense (New York, Rand McNally, 1957), 178.
79.   "the effect of blast": Fairbanks Daily News-Miner, 1959 Progress Edition.
79.   "welcome new weapon": Time, March 16, 1959.
81.   "bullet with a bullet": Los Angeles Times, December 30, 2001.
82.   "If these attacks were followed up": New York Times, December 4, 1959.
81.   "There is no better place": Anchorage Times, August 1, 1959.
82.   "As he no doubt expected": William Egan papers, University of Alaska Fairbanks Rasmuson Library, July 28, 1961 speech, Box 70, Folder 47.
83.   "foolhardy, if not irresponsible": Fairbanks Daily News-Miner, June 30, 1960.
83.   "have a strategic diversionary": New York Times, June 15, 1960.
85.   "being viewed with satisfaction": Fairbanks Daily News-Miner, June 30, 1960.
85.   "These areas, and these": New York Times, March 15, 1959.
85.   "defend every community": Ibid, April 26, 1959.
86.   "No other senator": U.S. News & World Report, September 29, 2007.
86.   "When you examine": Hedrick Smith, The Power Game: How Washington Works, (New York: Ballantine Books, 1996), 184.
87.   "The issue involved today": Anchorage Daily News, March 28, 2008.

CHAPTER 5

89. Within seconds after rising: Anchorage Times, March 26, 1965.
89. Scientists estimated that the energy: The Great Alaska Earthquake of 1964, Human Ecology (Washington, D.C.: National Academy of Sciences, 1970), ix.
93. "I figured something had gone wrong": Genie Chance, Chronology of the Physical Events of the Alaskan Earthquake, (Anchorage: University of Alaska, 1966), 133.
93. "Boy, it's some wind": Ibid, 146.
93. Outside West High School: Anchorage Times, March 26, 1974.
93. "I remember how reluctantly": Chance, 113.
96. "Residents in low-lying areas": The Great Alaskan Earthquake of 1964, 319.
96. "I saw people running": Chance, 35.
97. "All the homes had been swept": William Graves, National Geographic, July 1964.
97. "With the recent misfortunes": William Egan papers, University of Alaska Fairbanks Rasmuson Library, correspondence, April 20, 1964.
101. "I wanted to send my Easter Basket": Congressional Record, September 30, 1964.
101. "I reject that without qualification": Bob Bartlett news release, April 1964.
101. "There is little equity": The Great Alaskan Earthquake of 1964, Human Ecology, 22.
102. "Had we been required to follow": Washington Post, October 30, 2006.
104. "What can there be but praise": Anchorage Times, March 26, 1965.
104. "It doesn't matter how well engineered": Sheila Ann Selkregg, The Decision and Rationale Which Led to Construction on High-Risk Land After the 1964 Alaska Earthquake - Analysis of Risk Based Cultural Dissociation, Ph.D. Dissertation, Portland State University 1994-95.

CHAPTER 6

107. The statehood land grant: Claus-M Naske, 103,350,000 Acres . . . the land Grant Provisions of Alaska Statehood Bills from 1916 Onward, Alaska Journal, Autumn, 1972, 21-23.
108. "Wanted—a crystal ball gazer": New York Times, January 18, 1959.
108. Given the slow pace: The Alaska Land Transfer Acceleration Act: Background and Summary, 2005, Library of Congress.
109. "a controversy of immense": Willie Hensley, What Rights to Land Have the Alaska Natives: The primary issue, constitutional law paper, University of Alaska, 1966.
109. "In retrospect, given the steadily": Edward Teller, Memoirs A Twentieth Century Journey in Science and Politics, (Cambridge, Mass.: Perseus Publishing, 2001), 449.
111. "The Alaskan Press threw": Harper's Magazine, April 1962.
111. No one, least of all the Atomic": Fairbanks Daily News-Miner, January 19, 1959.
111. "We the Inupiat have come": Claus-M Naske and Herman Slotnick, Alaska: A History of the 49th State, (Norman, Okla.: University of Oklahoma Press, 1979), 196.
111. "worthless harbor": Harper's Magazine, November 1962.
114. Supporters said the Rampart: William Egan papers, University of Alaska Fairbanks Rasmuson Library. Speech to Alaska Rural Electric Cooperative, August 11, 1961. Box 70, folder 49.
115. "Many Natives are only": Fairbanks Daily News-Miner, January 23, 1964.
115. The Plot to Drown Alaska: Atlantic Monthly, May 1965.
115. The Plot to Strangle Alaska: Ibid, July 1965.
118. "Claims were laid": Dermot Cole, Fairbanks: A Gold Rush Town that Beat the Odds, (Fairbanks: Epicenter Press, 1999) 184.
119. The official, Newton Edwards: Donald Mitchell, Take My Land, Take My Life: The Story of Congress's Historic Settlement of Alaska Native Land Claims, 1960-1971, (Fairbanks: University of Alaska Press, 2001), 94.

119.   "I saw my first white man": Lael Morgan, Art and Eskimo Power: The Life and Times of Alaskan Howard Rock, (Fairbanks: Epicenter Press, 1988), 221.

120.   "I'm talking about our original": Alaska Native Corporations CEO report, 2006, 15.

120.   "People can quibble": Fairbanks Daily News-Miner, October 18, 1988.

120.   The idea that the land: Mitchell, 158.

121.   "transactions were instrumental": James Linxwiler, The Alaska Native Claims Settlement Act at 35: Delivering on the Promise,.Paper 12, 53rd Annual Rocky Mountain Mineral Law Institute, 2007, 156.

121.   "The economic clout": Fairbanks Daily News-Miner, December 16, 1991.

CHAPTER 7

123.   "Meals were served": Jack Roderick, Crude Dreams: A Personal History of Oil & Politics in Alaska (Fairbanks: Epicenter Press, 1997) 276.

128.   There was only one limitation: Anchorage Daily News, September 11, 1969.

128.   "We'd be in a hell": Saturday Evening Post , October 12, 1963.

128.   "Tomorrow we reach out": Anchorage Daily News, September 10, 1969.

128.   An Oklahoma company: Anchorage Times, September 9, 1969.

128.   "future untroubled": Ibid, September 11, 1969.

130.   The oilmen and journalists: Hugh Gregory Gallagher, Etok: A Story of Eskimo Power (New York: G.P. Putman's Sons, 1974) 184.

131.   "it appears that all": Anchorage Times, September 10, 1969.

131.   "For the industry": Anchorage Daily News, September 12, 1969.

132.   "Whether this is the last": Anchorage Times, September 24, 1969.

132.   "I have already been confronted": Anchorage Daily News, September 12, 1969.

133.   One of the advocates: Ibid, September 10, 1969,

133.   "The field resulted": Gill Mull, Alaska's Oil/Gas and Minerals Industry, Alaska Geographic Quarterly 9, no. 4 (1982), 187,

133.   "remedy future serious": Fairbanks Daily News-Miner, January 14, 1964.

136.   "We used that as a": Transcript of oral history interview with Roscoe Bell, University of Alaska Fairbanks Rasmuson Library by Paul McCarthy, May 1985, 69.

136.   "Made solely to solve": Roderick, 172.

137.   "But tomorrow?": Oil & Gas Journal, August 22, 1966.

140.   "I don't know why": Fairbanks Daily News-Miner, May 3, 1967.

140.   "There'll be oil for Christmas": Ibid.

142.   "My information is that": Jessen's Weekly, March 15, 1968,

142.   "We have enough contracts": U.S. News & World Report, December 9, 1968.

142.   Other proposals for shipping: New York Times, December 17, 1969.

CHAPTER 8

145.   As the tally took place: New York Times, July 18, 1973.

148.   "His failure to act": Jim Magoffin, Triumph Over Turbulence: Alaska's Luckiest Bush Pilot, (Fairbanks: Self-published, 1993), 245.

148.   "They're talking about burying": Fairbanks Daily News-Miner, June 26,1970.

148.   "build it now": Ibid.

148.   "We are going to do everything": Seattle Post-Intelligencer, February 20, 1971.

149.   "Rest assured": New York Times, February 17, 1971,

149.   "In Canada, you don't": Harper's Magazine, May 1970.

152.   "This thing has to be viewed": Robert Douglas Mead, Journeys Down the Line: Building the Trans-Alaska Pipeline, (New York: Doubleday & Co., 1978) , 209.

152.   "Many of the abuses that": Dermot Cole, Amazing Pipeline Stories: How Building the Trans-Alaska Pipeline Transformed Life in America's Last Frontier, (Fairbanks: Epicenter Press, 1997) , 29.

154. "If one thing is missing": Mead, 211.

154. "I enjoyed the company": Cole, 167.

154. Fairbanks Becomes Wild City: All-Alaska Weekly, July 25, 1975.

155. It seems that Alaska is not so": Fairbanks Daily News-Miner, Progress Edition, 1975.

158. Carr, whose empire: Jay Hammond, Tales of Alaska's Bush Rat Governor, (Fairbanks: Epicenter Press, 1994), 213.

158. "This time I saw eleven": Anchorage Times, June 22, 1975.

158. "sudden and unexpected wealth": Cole, 119.

159. "If there has ever been a greater": Hammond, 177.

159. "We've fetched up hard aground": Alaska Oil Spill Commission Final Report, 1990, 13.

164. Exxon sold the tanker: Anchorage Daily News, February 25, 2008.

164. After nearly two decades: Ibid, June 26, 2008.

CHAPTER 9

167. "present and future generations": Alaska National Interest Lands Conservation Act, Public Law 96-487 (94 Stat. 2371) December 2, 1980.

170. "They had four pictures on the wall": The American Presidency Project, remarks on signing H.R. 39 into law, University of California at Santa Barbara, www.presidency.ucsb.edu.

170. "It was the most important": Anchorage Daily News, July 7, 2005.

170. "Over half of the federal lands": The American Presidency Project, remarks on signing H.R. 39 into law, University of California at Santa Barbara, www.presidency.ucsb.edu..

171. The Great Alaska Feud: Washington Post, September 30, 1979,

171. "I believe Alaska has suffered": Anchorage Daily News, September 4, 2007.

173. "I don't want to get personal": Washington Post, September 30, 1979.

179. "It's not something I would": Anchorage Daily News, December 17, 2005.

179. "turbulence is the norm": Frank Norris, Alaska Subsistence: A National Park Service Management History, (Diane Publishing, 2002) Chapter 10.

179. "The court said the state": Kenai Peninsula Clarion, December 29, 2006.

CHAPTER 10

183. Barely two decades: State of Alaska, Division of Elections, August 26, 1980.

183. "latest American bombshell": Jay S. Hammond, speech to Allied Newspaper Publishers, September 15, 1980, Juneau.

184. "resist the federal drive": Alaska Statehood Commission Final Report, More Perfect Union: A Plan for Action, Juneau 1983.

185. "Theodore Stevens gets promotion": Juneau Empire, January 5, 1959.

185. "most extreme case of clout": Roll Call, May 6, 1993.

185. "About a third of all jobs": Scott Goldsmith, Insitute of Social and Economic Research, University of Alaska Anchorage, July 2008.

187. "As a former chairman": Los Angeles Times, August 7, 2007.

190. "However, for the long term": Hammond speech, September 15, 1980.

191. "We have gotten ourselves into": Fairbanks Daily News-Miner, May 4, 1977.

191. "I believe we can structure": Ibid, August 9, 1982.

192. "Alaska is America's fastest": Anchorage Daily News, March 16, 1986.

192. "Too many people and institutions": Terrrence Cole, Banking on Alaska: The Story of the National Bank of Alaska, Vol. 1 (Anchorage: Rasmuson Foundation, 2000), 425.

193. "What's our plan for increasing": Fairbanks Daily News-Miner, January 27, 2003.

APPENDIX

ALASKA, STATE OF

Economic Development

LARGE DEVELOPMENT PROJECTS
Project Chariot

In 1958, under the prodding of Dr. Edward Teller, the Hungarian physicist considered one of the fathers of the hydrogen bomb, the U.S. Atomic Energy Commission proposed blowing up a string of nuclear devices to create a giant artificial harbor at Alaska's Cape Thompson. Cape Thompson lies twenty-six miles southeast of Point Hope at the northern headland of the Chukchi Sea in Arctic Alaska.

Teller traveled the new state to promote the project. Teller and other promoters of nuclear power saw creating a harbor in Alaska as a way to prove that like those from dynamite, nuclear explosions had peaceful uses transforming the face of the globe in ways useful to humanity.

Teller's immense prestige helped move Alaska's political and press establishments to champion the project for which no one could figure out an immediate Alaskan use but which promised to spend a lot of federal money in Alaska and which also promised, proponents said, to provide a major new port for Alaska and perhaps the world.

The Inupiat at the small village of Point Hope objected that the project would destroy sources for their subsistence way of life and perhaps their way of life entirely. In this era before the passage of national environmental protection acts, some scientists objected immediately about the great nuclear blast or blasts spreading perilous and long-lasting radioactivity over the Arctic and perhaps populated areas of Europe, Asia, and North America. Soon the Wilderness Society, the Sierra Club, and eminent environmentalist Barry Commoner joined the battle against the project.

In 1962, unused to vast public objections, the Atomic Energy Commission announced it would delay the project. It has never formally been canceled but few think it has any prospects.

-John de Yonge

Sources

The Firecracker Boys, Dan O'Neill, Basic Books, 2007
Alaska: A History of the 49th State, Claus-M. Naske and Herman E. Slotnick, University of Oklahoma Press, 1994
Environmental Conflict in Alaska, Ken Ross, University Press of Colorado, 2000

Rampart Dam

In the 1950s, one of the periods of great dam building by the federal government, when the U.S. Army Corps of Engineers competed with the U.S. Bureau of Reclamation in building dams and other water projects, the Corps proposed building the Rampart Dam on the Yukon River, at Rampart Canyon and close to the town of Rampart.

The dam would have been the largest in North America, perhaps the world, granting that at the time in the midst of the Cold War, the Soviet government kept secret the sizes and capacities of some of its giant water projects on the Volga River and elsewhere.

The project, which would take a decade to finish, perhaps more, would create an another great lake, this one a 400-mile-long reservoir larger than Lake Erie and flooding the Yukon way back into Canada, which had not been asked about the project. The lake would take twenty-two years to fill.

The dam's economic justification was to generate 5,000 megawatts of electricity, two and one-half times more juice than was being used in all of Alaska then. A long and vast array of high-tension lines would have to be built to plug the dam's electricity into anything but the village of Rampart.

The corps' report allowed that turning the Yukon into a giant lake would kill off the Yukon's giant salmon runs upstream of Rampart, drown vast numbers of moose, bears, beavers, muskrats and other animals, inundate a large part of the breeding and nesting grounds of ducks, geese and swans and other birds, and otherwise have major impacts on the lives of Natives living along or otherwise depending on the Yukon for their sustenance and way of life. Those Natives in the way of rising Rampart Dam waters would have to leave, like it or not. The idea did not please them.

Until statehood came to Alaska in 1959, few paid attention to the Rampart Dam. Then U.S. Sen. Ernest Gruening, a Democrat and New Dealer, took up the cause of building it.

Gruening touted the Rampart Dam as being equal to or better than Soviet dams and therefore necessary if for nothing else than American prestige. He also foresaw vast economic development coming to Alaska, especially the Interior, with smelters smelting away, factories humming, electricity flowing to power new mines and other projects. Other proponents began to cluster around the project, including those seeing it as grand allure for tourists.

The U.S. Fish and Wildlife Service from the beginning opposed the dam because of all the fish and wildlife it would eradicate. In the days before national environmental laws, such Fish and Wildlife Service opposition to water projects counted for little.

Alaska Natives, more than a decade before Congressional passage of the Alaska Native Land Claims Act, began to organize opposition, seeing the project as another white man's way of taking Native lands and resources and displacing and destroying Native cultures without so much as a thank you. They noted the dam would not only displace people living along the river, but to build it new highways would lace through Native hunting and fishing areas, bringing with them the possibility of an influx of non-Native settlers and hunters and fishers.

Leading Alaskan environmentalists such as Cecila Hunter took notice of the project and mustered opposition among national environmental organizations. The national press began writing critical, often mocking reports.

The Canadian government signaled it was distinctly not interested in having its part of the Yukon turned into an American power reservoir.

Even the tourist industry reckoned that a Yukon lake of frigid waters and wind-whipped waves would not create much of a draw for water sports.

Senator Gruening knew how to count and he came to realize the dream of the dam was turning into a damned dream as far as Congress was concerned. The votes did not exist for it.

By the time Lyndon Johnson became President, the Rampart Dam had lost impetus and finally evaporated from national consciousness, though from time to time it gets talked about as a possible passport into an industrial future for Alaska.

-John de Yonge

Sources

"Alaska's Megaproject Mentality," article, Brian Yanity, Insurgent49, online publication, 2007

http://www.insurgent49.com/yanity_megaproject_two.html

Alaska Native Land Claims Act, 1971

Alaska Native Foundation

Trans-Alaska Pipeline

Atlantic Richfield Company discovered oil on state land at Prudhoe Bay on the far north shore of Alaska in 1968 and Prudhoe Bay soon proved to be the biggest oil field ever discovered in North America. Constructing oil-field facilities began soon after, creating one of the biggest economic booms ever experienced in Alaska, especially in Fairbanks, then and now a chief staging area for moving workers and supplies to the oil field.

Oil would be moved south from Prudhoe to Valdez via the 800-mile trans-Alaska pipeline.

The eight oil companies seeking to build and operate the pipeline—Humble Pipeline (now Exxon), Atlantic Richfield (later ARCO), BP, Amerada Hess, Home Pipeline, Mobile Pipeline, Philips Petroleum, and Union Oil—had to await federal resolution of land claims by Native Alaskans before starting construction. The Native claims included land over which the oil companies sought a right-of-way.

Congress settled the Native claims with passage of the Alaska Native Claims Settlement Act in 1971. President Richard Nixon signed the Trans-Alaska Pipeline Authorization act in 1973.

The project required more than three million tons of construction material, consumed seventy-three million cubic yards of gravel, and employed more than 70,000 workers over its lifespan, with a peak of 28,072 employed in October, 1975.

The pipeline crosses three mountain ranges and more than 500 rivers and streams. Other pipeline facts:

Diameter: 48 inches

Cost: $8 billion in 1977; largest privately funded construction project at that time

Start of construction: March 27, 1975

Completion: May 31, 1977

First tanker to carry oil: ARCO Juneau, August 1, 1977

Tankers loaded at Valdez: 19,625 through April 2008

Oil transport: More than 15 billion barrels as of 2008

-Sam Travis

Sources

Alyeska Pipeline Service Company

http://www.alyeska-pipe.com/pipelinefacts.html

Trans-Alaska Pipeline System, Environmental Impact Survey, renewal information, U.S. Department of the Interior, Bureau of Land Management, 2008

http://tapseis.anl.gov/documents/docs/Section_13_May2.pdf

TOURISM

Summer visitors to Alaska, 2001-2007

2001: 1,202,800

2002: 1,275,000

2003: 1,310,100

2004: 1,447,400

2005: 1,632,000

2006: 1,631,000

2007: 1,714,100

Add to these numbers another 250,000 visitors in the winter months, increasing the estimated total for 2007 to 1,964,000.

Alaska's permanent population is estimated at 627,000. That means more than three times as many people visit Alaska each year as live in the state.

In 2007, summer visitors added $1.8 billion to the state's economy, according to the Alaska Travel Industry Association.

Sources

2001-04 data from "Alaska Visitor Arrivals Studies" conducted by Northern Economics, Inc.

2005-07 data based on 2006 visitor/resident ratios obtained by McDowell Group, Inc.

Anchorage Daily News

http://www.adn.com/money/industries/tourism/story/81884.html

Government

EXECUTIVE
Alaska State governors since 1959:
1959-1966, William A. Egan, Democrat
1966-1969, Walter J. Hickel, Republican
1969-1970, Keith H. Miller, Republican
1970-1974, William A. Egan, Democrat
1974-1982, Jay S. Hammond, Republican
1982-1986, William J. Sheffield, Democrat
1986-1990, Steve C. Cowper, Democrat
1990-1994, Walter J. Hickel, Independent
1994-2002, Tony C. Knowles, Democrat
2002-2006, Frank H. Murkowski, Republican
2006-, Sarah H. Palin, Republican

Sources
Alaska State Legislature
http://w3.legis.state.ak.us/pubs/pubs.php
Alaska State Legislature's Majority Organization
http://www.akrepublicans.org/pastlegs

JUDICIARY
Alaska Supreme Court justices since 1959:
1959-1970, Buell Nesbett; chief justice, 1959-62
1959-1971, John H. Dimond; chief justice, 1962-65
1959-1960, Walter H. Hodge
1960-1965, Harry O. Arend
1965-1997, Jay A. Rabinowitz; chief justice, 1991-94
1968-1983, Roger G. Connor
1968-1972, George F. Boney; chief justice, 1969-72
1970-1977, Robert C. Erwin
1972-1980, Robert Boochever; chief justice, 1975-78
1972-1975, James M. Fitzgerald
1975-1993, Edmond W. Burke
1977-, Warren W. Mathews; chief justice, 1987-90 and 1997-2000
1980-1998, Allen T. Compton; chief justice, 1994-97
1983-1995, Daniel A. Moore, Jr.
1994-, Robert L. Eastaugh
1996-, Dana Fabe; chief justice, 2000-2003 and 2006-present
1997-2007, Alexander O. Bryner; chief justice, 2003-2006
1998-, Walter L. Carpeneti
2008-, Daniel E. Winfree
Note: The five members of the Supreme Court elect from among themselves a chief justice to serve a three-year term. A justice may serve more than once as chief justice, but not consecutively.

Sources
Alaska Court System
http://www.state/ak.us/courts
Alaska Judicial Council
http://www.ajc.state.ak.us/Selection/apptlog3.htm

LEGISLATIVE
House of Representatives
Speakers of the House of Representatives since 1959:
1959-1962, Warren A. Taylor, Democrat, Fairbanks
1963-1964, Bruce Kendall, Republican, Anchorage
1965-1966, Mike Gravel, Democrat, Anchorage
1967-1968, William K. Boardman, Republican, Ketchikan
1969-1970, Jalmar M. Kertulla, Democrat, Palmer
1971-1972, Gene Guess, Democrat, Anchorage
1973-1974, Tom Fink, Republican, Anchorage
1975-1976, Mike Bradner, Democrat, Fairbanks
1977-1978, Hugh Malone, Democrat, Kenai
1979-1980, Terry Gardiner, Democrat, Ketchikan
January-June 15, 1981, Jim Duncan, Democrat, Juneau
June 16, 1981-1984, Joe L. Hayes, Republican, Anchorage
1985-1988, Ben F. Grussendorf, Democrat, Sitka
1989-1990, Samuel R. Cotton, Democrat, Eagle River
1991-1992, Ben F. Grussendorf, Democrat, Sitka
1993-1994, Ramona L. Barnes, Republican, Anchorage
1995-1998, Gail Phillips, Republican, Homer
1999-2002, Brian S. Porter, Republican, Anchorage
2003-2004, Pete Kott, Republican, Eagle River
2005-, John Harris, Republican, Valdez

Senate
Presidents of the Alaska State Senate since 1959
1959-1960, William E. Beltz, Democrat, Unalakleet
1961-1964, Frank Peratrovich, Democrat, Klawock
1965-1966, Robert J. McNealy, Democrat, Fairbanks
1967-1968, John Butrovich, Jr., Republican, Fairbanks
1969-1970, Brad Phillips, Republican, Anchorage
1971-1972, Jay S. Hammond, Republican, Naknek
1973-1974, Terry Miller, Republican, Fairbanks
1975-1976, Chancy Croft, Democrat, Anchorage
1977-1978, John L. Rader, Democrat, Anchorage
1979-1980, Clem V. Tillion, Republican, Homer
1981-1984, Jalmar M. Kerttula, Democrat, Palmer
1985-1986, Don Bennett, Republican, Fairbanks
1987-1988, Jan Faiks, Republican, Anchorage
1989-1990, Tim Kelly, Republican, Anchorage

1991-1992, Richard I. "Dick" Eliason, Republican, Sitka
1993-1994, Rick Halford, Republican, Chugiak
1995-1996, Drue Pearce, Republican, Anchorage
1997-1998, Mike W. Miller, Republican, North Pole
1999-2000, Drue Pearce, Republican, Anchorage
2001-2002, Rick Halford, Republican, Chugiak
2003-2004, Gene Therriault, Republican, North Pole
2005-2006, Ben Stevens, Republican, Anchorage
2007-2008, Lyda Green, Republican, Wasilla

Sources
Alaska State Legislature http://w3.legis.state.ak.us/pubs/pubs.php
Alaska State Legislature's Majority Organization http://www.akrepublicans.org/pastlegs

Political issues

CAPITAL MOVE
A timeline of major events:

1884: Organic Act passed by Congress creating the new office of appointed governor, who resided in Sitka.

1900: Capitol move to Juneau from Sitka mandated by Congress, completed in 1906.

1931: The Alaska State Capitol building opens in Juneau.

1960: General election voters turn down, by a vote of 18,000 for and 23,000 against, an initiative to relocate the capital from Juneau to the Cook Inlet–Railbelt area.

1962: Voters reject an initiative to move the capital to western Alaska, at least thirty miles from Anchorage. The initiative failed, 26,000 for to 32,000 against.

1974: Voters pass an initiative to relocate the capital to one of three sites in western Alaska, at least thirty miles from both Anchorage and Fairbanks. A selection committee offers Larson Lake, Mount Yenlo, and Willow as possible locations.

1976: Voters choose Willow as the new capital site.

1978: Voters pass an initiative to determine the cost of moving the capital before moving it. However, a $996 million bond proposal fails 31,000 for to 88,000 against, resulting in a repeal of the 1974 initiative.

1982: Voters reject paying $2.843 billion to move the capital to Willow, 91,000 for to 102,000 against. Proponents abandon relocating the capital to Willow.

1994: A new initiative calls for a relocation to Wasilla. At the same time the FRANK organization (Fiscally Responsible Alaskans Needing Knowledge) places an initiative on the ballot to require the state to announce total costs of any attempt to move the state capital or legislature. This measure also gives voters the right to approve any bonds for those costs. The relocation initiative fails. The FRANK Initiative passes 159,000 for to 46,000 against.

2002: On a statewide vote of 74,000 yes to 153,000 no, voters reject an initiative to repeal the FRANK Initiative and to move legislative sessions to the Matanuska-Susitna Borough, or to Anchorage if appropriate buildings can't be found in Mat-Su.

To date: The Alaska capital remains in Juneau.

Sources
Bill McAllister, article, "Alaska dreams of a new Capitol, but where," Stateline.org: http://www.stateline.org/live/
ViewPage.action?siteNodeId=136&languageId=1&contentId=15936
Fiscally Responsible Alaskans Needing Knowledge http://www.frankinitiative.net/your_rIghts/HOME.html

STATEHOOD REVIEW
By law, the Alaska Statehood Commission gathered in Constitution Hall at the University of Alaska Fairbanks on October 22, 1980, to begin studying the relationship of Alaska's citizens to the United States and to recommend possible changes in that relationship. Recent federal legislation setting off large amounts of Alaska for national parks, wildlife areas and other uses stimulated the Alaska Legislature to create the commission.

The commission had eleven members: five appointed by the governor, two by the president of the state Senate, two by the speaker of the House of Representatives, and two by the Alaska Legislative Council.

Over the next twenty-seven months the commission requested public comments from Alaskans, with hearings across the state. It commissioned fourteen expert studies ranging in subject from the history of the statehood movement to the flow of funds between Alaska and the federal government, the status and well-being of Alaska's Natives, and the relative success of the Alaska Statehood Act.

In 1981, it published "More Perfect Union: A Preliminary Report," invited additional public comment, and then gathered to draft its final conclusions.

The commission's 1982 final report, "A More Perfect Union: A Plan for Action," issued twenty recommendations for the state's relationship to the United States.

The commission's members were Jack Coghill of Nenana, H.A. "Red" Boucher of Anchorage, Ruth Burnett of Fairbanks, Nelda Calhoun of Homer, Evelyn Conwell of Kotzebue, John Dapcevich of Sitka, Miles Davic of Anchorage, Gregg Erickson of Juneau, Sue Greene of Juneau, Edward Merdes of Fairbanks, and Brian Rogers of College.

Their report recommended the following:

1. "Alaska should become an activist state. It should take a lead among states to define the boundaries of state powers in our union."

2. "Repeal of the Jones Act will serve Alaska's and the nation's interest, and Alaska should seek repeal. In the short term, the state should dedicate itself to getting the Jones Act amended to allow the use of foreign-built ships in Jones Act trade."

3. "Alaska and our congressional delegation should vigorously oppose the extension of that portion of the Export Administration Act of 1979 which bans the export of Alaska North Slope oil. This law expires in 1983."

4. "Alaska must act immediately to create in Washington, D.C., a research and advocacy institute and ask other resource states to join in supporting it. The institute would combat efforts in Congress to limit or tax state resource revenues."

5. "The state Board of Education and Alaska school districts should require the teaching of Alaskan history, citizenship, and culture."

6. "The Alaska State Legislature should pass a resolution applying to Congress under Article V of the U.S. Constitution for the calling of a national constitutional convention. The convention's sole duty would be to define procedures governing all future constitutional conventions called by the states."

7. "Alaska should take the initiative to establish a legal action fund for the states. Lawyers for this fund would sue to oppose illegal and coercive federal restrictions, regulations, burdensome to state and local government, and excessive use by Congress of its commerce powers to override state and local laws."

8. "Alaska should provide seed money to the National Governors' Association or like organization to sponsor a national convocation on federalism in the United States."

9. "Alaska and other states should consider amending the U.S. Constitution to strengthen the role of the states."

10. "The governor of Alaska should prepare the political impact statements on proposed major federal actions. Eventually, the National Governors' Association should prepare them on behalf of all states."

11. "Alaska's governor should invite the leaders of northwestern states and the western Canadian provinces and territories to join Alaska in establishing a conference modeled after the New England Governors and Eastern Canadian Premiers Conference. The governor should establish in the executive branch an interagency task force on foreign relations."

12. "The Legislature and the governor should immediately invite representatives from Hawaii and the noncontiguous possessions to meet with them to explore setting up a permanent coalition to deal with such common interest problems as the effects of discriminatory transportation laws."

13. "Alaska must vigorously police federal implementation of the Alaska Statehood Act. We should insist that the remaining land transfers be completed within four years, and we must guard against congressional attempts to unilaterally change the Statehood Act or Alaska Constitution. The Legislature should authorize and direct the lieutenant governor to place all such attempted changes in the Statehood Act or Alaska Constitution before Alaskans vote in a ballot proposition."

14. "Alaska should consider two amendments to the state constitution which will clarify Alaska's powers as a sovereign state and its authority to engage in foreign relations."

15. "State officials should refuse federal grants carrying particularly burdensome requirements."

16. "The Legislature should fund the Department of Revenue or other appropriate agency to make an annual study of and report on the flow of federal spending and revenues in Alaska."

17. "The governor should establish an office of external relations on his staff, to be headed by a special assistant charged with coordinating Alaska's expanded relations with other states and with foreign nations."

18. "The State of Alaska should explore with the federal government and Native organizations the establishment of a permanent joint fact-finding and advisory body to air and help reconcile problems that arise over land, resources and other interests."

19. "The Legislature, in order to give all Alaskans the greatest measure of home rule, should divide Alaska's single unorganized borough into regional unorganized boroughs in accordance with the intent of the state constitution."

20. "The state should establish an Alaska information office under the governor's direction to produce clear, objective, precise information about Alaska for nationwide distribution and to arrange for visits to Alaska by members of the national press corps, members of government and other opinion-makers."
-John de Yonge

Sources
Alaska Statehood Act, Public Law 85-508, July 7, 1958.
Session Laws and Resolves, 11th Alaska Legislature, 1980,
"A More Perfect Union: A Plan for Action, Final
Report," Alaska Statehood Commission, 1982

SUBSISTENCE HUNTING & FISHING
A timeline of major events:

1925: Territorial law allows "any Indian or Eskimo, prospector or traveler" to take animals, birds or game fish during closed seasons or when in need of food.

1959: The new state's constitution reserves fish and wildlife for "common use" by all Alaskans.

1960: The federal government transfers authority over fish and game to the new state.

1964: To protect sockeye salmon, state resource managers move Katie John, an Ahtna Native, from her family's ancestral fish camp at Batzulnetas on the upper Copper River.

1971: Congress passes the Alaska Native Claims Settlement Act (ANCSA). Alaska Natives give up claims to aboriginal lands and hunting and fishing rights in exchange for forty-six million acres and $962 million. The conference report states the State of Alaska and the U.S. Department of Interior will protect Native subsistence and subsistence lands.

1973: Congress begins considering what will be the Alaska National Interest Lands Conservation Act of 1980.

1974: The state Board of Game gets authority to set up subsistence hunting areas and to open and close seasons to protect subsistence.

1975: When caribou numbers in the Western Arctic herd crash, the state designs a system to award permits to hunters most dependent on the herd. A Fairbanks sportsmen's group successfully challenges the system in court, spurring efforts to include subsistence protections in federal law.

1978: Watching and anticipating congressional action on Alaska subsistence, the Alaska Legislature passes the state's first subsistence law. It defines subsistence as "customary and traditional" uses and establishes subsistence as the highest priority use of fish and wildlife. It directs the Boards of Fisheries and Game to develop regulations to allow for subsistence harvests whenever a biological surplus exists. It creates the Division of Subsistence within Alaska Department of Fish and Game. The law does not define subsistence users.

1980: Congress passes the Alaska National Interest Lands Conservation Act (ANILCA), creating new national parks, preserves, and wildlife refuges on 104 million of Alaska's 375 million acres. ANILCA requires a subsistence priority for rural residents on federal public lands. It also says the State of Alaska can manage fish and game on federal public lands *if* it enacts a law granting a subsistence priority to rural residents, in compliance with ANILCA. Congress also designates federal district courts to hear claims that the state is not implementing the subsistence priority.

1982: The state Boards of Fisheries and Game adopt regulations creating a "rural" subsistence priority to achieve consistency with ANILCA.

1982: Gov. Bill Sheffield appoints a commission to resolve subsistence controversies.

1983: A Fairbanks hunting group, Alaskans for Equal Hunting and Fishing, collects 20,000 signatures to put an initiative on the ballot to repeal the 1978 subsistence law. Voters reject the measure.

1983: Anchorage resident Sam McDowell sues the state over its subsistence law, saying it denies subsistence to some urban residents who have historically depended on it, while granting privileges to some rural residents who don't.

1984: Katie John and fellow villagers petition the Wrangell-St. Elias National Park and Preserve to resume fishing on the upper Copper River. When denied, John sues the federal government, claiming it failed to ensure her subsistence rights guaranteed under ANILCA.

1985: The Alaska Supreme Court, in the *Madison* decision, rules that state regulations limiting subsistence to rural residents aren't consistent with the state's 1978 subsistence law. The state falls out of compliance with ANILCA.

1986: The Alaska Legislature adopts a law limiting subsistence to rural residents. The new law defines rural as areas where "non-commercial, customary, and traditional use of fish and game is a principal characteristic of the economy." The law also requires the state Boards of Fish and Game to identify resources that are "customary and traditional" for subsistence.

1986: In state Superior Court, the Sam McDowell lawsuit is amended to challenge the state's new subsistence law.

1986: Kenai Peninsula Kenaitze subsistence fishers sue the State of Alaska in federal court after the Boards of Fish and Game determine most of the Kenai Peninsula to be "non-rural," making residents ineligible for subsistence fishing and hunting. The Kenaitze claim the state's definition of rural violates Title VIII of ANILCA.

1986: A federal judge rules against the Kenaitze, saying the definition of rural under state law jibes with ANILCA.

1986: A state superior court holds that the 1986 subsistence law, including the rural priority, is constitutional.

1988: The Ninth U.S. Circuit Court of Appeals reverses the Kenaitze decision, finding that the state's definition of rural is not consistent with ANILCA. The court suggests that a definition of rural hinges on demographic characteristics and orders the federal court in Alaska to establish a subsistence fishery for the Kenaitzes. The U.S. Supreme Court ultimately denies review.

1989: Under the direction of a federal district court, the state and the Kenaitze tribe agree to a one-year, educational fishery, pending a more permanent solution.

1989: A U.S. District Court, in *Bobby (Lime Village) v. State*, rules that the standard for subsistence hunting regulations is customary and traditional use of game and that seasons and bag limits generally are inappropriate for regulating subsistence.

1989: The Alaska Supreme Court, in *McDowell v. State*, rules that Alaska's subsistence law granting a priority based solely on residency is inconsistent with the "common use" clause and other sections of the Alaska State Constitution. The court grants a stay of the decision until June, 1990.

1990: With the State of Alaska out of compliance with ANILCA, the federal government publishes temporary federal subsistence regulations containing minimal changes to the state program.

1990: Seeking to avoid the extension of federal authority over subsistence, the Alaska Legislature considers alternatives, including a constitutional amendment from Gov. Steve Cowper. The House amends Cowper's proposed amendment, then rejects it. The Senate never votes on the amendment.

1990: Governor Cowper introduces a constitutional amendment to set a statewide vote aimed at holding off federal management and buying time to amend ANILCA or challenge its constitutionality. Amended by the Alaska Senate, the measure fails in the state House to get the required two-thirds vote.

1990: After the McDowell decision is remanded to the lower courts for implementation, a state judge determines that the rural criteria can be removed from state law. This leaves the state with a subsistence priority not limited to rural residents.

1990: On July 1, the secretaries of Interior and Agriculture assume subsistence management on federal public lands (not including navigable waters), adopting temporary regulations that generally mirror those of the state. The federal agencies lay out a two-year timetable for establishing a subsistence management program.

1990: A U.S. District Court authorizes an emergency caribou hunt for Kwethluk residents. The court overrules the state game board's denial of an emergency hunt, saying the board's decision lacked scientific standards that would offset the subsistence needs of Kwethluk residents.

1990: Sam McDowell, who successfully challenged the state's rural subsistence priority, sues the federal government in U.S. District Court, claiming the rural preference violates the Constitution's "equal protection" clauses and the Alaska Statehood Act, and threatens the state's ability to manage wildlife populations with sound biological principles. The state declines to intervene.

1990: The state Board of Game holds an emergency meeting to revise hunting regulations in anticipation of an increase in hunters, given that all Alaskans now are eligible for subsistence. Non-residents are excluded from many hunts.

1990: The state Department of Law opines that all Alaskans must be considered potential subsistence users in areas under state jurisdiction.

1990: Two regional Native corporations, NANA and AHTNA, close their lands to all except corporation shareholders, to protect Natives' subsistence use.

1990: Federal land management agencies assume management of subsistence uses on federal public lands.

1990: Katie John requests a federal subsistence priority for harvesting sockeye salmon at her traditional fish camp on the upper Copper River. The National Park Service recommends the appeal be denied. John sues the Secretaries of Interior and Agriculture in federal court.

1990: Three Native groups—the Association of Village Council Presidents, Tanana Chiefs Council, and Rural Alaska Resource Association—seek inclusion of "navigable waters" in the federal definition of public lands.

1990: The state Board of Fisheries adopts a policy to address subsistence fishing proposals only if subsistence needs aren't being met, or if conservation is a concern.

1990: The Arctic Regional Fish and Game Council in U.S. District Court challenges federal temporary subsistence regulations, arguing they are inconsistent with Native customs and traditions.

1990: Gov. Steve Cowper names thirteen to a commission on subsistence, created during special legislative session on subsistence.

1990: The Federal Subsistence Board designates non-rural communities.

1991: The Kenaitzes appeal the non-rural determinations for Kenai, Homer, and Seward. The appeal is denied.

1991: Gov. Walter Hickel appoints a subsistence council to build a program to enable the state to implement its subsistence law.

1991: The Alaska Department of Fish and Game seeks deletion of provisions of federal subsistence regulations about federal jurisdiction over certain marine and navigable waters. The state says assertion of federal authority over fish in state waters is contrary to the Statehood Act and ANILCA.

1991: Governor Hickel drafts legislation to amend the state's subsistence law. The Legislature fails to act on the bill.

1992: The Federal Subsistence Management Program becomes effective July 1. The program applies to federal public lands and non-navigable waters on those lands.

1992: Gov. Walter Hickel calls a special legislative session to address subsistence. The Legislature approves changes to state management of subsistence, including extension of eligibility to all Alaskans.

1992: The joint Boards of Fish and Game establish non-subsistence areas around Fairbanks, Anchorage-Mat-Su-Kenai, Juneau, and Ketchikan. Five months later, Valdez is added to the list.

1992: Alaska sues to challenge federal authority to manage fish and wildlife on Alaska's federal lands. The case, *Alaska v. Babbitt*, is consolidated with *Katie John v. U.S.*

1992: U.S. District Court Judge Russell Holland upholds ANILCA's rural preference in *McDowell, et al v. USDI*. Holland rejects McDowell's claim that the law violates the equal protection clause of the Fifth Amendment of the U.S. Constitution.

1993: The secretary of the interior approves ten charters, establishing the Alaska Subsistence Advisory Councils as provided for by Section 805 of ANILCA.

1993: Alaska Superior Court Judge Dana Fabe, in *Kenaitze vs. Alaska*, rules that non-subsistence areas established by 1992 state law were unconstitutional. In theory, all Alaskans are again eligible for subsistence hunting and fishing.

1993: Sen. Ted Stevens urges state leaders to comply with ANILCA to keep the Clinton administration from taking over management of subsistence fisheries in Alaska.

1994: Sen. Frank Murkowski, speaking to a joint session of the Alaska Legislature, predicts a 1995 federal takeover of fisheries for subsistence management.

1994: U.S. District Court Judge Holland rules for Katie John, concluding that the federal government, not the State of Alaska, is entitled to manage fish and wildlife on public lands in Alaska for purposes of Title VIII of ANILCA. He also rules that "public lands" include all navigable waters in Alaska inside the three-mile limit. The state and federal governments file appeals.

1994: Secretary of the Interior Bruce Babbitt informs Governor Hickel that if the state does not adopt a certifiable program before judicial stays are lifted, the United States will assume the management of subsistence fishing in Alaska pursuant to direction of the federal courts.

1994: Bills for a constitutional amendment establishing rural priority for subsistence fail in the Legislature.

1995: Gov. Tony Knowles drops the State's 1992 lawsuit, *Alaska v. Babbitt*, which challenges the federal government's authority to manage subsistence hunting and fishing on federal lands in Alaska.

1995: The Alaska Legislature passes a resolution urging Governor Knowles to continue the lawsuit, *State v. Babbitt*, and to pursue the state's position that the Secretary of the Interior and Secretary of Agriculture do not have the authority to assume management of fish and wildlife on public lands in Alaska. The Legislature's petition to intervene in the appeal is denied by the Ninth Circuit Court of Appeals.

1995: The Ninth Circuit Court of Appeals, ruling on *State v. Babbitt* and *Katie John v. U.S.*, reverses and remands the March 30, 1994, federal District Court decision. Ninth Circuit rules that public lands include those navigable waters in which the U.S. has an interest by virtue of the reserved water rights doctrine. The court further directs federal agencies that administer the subsistence priority to identify those waters. The court directs that in determining whether the reserved water rights doctrine applies, it must be determined whether the U.S. intended to reserve unappropriated waters.

1995: The Alaska Supreme Court, in *Kenaitze v. State*, overturns the Alaska Superior Court's earlier ruling that non-subsistence areas were unconstitutional. Previously established "non-subsistence" areas are automatically reinstated. The court also finds that the "proximity" criterion for determining qualification for the state's "Tier 2" subsistence uses violates the Alaska constitution. The proximity criterion is subsequently deleted from state law.

1995: The Alaska Supreme Court, in *Totemoff v. State*, finds the state has authority to enforce hunting and fishing laws on federal land if state and federal laws or regulations don't conflict. In direct opposition to the ruling of the Ninth Circuit Court of Appeals in *Katie John*, the court rules that the federal government doesn't have jurisdiction over navigable waters in Alaska.

1995: The U.S. Supreme Court rejects the Alaska State Legislature's and Alaska Outdoor Council's requests to intervene in the appeal of the Katie John lawsuit.

1995: The Southcentral Alaska Federal Subsistence Regional Advisory Council recommends finding the entire Kenai Peninsula rural for subsistence purposes.

1996: The U.S. Supreme Court denies the State of Alaska's petition to review the *Katie John* decision.

1997: Governor Knowles appoints a Subsistence Task Force to forge a subsistence solution and recommend changes to the Alaska Constitution, Alaska statutes, and ANILCA.

1998: Sen. Ted Stevens negotiates a one-year moratorium on implementation of the *Katie John* decision, effectively holding off federal management of subsistence fisheries until 1999.

1998: The Alaska Legislative Council and seventeen Alaska legislators sue in Federal District Court, challenging federal subsistence regulations on public lands. The court dismisses the case.

1998: Governor Knowles proposes a state constitutional amendment and amendments to ANILCA to resolve the subsistence conflict and head off a federal takeover of subsistence. The Legislature fails to pass the measure in two special sessions over the issue.

1999: Senator Stevens again negotiates a moratorium on extension of federal management to fisheries on federal public lands. Federal management is set to begin October 1.

1999: Governor Knowles calls a special session of the Legislature to amend the state constitution on subsistence. The Legislature refuses to act.

1999: The federal government takes over subsistence management of fisheries on federal public lands October 1. Waters now under federal subsistence management include fresh waters that run into or adjacent to national parks, forests, refuges, and reserves, and Wild and Scenic Rivers. These include all the rivers of the Tongass National Forest, most rivers on the Kenai Peninsula and large sections of the Yukon and Kuskokwim Rivers.

2000: The Federal Subsistence Board finds the entire Kenai Peninsula to be rural, increasing the number of federally qualified subsistence users from 14,000 to 49,000.

2000: The Federal Subsistence Board creates a new subsistence fishery for coho salmon and steelhead trout on Prince of Wales Island, and for cutthroat and rainbow trout throughout Southeast Alaska. Other deviations from state management include a general allowance for cash sales (customary trade) of subsistence-caught fish.

2001: The Ninth Circuit Court of Appeals, on an 8-3 vote, reaffirms its 1995 decision in *Katie John v. U.S.* that the federal subsistence jurisdiction extends to navigable waters on federal public lands.

2001: The Federal Subsistence Board, on reconsideration, finds Homer, Seward and Kenai and adjoining communities non-rural for federal subsistence. The decision reduces eligible federal subsistence users on the Kenai Peninsula from 49,000 to about 5,000.

2001: Governor Knowles announces a "subsistence summit" in Anchorage aiming at restoring state subsistence management; protecting rural subsistence rights, and unifying Alaskans.

2001: Governor Knowles' Subsistence Leadership summit adjourns, calling for a state constitutional amendment guaranteeing a rural subsistence priority, co-management of fish and game by Native and rural residents, and possible improvements to ANILCA.

2001: State Superior Court Judge Mark Rindner rules that the State of Alaska too quickly placed villages like Eklutna, Knik and Ninilchik in nonsubsistence zones, a ruling that challenges the state's subsistence management model in Southcentral Alaska.

2001: Governor Knowles announces the state will not appeal the landmark Katie John decision to the U.S. Supreme Court and says he is ready to call a special session of the Legislature to take up subsistence.

2001: Governor Knowles appoints a Subsistence Drafting Group to draft a constitutional amendment and recommendations for the Legislature to implement it

2001: The Subsistence Drafting Group issues recommendations, including, first, a constitutional amendment making subsistence by rural residents the top priority over other uses of fish and game and, second, an allowance for creating a "second priority" for individuals who show a long-term, consistent pattern of subsistence and for communities with subsistence traditions. Recommendations include guidelines on how a revised state subsistence law might be worded.

2001: The Federal Subsistence Board establishes a new subsistence fishery on federal sections of the Kenai River, the first such fishery in fifty years. It also creates a region-wide subsistence coho fishery in Southeast Alaska.

2002: Governor Knowles introduces in the Legislature a resolution for a state constitutional amendment on subsistence, incorporating a rural subsistence preference and allowance of a "secondary preference" for urban Alaskans who can demonstrate a customary and traditional use of subsistence resources.

2002: By a nearly 3 to 1 margin, Anchorage voters say "yes" to the following advisory question: "Shall the citizens of Anchorage urge the Alaska Legislature to resolve the subsistence issue by placing a constitutional amendment before the qualified voters at the November 2002 general election?"

2002: Citing the results of the Anchorage advisory vote, Knowles calls a special session of the Legislature to solve Alaska's subsistence dilemma.

2002: The legislative special session focuses on budget and school-funding questions. One committee hearing is held on subsistence. Lawmakers call for private meetings with Natives and outdoorsmen to find agreement. Alaska Federation of Natives declines to participate, and the private meeting idea is scrapped.

2007: Federal court holds that federal law gives the U.S. Department of Interior and the U.S. Department of Agriculture the authority to regulate and protect Native subsistence rights. Gov. Sarah Palin, contrary to advice from the head of the Alaska Law Department, uses a private law firm to appeal this decision to the U.S. Ninth Circuit Court of Appeals.

2008: The Palin administration and the federal government remain opposed on subsistence, with the governor holding that all Alaskans have the right to subsistence hunting and fishing and the federal agencies and courts holding that subsistence applies only to rural residents as defined by federal procedures.

Sources
United Fishermen of Alaska, Subsistence Management Information, 2008
http://www.subsistmgtinfo.org/fvss.htm
Anchorage Daily News

History

BOOKS
In 2006, the Alaska Historical Society compiled a list of the sixty-seven "best history books" about Alaska history. The number was settled on by historian Frank Norris and librarian Bruce Merrell, society president, in recognition of the year the United States

acquired the Alaska territory – 1867. A six-member committee reviewed 771 nominations. These were the final selections, in alphabetical order.

Berton, Pierre, *The Klondike Fever: The Life and Death of the Last Great Gold Rush*, 1958

Black, Lydia T., *Russians in Alaska, 1732-1867*, 2004

Bockstoce, John R., *Whales, Ice and Men: The History of Whaling in the Western Arctic*, 1986

Bowkett, Gerald E., *Reaching for a Star: The Final Campaign for Alaska Statehood*, 1989, 2008

Catton, Theodore, *Inhabited Wilderness: Indians, Eskimos, and National Parks in Alaska*, 1997

Chandonnet, Fern, editor, *Alaska at War, 1941-1945: The Forgotten War Remembered*, 1995

Coates, Ken, and Bill Morrison, *The Sinking of the Princess Sophia: Taking the North Down With Her*, 1991

Coates, Peter A., *The Trans-Alaska Pipeline Controversy: Technology, Conservation, and the Frontier*, 1991

Cole, Terrence, *E.T. Barnette: The Strange Story of the Man Who Founded Fairbanks*, 1981

Cooley, Richard A., *Politics and Conservation: The Decline of the Alaska Salmon*, 1963

Durbin, Kathie, *Tongass: Pulp Politics and the Fight for the Alaska Rain Forest*, 1999

Fisher, Raymond H., *Bering's Voyages: Whither and Why*, 1977

Fitzhugh, William W. and Aron Crowel, *Crossroads of Continents: Cultures of Siberia and Alaska*, 1988

Fortuine, Robert, *Chills and Fever: Health and Disease in the Early History of Alaska*, 1989

Garfield, Brian, *Thousand-Mile War: World War II in Alaska and the Aleutians*, 1969

Giddings, J. Louis, *Ancient Men of the Arctic*, 1967

Gruening, Ernest, *Many Battles: The Autobiography of Ernest Gruening*, 1973

Hammond, Jay S., *Tales of Alaska's Bush Rat Governor: The Extraordinary Autobiography of Jay Hammond, Wilderness Guide and Reluctant Politician*, 1994

Harkey, Ira, *Pioneer Bush Pilot: The Story of Noel Wien*, 1974

Haycox, Stephen W., *Alaska: An American Colony*, 2002

Hayes, Derek, *Historical Atlas of the Pacific Northwest: Maps of Exploration and Discovery*, 1999

Hinckley, Ted C., *The Americanization of Alaska, 1867-1897*, 1972

Hudson, Ray, *Moments Rightly Placed: An Aleutian Memoir*, 1998, 2008

Hunt, William R., *North of 53: The Wild Days of the Alaska-Yukon Mining Frontier, 1870-1914*, 1974

Huntington, Sidney, as told to Jim Rearden, *Shadows on the Koyukuk: An Alaskan Native's Life along the River*, 1993

Kent, Rockwell, *Wilderness: A Journal of Quiet Adventure in Alaska*, 1920

Kizzia, Tom, *The Wake of the Unseen Object: Among the Native Cultures of Bush Alaska*, 1991

Langdon, Steve J., *The Native People of Alaska*, 1987

Malloy, Mary, *Souvenirs of the Fur Trade: Northwest Coast Indian Art and Artifacts Collected by American Mariners, 1788-1844*, 2000

Mangusso, Mary Childers, and Stephen W. Haycox, *Interpreting Alaska's History: An Anthology*, 1989

Marshall, Robert, *Arctic Village*, 1933

McPhee, John A., *Coming Into the Country*, 1977

Mergler, Wayne, ed., *The Last New Land: Stories of Alaska, Past and Present*, 1996

Miller, Orlando W., *The Frontier in Alaska and the Matanuska Colony*, 1975

Mitchell, Donald Craig, *Sold American: The Story of Alaska Natives and Their Land, 1867-1959, The Army to Statehood*, 1997

Mitchell, Donald Craig, *Take My Land, Take My Life: The Story of Congress's Historic Settlement of Alaska Native Land Claims, 1960-1971*, 2001

Moore, Terris, *Mt. McKinley: The Pioneer Climbs*, 1967

Morgan, Lael, *Art and Eskimo Power: The Life and Times of Alaskan Howard Rock*, 1988, 2008

Muir, John, *Travels in Alaska*, 1915

Murie, Margaret E., *Two in the Far North*, 1962

Murphy, Claire Rudolf, and Jane G. Haigh, *Gold Rush Women*, 1997

Naske, Claus-M., *Edward Lewis "Bob" Bartlett of Alaska: A Life in Politics*, 1979

Nelson, Daniel, *Northern Landscapes: The Struggle for Wilderness Alaska*, 2004

Nelson, Richard K., *Make Prayers to the Raven: A Koyukon View of the Northern Forest*, 1983

Neufeld, David, and Frank Norris, *Chilkoot Trail: Heritage Route to the Klondike*, 1996

Oliver, Ethel Ross, *Journal of an Aleutian Year*, 1988

O'Neill, Dan, *The Firecracker Boys*, 1994, 2007

Orth, Donald J., *Dictionary of Alaska Place Names*, 1967

Pierce, Richard A., and Alton S. Donnelly, eds., *Russian America: A Biographical Dictionary*, 1990

Potter, Jean, *The Flying North*, 1947

Rawson, Timothy, *Changing Tracks: Predators and Politics in Mt. McKinley National Park*, 2001

Ray, Dorothy Jean, *The Eskimos of Bering Strait, 1650-1898*, 1975

Rogers, George William, *The Future of Alaska: Economic Consequences of Statehood*, 1962

Salisbury, Gay, and Laney Salisbury, *The Cruelest Miles: The Heroic Story of Dogs and Men in a Race against an Epidemic*, 2003

Sherwood, Morgan B., *Big Game in Alaska: A History of Wildlife and People*, 1981

Sherwood, Morgan B., *Exploration of Alaska, 1865-1900*, 1965

Smithsonian Institution, *Handbook of North American Indians, Volumes 4-7*, 1981-1990

Steller, Georg Wilhelm, *Journal of a Voyage with Bering, 1741-42*, 1988

Stuck, Hudson, *Ten Thousand Miles with a Dog Sled*, 1914

Tabbert, Russell, *Dictionary of Alaskan English*, 1991

Tower, Elizabeth A., *Icebound Empire: Industry and Politics on the Last Frontier, 1898-1938*, 1996

U.S. Senate Committee on Military Affairs, Compilation of Narratives of Explorations in Alaska, 1900

Webb, Melody, *The Last Frontier: A History of the Yukon Basin of Canada and Alaska*, 1985

White, Stroller, edited by R.N. DeArmond, *Tales of a Klondike Newsman*, 1969

Wickersham, James, *Old Yukon: Tales-Trails—Trials*, 1938

Wilson, William H., *Railroad in the Clouds: The Alaska Railroad in the Age of Steam, 1914-1945*, 1977

Young, George O., *Alaskan Trophies Won and Lost*, 1928

Source
Alaska Historical Society

TIMELINE, 1959-2009

1959: Statehood proclaimed; Sitka pulp mill opens; U.S. Court of Claims issues judgment favoring Tlingit and Haida claims to Southeast Alaska lands.

1960: Three oil companies announce a wildcat well on Kenai Peninsula, producing 1,870 barrels per day, confirming the region's commercial oil potential; six banks merge to form the National Bank of Alaska; state oil revenues exceed estimates by $6 million.

1961: Population of Anchorage reaches 43,753; Alaska Methodist University opens; Joe Redington Jr. wins junior sled dog racing event at the Anchorage Fur Rendezvous; Ladd Field in Fairbanks renamed Fort Wainwright.

1962: Matanuska Valley Farmers Cooperative Association changes its name to Matanuska Maid, the largest distributor of local produce; Northwest Orient Airlines closes its refueling base on Shemya Island as the new jets do not need to stop on trans-Pacific flights; thanks to electric lights, the last U.S. Coast Guard lamp lighter retires in Alaska.

1963: Telephone service arrives in Kake and Angoon; Chester Noongwook of Savoonga, the last dog team mail carrier, finishes his final 100-mile run on St. Lawrence Island; discovery of the Beluga gas field confirmed; refinery opens at Nikiski.

1964: Earthquake devastates Southcentral Alaska at 5:36 p.m. on March 27; former University of Alaska president Terris Moore completes a series of donations to the university equal to the total amount of salary he received during his four years as president; herring roe shipped to Japan for first time.

1965: Coin-operated laundry opens in Kotzebue; first building to be built at new site of Valdez after the earthquake is an elementary school; Japan agrees to cut its king crab catch in the Bering Sea.

1966: Alaska Federation of Natives organized; Interior Secretary Udall imposes a "land freeze" to protect Native use and occupancy of Alaska lands; fire destroys twenty-one businesses in the heart of Sitka; Walter J. Hickel elected governor.

1967: Plans for an underground nuclear test draw protests from AFN and the Arctic Slope Native Association; Alaska celebrates the centennial of the purchase from Russia; Fairbanks suffers devastating flood; Sheldon Jackson closes its high school branch in Sitka; Bristol Bay has its worst fishing season in decades.

1968: Largest oil field in North America discovered at Prudhoe Bay; Hickel establishes Alaska Lands Claims Task Force that recommends a forty million acre land settlement for Alaska Natives; first parking garage opens in Anchorage at J.C. Penney's;

Alaska Marine Highway System expands to Puget Sound and traffic grows; commission recommends rail link to North Slope.

1969: North Slope Oil lease sale brings $900 million; first live satellite telecast in Alaska; oil companies propose 800-mile buried pipeline to Valdez at an estimated cost of $900 million; snowmobiles grow in popularity.

1970: Work begins on Snettisham hydroelectric project near Juneau; Anchorage and Fairbanks boom in anticipation of oil pipeline, but court delays and environmental challenges mount; federal government considers selling Alaska Railroad; Alaska Communications System to be sold to RCA.

1971: Record low temperature of 80 below recorded at Prospect Creek, a site on the proposed pipeline; Gov. Bill Egan proposes creation of new Department of Environmental Conservation; Alaska Native Claims Settlement Act signed into law; Anchorage sees first live network sports broadcast of NFL playoff game and Super Bowl.

1972: Eva McGown, hostess of Fairbanks, is one of four people to die in the fire that destroyed the Nordale Hotel; Alaska Constitution amended to prohibit sexual discrimination; pipeline cost estimate increases to $3 billion.

1973: Congress passes the Trans-Alaska Pipeline Authorization Act; salmon fisheries limited entry program becomes law; Congressman Nick Begich, House Majority Leader Hale Boggs and two others lost in crash of Cessna 310 on flight to Juneau; Dick Wilmarth wins first Iditarod Trail Sled Dog Race from Anchorage to Nome in twenty days.

1974: Estimated pipeline cost increases to $4.5 billion; construction begins on haul road; Anchorage, Fairbanks and Valdez boom; Alaska voters approve capital move initiative; homesteading officially ends; $5.7 billion natural gas pipeline to Lower 48 proposed.

1975: Alaska Legislature appropriates funds to initiate purchase and installation of 100 satellite earth stations for establishment of statewide satellite communications network; Yukon River Bridge is completed and pipeline construction enters most hectic phase.

1976: Natural gas pipeline proposals filed; Alaska voters pick Willow as new capital site; voters approve constitutional amendment establishing Alaska Permanent Fund to receive "at least 25 percent" of all state oil revenues and related income.

1977: Trans-Alaska Pipeline completed from Prudhoe Bay to Valdez; Pump Station eight destroyed by explosion that claims one life; Alaska economy slows after pipeline frenzy.

1978: Legislature approves Delta Barley Project proposed by Gov. Jay Hammond, creating farms averaging 2,700 acres that were envisioned as the start of a new agriculture industry; President Jimmy Carter proclaims seventeen national monuments covering 56 million acres, leading to protests in Alaska; Sen. Ted Stevens survives Anchorage plane crash that claims the life of his wife Ann and four others.

1979: State challenges Antiquities Act withdrawals in court; debate continues on legislation to place more than 100 million acres of Alaska in parks, refuges and other conservation units, provoking intense opposition in Alaska and some support from a local environmental movement; *Spirit of the Wind*, a movie about mushing legend George Attla, premieres.

1980: Alaska Legislature increases Permanent Fund share of oil revenues from 25 to 50 percent, repeals Alaska personal income tax, establishes Alaska Dividend Fund to distribute Permanent Fund earnings to Alaska residents. Congress passes Alaska National Interests Lands Conservation Act (ANILCA).

1981: State treasury swells with oil revenues as world prices increase; $1.8 billion deposited into Alaska Permanent Fund.

1982: Alaska voters repeal law relocating capital to Willow and oil revenue peaks at more than $4 billion; first Permanent Fund dividends of $1,000 per person distributed; Bill Sheffield elected governor.

1983: Time zone shift: all of Alaska except westernmost Aleutian Islands move to Alaska Standard Time, one hour west of Pacific Standard Time; crab stocks so low that most commercial seasons are canceled; Legislature raises drinking age from 19 to 21.

1984: State celebrates 25th anniversary of Alaska statehood; future Gov. Sarah Palin named "Miss Wasilla"; Frank Turpin named president of Alaska Railroad; labor and financial problems ground Wien Air Alaska.

1985: State purchases Alaska Railroad from the federal government for bargain price of $22 million; declining oil prices begin to create budget problems that would lead to steep recession and loss of thousands of jobs.

1986: Price of oil drops below $10 per barrel, causing Alaska oil revenues to plummet; legislature passes a new bill governing subsistence hunting and fishing.

1987: The average phone call from Alaska to the Lower 48 drops from $3.50 to $3.11. A $10 call made in 1971 could be made for $2.37, though Alaskans still paid about 11 percent more than the rest of the nation; low oil prices trigger a collapse of the real-estate market and steep rise in foreclosures; a new light infantry division begins to arrive at Fort Wainwright in Fairbanks.

1988: Anchorage Mayor Tony Knowles leaves office after eight years during which Anchorage had its ups and downs because of oil prices; Anchorage loses 30,000 in population; the Soviets allow a one-day visit of a group of Alaskans to the Siberian port city of Provideniya.

1989: *Exxon Valdez* runs aground on Bligh Reef, spilling eleven million gallons of oil into Prince William Sound; the Permanent Fund passes the $10 billion mark; Alaska Supreme Court throws out Alaska's rural preference law.

1990: Alaska Legislature struggles to resolve the subsistence issue but is unable to do so; federal authorities take over subsistence management on federal lands; oil prices temporarily double after Iraq's invasion of Kuwait; population tops 550,000; Walter Hickel makes a political comeback with lieutenant governor candidate Jack Coghill on an Alaskan Independence Party ticket to win the gubernatorial race.

1991: An amended *Exxon Valdez* settlement wins judicial approval; Congress effectively closes the Arctic National Wildlife Refuge to oil development; Bristol Bay fisherman strike over low salmon prices.

1992: Final repercussions of Alaska's recession are felt as oil industry retrenches with major job losses; the *Anchorage Times*, once Alaska's largest newspaper folds; Spurr Volcano erupts three times, one blast dumping ash on Anchorage; Juneau's Hillary Lindh wins Olympic Silver Medal in downhill skiing.

1993: Alaska Legislature passes largest capital works appropriation in ten years; Greens Creek Mine near Juneau closes due to low silver, zinc, and lead prices; Sitka Pulp Mill announces indefinite suspension of mill operations, affecting 400 workers; Alaskan Independence Party Chairman Joe Vogler is murdered.

1994: Binky the polar bear gains worldwide fame after two unfortunate visitors to the Alaska Zoo climb into his quarters and are bitten. Exxon appeals a $5 billion punitive damages award stemming from the Prince William Sound oil spill, the largest in U.S. history and no one knows how long before the case is settled.

1995: The salmon fishing is so good that the market for pinks and reds crashes, creating unexpected economic woes for fishermen; oil production on the North Slope continues to decline and BP and ARCO say they won't do costly exploration work, but instead will try to coax more oil from existing fields; oil industry finds warmer reception in Juneau than in years past; experimental Healy Clean Coal Project starts; more than one million tourists visit the state.

1996: The use of photo radar units in Anchorage leads to issuance of nearly 20,000 speeding tickets, but political opposition to their use continues to grow; the Miller's Reach fire becomes the most destructive in Alaska history, destroying more than 400 homes and forcing 1,000 to evacuate; residents of Ruby mourn the loss of postmistress Agnes Wright; former Alaskan Jewel hits the bestseller charts with her first album, "Pieces of You"; Congress allows export of Alaska oil.

1997: More than 200 Canadian fishing boats block passage of an Alaska state ferry in a dispute over salmon fishing that angered Alaskans; Soprano Vivica Genaux, twenty-eight, who grew up in Fairbanks, gets her big break in the opera world when she is called upon, as a backup, to sing the role of Rosina for the New York Metropolitan Opera; the Fairbanks Municipal Utilities System is sold to three private firms; the Williams Company buys the MAPCO refinery in Fairbanks.

1998: Bill Oefelein becomes Alaska's first astronaut. He pilots the space shuttle *Discovery* on a mission eight years later; Tesoro stops buying state-owned royalty oil for its Nikiski refinery; Anchorage has its biggest building season in more than a decade, reporting $500 million in residential and commercial projects; state adopts moose as its official land mammal; Seward Sea Life Center opens; U.S. Supreme Court rules that Venetie lands are not "Indian Country."

1999: BP and ARCO announce plans to merge; Anchorage banker decides to donate $90 million to help expand the Anchorage Museum of History and Art and to enhance the work of the Rasmuson Foundation; Wells Fargo buys National Bank of Alaska; state undertakes major educational effort about the "Y2K computer glitch" and the need to be prepared for computer problems on January 1, 2000; Sen. Ted Stevens named "Alaskan of the Century."

2000: Native leader Morris Thompson and 87 others die in an Alaska Airlines jet crash off the California coast; BP takes over ARCO, but the Alaska operations are sold to Phillips Petroleum under an arrangement designed to allay anti-trust concerns; U.S. Census shows a state population of 626,932, moving Alaska to 47th in population ranking among the states.

2001: Like so many others across America, Alaskans mourn friends and relatives killed in the terror attacks of September 11th, and join in the October assault on al-Qaeda and Taliban targets in Afghanistan; the year starts on a sad note with paint-ball shootings of Alaska Natives in Anchorage. The assailants are prosecuted with their own videotape and Gov. Tony Knowles creates a commission on tolerance; the year saw other developments in Native issues. Governor Knowles declines to appeal the Katie John subsistence case and holds a summit on subsistence; in December Point Hope Alaska Native Jesse Frankson sets a Guinness World Record for the highest martial arts kick.

2002: St. Patrick's Day brings Anchorage a record-setting snowfall of 28.6 inches of wet snow; rescuers from North Slope Search and Rescue use helicopters to pluck eighteen seal hunters from broken sea ice; the Bush administration, with support from Congress, pushes ahead with making Fort Greely into a site for the missile defense system, designed to stop an attack on the United States; Interior Alaska is shaken by a 7.9 earthquake centered ninety miles south of Fairbanks; the seventy-five-year-old Ward Cove Packing Company is shut down.

2003: Minimum wage rises from $5.65 to $7.15, the highest on the West Coast; decision by Board of Fish and Game to allow wolf control leads to threats of a tourism boycott; bears kill Timothy Treadwell and his companion Amie Huguenard in Katmai National Park and Preserve.

2004: Thick smoke from Interior fires reduces visibility to a quarter-mile or less for weeks in Fairbanks, forcing many residents to stay indoors with their windows closed. All told, 708 fires burn more than 6.7 million acres and cost more than $106 million; the U.S. Senate race between Lisa Murkowski and Tony Knowles turns into Alaska's costliest contest, with expenditures topping $11 million.

2005: Four Alaska Boy Scout leaders die in an accident at the Boy Scout National Jamboree when a dining tent pole strikes power lines; Gov. Frank Murkowski fires state Natural Resources Commissioner Tom Irwin over a policy disagreement on the gas pipeline; six of Irwin's staff members resigned in protest; Former Gov. Jay Hammond dies at 83; Explorer Norman Vaughan dies at 100.

2006: Former Wasilla Mayor Sarah Palin wins the governor's race; corrosion in pipes on Alaska's North Slope leads to a spill of 267,000 gallons and a discovery that there are numerous pipes in danger of leaking, prompting a reduction in oil production and a major rehab program; FBI raids the offices of six lawmakers, part of a far-reaching corruption investigation.

2007: VECO executives Bill Allen and Rick Smith plead guilty to bribery and become central witnesses in a growing legislative corruption scandal that sends former legislators Pete Kott and Vic Kohring to jail; Maggie the elephant, long a resident of the Anchorage Zoo, is moved to a new home in California, with the help of the U.S. Air Force; cancer survivor Lance Mackey defies the odds by winning both the Yukon Quest and the Iditarod in the same year.

2008: Sen. Ted Stevens is indicted on charges that he accepted gifts from VECO Corporation boss Bill Allen, but did not report them on his U.S. Senate disclosure form; Sen. John McCain selects Governor Palin to serve as his vice presidential running mate; Alaska marks the 50th anniversary of the passage of the Alaska Statehood Act.

Sources
Alaska Blue Book 1991-92, 9th Edition, 1991, State of Alaska, Department of Education, Juneau, Alaska
State Library Electronic Doorway, http://sled.alaska.edu/akfaq/akchron.html
Anchorage Daily News
Fairbanks Daily News-Miner

Miscellaneous

FACTS ABOUT ALASKA
Capital: Juneau
Motto: "North to the Future"
Flower: Forget-me-not
Fish: King Salmon
Bird: Ptarmigan
Tree: Sitka Spruce
Mineral: Gold
Gem: Jade
Sport: Dog Mushing
Insect: Dragonfly

Fossil: Woolly Mammoth
Mammal: Moose

STATE HOLIDAYS
Seward's Day, last Monday of March, commemorates the purchase of Alaska from Russia in 1867.

Alaska Day, October 18, commemorates the official transfer of the territory into U.S. hands and the raising of the flag at Sitka on October 18, 1867.

While they are not legal holidays, the state has designated several other days to honor prominent historical figures: Ernest Gruening Day, February 6; Elizabeth Peratrovich Day, February 16; Susan Butcher Day, first Saturday in March; Bob Bartlett Day, April 20; James Wickersham Day, August 24; William A. Egan Day, October 8; Anthony J. Dimond Day, November 30.

1964 EARTHQUAKE
The "Good Friday" earthquake hit near Prince William Sound at 5:36 p.m. Alaska Standard Time on Friday, March 27, 1964.

Seismographs recorded the quake's magnitude at between 8.4 and 8.6 on the Richter scale. This measurement was revised to 9.2 after the introduction of the Moment Magnitude scale in 1979, making it the largest earthquake ever recorded in North America and the second-most powerful ever recorded anywhere.

The force of the earthquake spawned a tsunami along the Gulf of Alaska. Together the quake and wave caused 128 deaths (113 caused by the tsunami) and about $311 million worth of property damage. Anchorage sustained severe quake damage; department stores and schools were destroyed, streets wrecked; landslides in Turnagain Heights devastated 75 homes. The tsunami hit Valdez and Chenega on Prince William Sound the hardest, killing fifty-five people in those locations alone. Both communities have been relocated.

-Sam Travis

Sources
U.S. Geological Survey
http://earthquake.usgs.gov/regional/states/events/1964_03_28.php
National Oceanic and Atmospheric Administration & Alaska Tsunami Warning Center, Palmer, Alaska,
http://wcatwc.arh.noaa.gov/64quake.htm

POPULATION
Population by decade, 1960-2010
1960-226,167
1970-300,382
1980-401,851
1990-550,043
2000-626,932

2010 (estimate)-694,109

Source
U.S. Census Bureau,
http://quickfacts.census.gov/qfd/states/02000.html

Natural resource development

FISHING (COMMERCIAL)

Most Americans have heard of Alaska's prodigious wild salmon runs, first exploited in the late 19th Century to create a yearly pack of 1 million cases of canned salmon. Thanks to commercial salmon catches in Washington, Oregon, California, British Columbia, and Alaska, salmon became the poor peoples' protein across the world. Canned salmon became a standard ration for soldiers around the world, a practice that continued well into the 20th Century.

In the early 20th Century, the salmon catch in Alaska alone amounted to 60 percent of Alaska's revenues, thanks to a small tax per case of fish canned.

Today wild Pacific salmon for market mainly come from Alaska and when fresh, fetch prices undreamed of in the past. It is not unusual in Lower 48 states and Alaskan fish markets to see freshly caught ocean Chinook salmon selling for well over $25 a pound. On the Yukon and other rivers, Japanese firms work with Native fishers to pack huge amounts of salmon eggs for sushi, bringing cash into cash-strapped economies.

The salmon fishery is still a big piece of Alaska's economy, if one discounts the impact of oil revenues. Statistics show the value of the salmon catch at about $250 million to $300 million a year, depending on the highly variable returns of the fish.

Trying to track these returns shows that run of pink salmon, the smallest salmon and least valuable, can range as high as 800 million annually, with runs of the most valuable, Chinook salmon, ranging as high as 200,000.

The single biggest salmon fishery of all, for sockeye salmon on Bristol Bay, annually takes millions of sockeye and involves thousands of fishers, packers, pilots, and other workers. This fishery, many Alaskans now believe, faces a serious threat from the Pebble and other immense open-pit gold mines proposed for the head of Bristol Bay.

As in all of Alaska's commercial fisheries, many agencies manage the salmon fisheries, the federal and state governments primarily, but with an eye in some fisheries to the Pacific Salmon Treaty with Canada and involving the other West Coast U.S. states on how many fish migrating through and out of Alaskan waters may be caught in Alaskan waters.

By now most Americans, thanks to television and movies, have become aware of the dangerous Bering Sea fisheries, especially those for King and other crab and for Pollock, a bottom fish manufactured into scores of fish products, including artificial crab.

This chiefly international fishery returns roughly $1 billion a year to the United States with a good part of that streaming into the Alaskan economy.

Many Alaskans and many non-Alaskans claim Alaskan commercial fishing as their chief economic activity. Much of the "Alaska" fishing fleet homeports in Washington State's Puget Sound or other ports, even in Oregon and California. Even so, thousands of

Alaskans, including many Natives along the Yukon and other rivers thrive thanks to the money they earn from salmon and other fisheries.

Few think of sports fisheries as part of the economy, but sports fishing in Alaska draws thousands of anglers from all over the world every summer and it's estimated that these spend upwards of $70 million a year following their passion. Alaskan economists have studied and noted the value of the sports fisheries for salmon, trout, sheefish and pike and so of the value of the pristine wild environments on which these fisheries depend.

-John de Yonge

Sources

Alaska Humanities Forum: History & Culture Studies, 2008

http://www.akhistorycourse.org/articles/article.php?artID=262

Alaska Department of Fish and Game

MINING

Mining made Alaska famous, first as a landing area for Stampeders hustling to the Klondike Gold Rush in Canada's Yukon Territory, then with gold rushes of its own at Nome and Fairbanks and elsewhere.

It also once gained famed for its copper mines.

Today it harbors thousands of mines, most of them small, but some of them among the largest existing or proposed in the world: The Red Dog Mine, near Kotzebue— zinc and lead; Chuitna Coal Project, near Anchorage—coal; Fort Knox Mine, near Fairbanks—gold; Pogo Mine, near Fairbanks—gold; Pebble Mine, proposed on Bristol Bay near Iliamna-copper-gold-molybdenum porphyry. These are all open pit, gigantic operations.

For most of the 1990s and early 2000s gold prices rose to new heights, causing the development of gold mines of all sizes. Though gold prices have declined recently, prices are still high enough to stimulate prospecting and development, especially by large, well-financed corporations.

There is opposition in Alaska and from elsewhere to large open pit mines, especially those proposed for Bristol Bay, home of the world's largest salmon runs.

In 2007, according to the Alaska Miners Organization, mining in Alaska produced $3.4 billion in gross revenues and provided 5,500 direct and indirect jobs.

-John de Yonge

Sources

Alaska Energy Careers, A Sitka Energy Project website, information program underwritten by state and federal grants

http://www.alaskaenergycareers.org/mining.html

Alaska Department of Natural Resources

http://www.dnr.state.ak.us/mlw/mining/largemine/fortknox/index.htm

Alaska Miners Association

http://www.alaskaminers.org/mcd07sum.pdf

Gold

Gold was first discovered in Alaska as early as 1847, well before the United States had purchased the territory from Russia. By 1880 significant gold deposits had been discovered in Juneau, and in 1897 the Klondike Gold Rush in neighboring Yukon Territory, Canada, put the soft, yellow metal firmly into the State's history.

Between 1890 and 1910 more than 30,000 people flooded into and through Alaska, bound for places like Valdez and Dawson, Fairbanks, and Ester.

World War II slowed gold mining in Alaska, however. After the war Alaska's gold production continued to decline. It wasn't until the 1980s, with gold prices soaring and new discoveries that gold production soared.

Gold production, 1959-2004, in thousands of Troy Ounces*:

1959 – 179,000
1960 – 168,000
1961 – 114,000
1962 – 165,000
1963 – 99,000
1964 – 58,000
1965 – 42,000
1966 – 27,000
1967 – 22,000
1968 – 21,000
1969 – unavailable
1970 – 34,000
1971 – 13,000
1972 – 8,000
1973 – 7,000
1974 – 9,000
1975 – 14,000
1976 – 22,000
1977 – 18,000
1978 – unavailable
1979 – 6,000
1980 – 9,000
1981 – 26,000
1982 – 30,000
1983 – 39,000
1984 – 19,000
1985 – 44,000
1986 – 48,000
1987 – 122,000
1988 – 135,000
1989 – 185,000
1990 – 103,000
1991 – 102,000
1992 – 160,000
1993 – 89,000
1994 – 145,000
1995 – 141,000

1996 – 161,000
1997 – 524,000
1998 – 588,000
1999 – 504,000
2000 – 501,000
2001 – 536,000
2002 – 543,000
2003 – 488,000
2004 – 456,000
2005 – 427,000
2006 – 499,000

*1 Troy Ounce = 31.1034768 grams
1,000 Troy Ounces = 31.1034768 kilograms = 68.5714285 lbs.

Sources
U.S. Bureau of Mines: *Mineral Yearbook*
http://minerals.usgs.gov/minerals/pubs/usbmmyb.html
U.S. Geological Survey: *Mineral Yearbook*
http://minerals.usgs.gov/minerals/pubs/state/ak.html

Oil & Gas
Commercial oil production began on Cook Inlet at Swanson River in 1959. It expanded between 1965 and 1972 with the construction of five additional Cook Inlet fields, and again in 1977 with the completion of the trans-Alaska Pipeline System that moved oil from the North Slope fields. By 2003, Cook Inlet area had produced 1.3 billion barrels of oil, and the North Slope 14.4 billion barrels.

Barrels of oil produced:
1959 – 1,000
1960 – 2,000
1961 – 17,000
1962 – 28,000
1963 – 29,000
1964 – 30,000
1965 – 30,000
1966 – 39,000
1967 – 80,000
1968 – 181,000
1969 – 203,000
1970 – 229,000
1971 – 218,000
1972 – 199,000
1973 – 198,000
1974 – 193,000
1975 – 191,000

1976 – 173,000
1977 – 464,000
1978 – 1,229,000
1979 – 1,401,000
1980 – 1,617,000
1981 – 1,609,000
1982 – 1,696,000
1983 – 1,714,000
1984 – 1,722,000
1985 – 1,825,000
1986 – 1,867,000
1987 – 1,962,000
1988 – 2,017,000
1989 – 1,874,000
1990 – 1,773,000
1991 – 1,798,000
1992 – 1,714,000
1993 – 1,582,000
1994 – 1,559,000
1995 – 1,484,000
1996 – 1,393,000
1997 – 1,296,000
1998 – 1,175,000
1999 – 1,050,000
2000 – 970,000
2001 – 963,000
2002 – 984,000
2003 – 974,000
2004 – 908,000
2005 – 864,000
2006 – 741,000
2007 – 719,000

Oil revenues account for 80 percent or more of Alaska's economy, depending on the world price of oil. In 2008 Alaska reaped record revenues that may increase that percentage amount. The oil revenues to Alaska for July, 2008, alone amounted to $596 million.

State income from oil over the past three decades has averaged about $2 billion a year and transformed state spending for schools, roads, satellite communications and other infrastructure, including in the "bush" villages, where previous to oil revenues hardly any good facilities existed.

Revenues from oil taxes and royalties gird the Alaska Permanent Fund, designed to capture revenues from nonrenewable sources, invest those revenues, and after safeguarding the fund from inflation, distribute dividends to state residents.

Income from oil counts so much in the state budget that Alaska long ago abolished its state income tax and property taxes. Much of that revenue annually gets distributed to local communities, many of which have abolished their sales taxes and property taxes. A consequence of this system is that in the rare times the world price for oil crashes, as it did in the mid-1980s, the Alaska state and local governments and school districts suddenly suffer intense pains from lack of tax income.

Sources

U.S. Energy Information Administration
http://www.eia.doe.gov/emeu/aer/petro.html
Alaska Division of Oil and Gas
http://www.dog.dnr.state.ak.us
Alaska Humanities Forum: History & Culture Studies, 2008
http://www.akhistorycourse.org/articles/article.php?artID=140

TIMBER

The timber industry in Alaska centers in Southeast Alaska, where nearly all of the commercial-grade timber stands, chiefly in the Tongass National Forest and on native corporation lands. Federal lands constitute 80 percent of the forest lands in Southeast Alaska.

The federal government for decades has largely subsidized the industry centered around Ketchikan by charging less than market rates for timber.

Political decisions and court actions have limited subsidies and the industry has suffered closures and bankruptcies, though surviving operations are posting small profits.

The timber industry once provided 4,000 jobs in Alaska. It now provides 450 jobs and that number probably will decline.

Sources

Alaska State Chamber of Commerce
http://www.alaskachamber.com/artman/publish/timber.html;Alaska
Anchorage Daily News, article on history of Southeast logging
http://www.adn.com/money/industries/timber/story/187046.html
Department of Commerce, Community, and Economic Development

FEDERAL GOVERNMENT

Armed Forces

Major Army, Navy, and Air Force installations in Alaska, 1959 to 2008:
1959
Army
Fort Richardson
Fort Greely

Air Force
Ladd Field (became an Army post, Fort Wainwright, in 1963)
Eielson Air Force Base
Elmendorf Air Force Base

Navy
Kodiak Naval Operating Base
Kodiak Naval Airfield
Kodiak Naval Communications Station
Buskin Lake Naval Radio Station
Holiday Beach Naval Radio Station
Chiniak Navy Security Guard Activity Site
Naval Arctic Research Lab, NARL, Barrow

2008

Army
Bassett Army Community Hospital
Camp Carroll (National Guard)
Cold Regions Test Center
Fort Greely
Fort Richardson
Fort Wainwright
Northern Warfare Training Center

Air Force
Eielson Air Force Base
Elmendorf Air Force Base

Navy
None

Sources
U.S. Army
http://www.army.mil

U.S. Army, Fort Wainwright
http://www.wainwright.army.mil/nwtc/index.html
U.S. Army, Fort Greely
http://www.greely.army.mil/sites/local/
U.S. Air Force
http://www.airforce.com/baselocator.php
U.S Navy
http://www.navy.mil/swf/index.asp
Fort Greely Morale Division http://www.fortgreelymwr.com/index.aspx
Fort Richardson Morale Division http://www.usarak.army.mil/framwr/
Eielson Air Force Base history
http://www.eielson.af.mil/
Elmendorf Air Force Base history http://www.elmendorf.af.mil/
Kodiak Military History Museum
http://www.kodiak.org/

Congress

SENATE
Senators from Alaska

1959-1968, E. L. "Bob" Bartlett, Democrat
1959-1968, Ernest Gruening, Democrat
1969-, Ted Stevens, Republican

1969-1980, Mike Gravel, Democrat
1981-2002, Frank H. Murkowski, Republican
2003-, Lisa Murkowski, Republican

Sources
Alaska State Legislature
http://w3.legis.state.ak.us/pubs/pubs.php
Alaska State Legislature's Majority Organization
http://www.akrepublicans.org/pastlegs

HOUSE OF REPRESENTATIVES
1959-1966, Ralph Rivers, Democrat
1967-1971, Howard Pollock, Republican
1971-1972, Nick Begich, Democrat
1973-, Don Young, Republican

Legislation

Key legislation passed by Congress affecting Alaska:

ALASKA STATEHOOD ACT
The Alaska Statehood Bill that Congress passed in July, 1958, and President Dwight Eisenhower signed soon after stemmed from a long political battle by resident Alaskans not just to control their own political destiny but to curb the rapacious appetites of the Guggenheims, the Morgans, and such lesser fry as the Seattle Salmon Kings for Alaska's gold, copper and other minerals, for its transportation (being provided at monopolistic, jacked-up prices) and of course for its salmon, crab and other marine resources.

After the Klondike, Nome and Fairbanks Gold Rushes flooded the virgin lands of Alaska in the late 19th and early 20th centuries with non-Native prospectors, merchants and lawyers, not to mention saloon keepers, sporting girls and bunco artists, thinking Alaskans realized that the chief answer to the lack of law and order, the lack of roads and railroads, the lack of hospitals, jails and mental facilities, and the desperation of many schools lay in achieving self-determination. That ultimately meant statehood under the U.S. federal system and an end to being ruled day to day by time servers in the Washington, D.C., offices of the U.S. Department of Interior, many of them infamously corrupt.

A series of scandals over land giveaways ultimately caused Present William Howard Taft in the final days of his presidency to recommend Congress give new powers of self-government to Alaska, and in 1912 Alaska became a U.S. Territory, still largely ruled from the Department of Interior, with a governor subject to Interior but appointed by the president. As a territory, however, Alaskans could elect their own house and senate, exercise considerable checks over the governor, lay taxes, write laws—all of which furthered the development of an Alaskan political culture bigger than each town's limits.

That bill granted Alaska one nonvoting delegate to the U.S. House of Representatives and Alaskans choose as delegate Alaska's leading political thinker and intellectual at the time, U.S. Federal Judge James Wickersham. Wickersham set the rule for the non-voting delegates to follow: Be persuasive, that's your only power. His abilities in that department soon had goods and services flowing to Alaska. They were perhaps paltry by standards elsewhere in the United States but they were considerably more than existed before, especially in establishing and maintaining law enforcement.

Wickersham proposed an Alaska statehood bill in 1916. It went nowhere. But it started Alaskans and power players in Washington, D.C., to think of the possibility of statehood.

Alaska as a place, however, dwelt rarely in the imaginations of most Americans and it remained exploited, by the Jones Act, named after U.S. Sen. Wesley Jones of Yakima, that made sure goods moving to and from Alaska had to move through Seattle, in U.S. ships controlled by Seattle families, thereby stiffing Alaskans with high prices; and by the White Act insuring that Seattle and other Outside salmon interests caught the fish and ran the canneries and allowed these interests to build large traps at river mouths to take all the salmon they wanted. (Alaska's state constitution bans fish traps.)

Alaskans complained about their territorial status, but few in Washington listened until the Second World War focused national attention on our nation's furthest north territory, thanks in large part to Japanese invasions of some Aleutian islands in hopes of diverting U.S. naval forces north and so away from a great Japanese naval air attack on Midway Island.

The diversion failed. A Japanese fleet was destroyed at Midway. Even so national honor demanded U.S. forces take back from the Japanese wet, foggy, cold, and icy properties mainly inhabited by birds and seals. The Alaskan Scouts, made up chiefly of Alaskan Natives, helped save the U.S. attack to expel the Japanese from the Aleutians from becoming a debacle.

Simultaneously the U.S. government, especially its military, understood Alaska's strategic geographical position as a shortcut to northern Asia and, more importantly, to our new but nerve-wracking ally, the Soviet Union. Within short order major military bases were being built: Ladd Field and then an air strip at what after the war became Eielson Air Force Base at and near Fairbanks, Elmendorf Air Force Base, and the U.S. Army's Fort Richardson at Anchorage, with lesser installations sprinkled hither and yon. By mid-war, thousands of fighters and light bombers arrived at Fairbanks to be turned over to Soviet pilots, who ferried them to Russia and the war with Hitler's Germany there. By the end of the war, the Pentagon had also assumed that our next enemy would be Stalin's Russia, and the Alaskan bases soon became equipped to carry nuclear war to the Russian mainland, including Western Russia and the Kremlin, if necessary.

By war's end and into the following years, stirred by Territorial governor Ernest Gruening and such major newspaper publishers as Robert Atwood of The *Anchorage*

Times and later William Snedden of the *Fairbanks Daily News-Miner*, the political and business establishments talked statehood. Chief opposition came from Southeast Alaska, especially Ketchikan, and from the vocal minority of nay-sayers who come and go in Alaska.

In 1946 an Alaska-wide vote led to the formation of the Alaska Statehood Association to promote statehood. In 1948 Bob Bartlett, Alaska's delegate to Congress, introduced a statehood bill in the House. It died. But to continue the effort, in 1949 the Alaska Statehood Committee formed and began what was to become one of the best and most effective propaganda exercises in 20th Century American politics.

That same year the House passed an Alaska statehood bill, which died in the Senate thanks to right-wing Republican and Southern, segregationist senators. The Republicans feared Alaska would put two more Democratic senators in Congress. The segregationists feared any senators from Alaska would help break the Southerner stranglehold on any legislation to stop racial discrimination and persecution and denial of rights in the U.S.

(Delegate Bartlett later, in order to get Southern senators to vote for statehood, had to promise that if he became a U.S. Senator — and he did — he would vote with them to maintain racial discrimination. Bartlett promised. After he became a U.S. senator, after much agony, he broke a political promise for the first time: He voted to end discrimination.)

Many of the chief Alaskan supporters of statehood were Republicans, and they began putting pressure on the Eisenhower White House to end its disregard for statehood and come to favor statehood. It took some years of effort, but it began to work. President Eisenhower never became a fervent supporter, but in the end he acquiesced. It helped that he had finally appointed a Secretary of the Interior, Fred Seaton, who became a fervent supporter of statehood, for Alaska and for Hawaii.

In 1955 Alaskans voted to hold a convention at the University of Alaska's only campus then, at Fairbanks, to write a constitution for a new State of Alaska to be presented to Congress. In early 1956 that convention, aided by the intellectual rigors of Dr. Donald Moberg, head of the university's Department of Political Science, produced a constitution regarded yet today as a model of clear rigorous organization.

Alaskans voted overwhelmingly to adopt it. And they approved what came to be known as the Tennessee Plan, modeled on a tactic Tennessee, more than a century earlier and many others states after, had used to attain statehood. The plan: Elect and send to Washington, D.C., making news stops all the way, two "U.S. senators" and one "U.S. representative" to knock on the doors of Congress and to ask admission. Former governor Gruening and Bill Egan, mayor of Valdez, were elected "U.S. senators" and Ralph Rivers, former mayor of Fairbanks, was elected "U.S. representative." The hoopla they created turned into excellent public relations, though Congress itself never let them in.

At the same time the statehood effort received considerable help from the newspaper magnate, William Randolph Hearst Jr. Hearst came to Alaska in 1957 and his contacts and friendships with fellow Republican publishers Atwood and Snedden caused him to bring the Hearst newspapers to join other major newspapers in editorializing in favor of statehood.

The pro-statehood forces also sought and received statehood endorsements from movie actors and other celebrities and Edna Ferber's potboiler novel about Alaska, *Ice*

Palace, soon to be made into a potboiler movie, helped galvanize statehood support in the Lower 48 states.

Congress passed the Alaska Statehood Act on July 7, 1958, to much indoor and outdoor rejoicing in Alaska, including impromptu parades and the hoisting of so many toasts that by noon the next day every aspirin in Alaska had been swallowed to allay statehood celebratory headaches.

President Eisenhower signed the bill soon thereafter and on January 3, 1959, he signed the official declaration announcing the addition of the 49th state to the union.

Sources

Alaska, a History of the 49th State, by Claus-M. Naske and Herman E. Slotnick, University of Oklahoma Press, 1994

"A Brief History of Alaska Statehood, 1967-1959," article, Eric Gislason, American Studies website, University of Virginia

http://xroads.virginia.edu/~CAP/BARTLETT/49state.html

Highlights of Alaska Statehood Act

The Alaska Statehood Act contains provisions echoing past Congressional acts admitting states to the union and provisions unique to Alaska.

The general provisions find that Alaska, per the constitution adopted by a vote of its citizens, is sufficient, and makes Alaska what is necessary, a democratic republic.

They define the territory of the new state and one provision later found bothersome by some citizens pining to make Alaska a new nation, a provision common to all statehood acts, states:

"The constitution of the State of Alaska shall always be republican in form and shall not be repugnant to the Constitution of the United States and the principles of the Declaration of Independence."

The act lays out a timetable for holding primary and general elections to elect two U.S. senators and one member of the U.S. House of Representatives and a new governor and other state officers before the president formally proclaims the new state.

It also schedules and details how the new state may choose from federal public lands those properties that will be used to sustain state government and schools. (Wisely, the new state under the direction of its first governor, William Egan, chose lands that included Prudhoe Bay, the richest oil field ever discovered in North America.)

Other provisions account for maintaining laws and ownership of real property and other matters pertaining to a transfer of authority from the federal to the new state government. Specified ownership of mineral rights pass to the state, including rights to oil, gold, coal, and other valuable minerals.

The act allows the president of the U.S. to withdraw lands in certain areas for national defense.

Provisions specify the U.S. retaining ownership of national parks and other federal preserves.

Great detail attends to transferring jurisdiction over civil and criminal laws and maintaining contracts, findings, ongoing court actions and so forth.

-John de Yonge

Source

Text of the Alaska Statehood Act

http://www.yale.edu/lawweb/avalon/statutes/ak_statehood.htm

ALASKA NATIONAL INTEREST LANDS CONSERVATION ACT

Known as the ANILCA; the Alaska National Interest Lands Conservation Act was first introduced to congress in 1977 and went through many revisions before finally being signed into law by President Jimmy Carter in 1980. Often regarded as one of the most significant conservation acts in the nation's history, the ANILCA established guidelines protecting more than 100 million acres of federal land.

Roughly one-third of the land was designated as protected wilderness, including Carter's famous Alaska National Wildlife Refuge (ANWR), and over forty-three million acres of the remaining claim was given to the Alaskan national park system, creating ten new national parks and expanding the borders of three already existing units.

Parks and Preserves created or expanded by the ANILCA:

Gates of the Arctic National Park

Kobuk Valley National Park

Noatak National Preserve

Wrangell–St. Elias National Park and Preserve

Yukon–Charley Rivers National Preserve

Denali National Park (formerly Mount McKinley National Park)

Lake Clark National Park and Preserve

Katmai National Park and Preserve

Aniakchak National Monument Preserve

Glacier Bay National Park and Preserve

Kenai Fjords National Park

Bering Land Bridge National Preserve

Sources

National Parks Conservation Association

http://www.npca.org/media_center/fact_sheets/anilca.html

U.S. Fish and Wildlife Service, Subsistence Management Program

http://alaska.fws.gov/asm/anilca/toc.html

Alaska Humanities Forum: Alaska History and Cultural Studies

http://www.akhistorycourse.org/articles/article.php?artID=256

ALASKA NATIVE CLAIMS SETTLEMENT ACT

Established in 1971, the Alaska Native Claims Settlement Act (ANCSA) extinguished the land claims of approximately 80,000 Alaskan natives in exchange for 44 million acres (about 9 percent of the state's total land) and $962.5 million in compensation. In a unique decision by Congress the act established thirteen regional corporations to oversee distribution of the settlement. It also included provisions for the establishment of some 200 village corporations, to be overseen by their respective regional bodies. Natives were encouraged to enroll in a region, village, or both, and would receive 100 shares of corporation for every enrollment.

Along with compensation, corporations were granted the right to earn income from their investments. Unfortunately, the bill did not specify whether proceeds were to be redistributed to shareholders or kept for further investment. The only provision regarding proceeds appears in section 7(i), and stipulates that 70 percent of revenue from resources within a regional corporation must be shared annually with the other corporations.

Section 17(d)(2) of the ANCSA requires the secretary to withdraw from development 80 million acres of significant federal land in Alaska, and was the result of conservationist concerns about the distribution of land within the state. These "d-2" lands formed a large part of the core discussion surrounding the Alaska National Interest Lands Conservation Act.

Regional Corporations created by ANCSA

Ahtna, Inc.
Sealaska Corp.
Aleut Corp.
Arctic Slope Regional Corp.
Bering Straits Native Corp.
Bristol Bay Native Corp.
Calista Corp.
Chugach Alaska Corp.
Cook Inlet Region, Inc.
Doyon Ltd.
Koniag, Inc.
NANA Regional Corporation, Inc.
The Thirteenth Regional Corporation

Sources
U.S. Fish and Wildlife Service
http://www.fws.gov/laws/lawsdigest/alasnat.html
"Alaska Native Claims Settlement Act," article, Alexandra J. McClanahan, LiteSite Alaska
http://litsite.alaska.edu/aktraditions/ancsa.html
"The Land Claims Settlement Act of 1971, article, Arctic Circle website, University of Connecticut, 2008
http://arcticcircle.uconn.edu/SEEJ/Landclaims/ancsa6.html

INDEX

*Page numbers in **bold** represent photographs.*

ABOUT THE AUTHOR

DERMOT COLE has been researching and writing about Alaska's history and its people for more than thirty years.

Originally from Pennsylvania, he traveled to Fairbanks in 1974 at age twenty-one to visit his identical twin, Terrence, his older brother, Patrick, and his sister, Maureen, all of whom had converged in Fairbanks to study at the University of Alaska.

Dermot had been in Fairbanks for ten minutes when a stranger on a motorcycle stopped him on the street, said "Hello Terrence," and offered him a ride. Cole never regretted that he forfeited the use of his return airline ticket to Montana, choosing instead to sample life in Alaska for a while.

Cole began work at the *Fairbanks Daily News-Miner* in 1976 as a sports writer. He has held almost every editing and reporting position at the paper and claims the unofficial state record for writing headlines announcing that the Alaska natural gas pipeline would be built soon.

The author was a Michigan Journalism Fellow and worked for the Associated Press in Seattle for a year, but he and his wife Debbie, also a writer, decided to move back to Fairbanks to raise their family. They have three children—Connor, Aileen, and Anne.

For more than fifteen years, Cole has written a newspaper column about life in Alaska. In 2006, he was honored by the governor of Alaska with a Distinguished Service to the Humanities Award.

Become a member of the

Alaska Historical Society

. . . or if you are already a member, sign up a relative or friend. Join the hundreds who want to stay in touch with historic Alaska through original scholarship in *Alaska History* and news of events and personalities in the quarterly *Alaska History News.*

Membership is $30 ($40 for a family). For fastest service, join on the web at the address listed below. Or you can send your check to:

Alaska Historical Society
P.O. Box 100299
Anchorage, Alaska 99510-0299

Visit us on the web at www.alaskahistoricalsociety.org.

READING RECOMMENDATIONS
for readers interested in the history of Alaska

ACCIDENTAL ADVENTURER
Memoir of the First Woman
to Climb Mt. McKinley
Barbara Washburn & Lew Freedman,
paperback, $16.95

ARCTIC BUSH PILOT
From Navy Combat to Flying
Alaska's Northern Wilderness
James Anderson & Jim Rearden,
paperback, $17.95

CHEECHAKO
The Personal Story of a
Famous Riverboat Captain
Charles W. Adams, paperback, $14.95

COLD CRIME
How Police Detectives Solved Alaska's
Most Shocking Cases
Tom Brennan, paperback, $14.95

CRUDE DREAMS
A Personal History of Oil & Politics in Alaska
Jack Roderick, paperback, $24.95

FATHER OF THE IDITAROD
The Joe Redington Story
Lew Freedman, paperback, $19.95

FLYING COLD
The Adventures of Russel Merrill,
Pioneer Aviator
Robert Merrill MacLean &
Sean Rossiter, oversized paperback, $19.95

GEORGE CARMACK
Man of Mystery Who Set Off
the Klondike Gold Rush
James Albert Johnson, paperback, $14.95

GOOD TIME GIRLS OF THE
ALASKA-YUKON GOLD RUSH
A Secret History of the Far North
Lael Morgan, paperback, $17.95

KAY FANNING'S ALASKA STORY
Memoir of a Pulitzer-Prize Winning
Newspaper Publisher
Kay Fanning, paperback, $17.95

MERCY PILOT
The Joe Crosson Story
Dirk Tordoff, paperback, $17.95

NORTH TO WOLF COUNTRY
My Life among the Creatures of Alaska
James W. Brooks, paperback, $17.95

SAVING FOR THE FUTURE
My Life & the Alaska Permanent Fund
Dave Rose & Charles Wohlforth,
paperback, $17.95

TALES OF ALASKA'S
BUSH RAT GOVERNOR
The Extraordinary Autobiography
of Jay Hammond, Wilderness Guide,
and Reluctant Politician
Jay Hammond, trade paperback, $17.95